Library of
Davidson College

Social Welfare Spending
Accounting for Changes from 1950 to 1978

Institute for Research on Poverty
Poverty Policy Analysis Series

Robert J. Lampman, *Social Welfare Spending: Accounting for Changes from 1950 to 1978*. 1984

Timothy Bates and William Bradford, *Financing Black Economic Development*. 1979

Joel F. Handler, *Protecting The Social Service Client: Legal and Structural Controls on Official Discretion*. 1979

Joel F. Handler, Ellen Jane Hollingsworth, and Howard S. Erlanger, *Lawyers and the Pursuit of Legal Rights*. 1978

Maurice MacDonald, *Food, Stamps, and Income Maintenance*. 1978

Robert H. Haveman, Editor, *A Decade of Federal Antipoverty Programs: Achievements, Failures, and Lessons*. 1977

Robert D. Plotnick and Felicity Skidmore, *Progress Against Poverty: A Review of the 1964—1974 Decade*. 1975

Social Welfare Spending
ACCOUNTING FOR CHANGES FROM 1950 TO 1978

Robert J. Lampman
Department of Economics
and
Institute for Research on Poverty
University of Wisconsin
Madison, Wisconsin

1984

ACADEMIC PRESS
(Harcourt Brace Jovanovich, Publishers)
Orlando   San Diego   New York   London
Toronto   Montreal   Sydney   Tokyo

This book is one of a series sponsored by the Institute for Research on Poverty of the University of Wisconsin.

Copyright © 1984 by the Board of Regents of the University of Wisconsin System on behalf of the Institute for Research on Poverty.

All rights reserved.

No portion of this book may be reproduced in any form by print, microfilm, or any other means without permission from Academic Press.

ACADEMIC PRESS, INC.
Orlando, Florida 32887

United Kingdom Edition published by
ACADEMIC PRESS, INC. (LONDON) LTD.
24/28 Oval Road, London NW1 7DX

Library of Congress Cataloging in Publication Data

Lampman, Robert J.
   Social welfare spending.

   (Poverty policy analysis series)
   Bibliography: p.
   Includes index.
   1. Income--United States. 2. Income distribution--United States. 3. Transfer payments--United States.
   I. Title. II. Series.
   HC110.I5L32 1984   339.2'2   84-2917
   ISBN 0-12-435260-X (alk. paper)

PRINTED IN THE UNITED STATES OF AMERICA

84 85 86 87   9 8 7 6 5 4 3 2 1

The Institute for Research on Poverty is a national center for research established at the University of Wisconsin in 1966. Its primary objective is to foster basic, multidisciplinary research into the nature and causes of poverty and means to combat it.

In addition to increasing the basic knowledge from which policies aimed at the elimination of poverty can be shaped, the Institute strives to carry analysis beyond the formulation and testing of fundamental generalizations to the development and assessment of relevant policy alternatives.

The Institute endeavors to bring together scholars of the highest caliber whose primary research efforts are focused on the problem of poverty, the distribution of income, and the analysis and evaluation of social policy, offering staff members wide opportunities for interchange of ideas, maximum freedom for research into basic questions about poverty and social policy, and dissemination of their findings.

To JoAnn Cockrell Lampman and our grandchildren

Contents

List of Figures   ix
List of Tables   xi
Foreword   xv
Acknowledgments   xvii

1. Introduction and Overview

Purposes of the Book   1
Policy Background   8
Overview   10
A Guide to Reading   12

2. The System of Interfamily Flows of Secondary Consumer Income

SCI as Distinct from Exchange Transactions
   and as Part of All Transfers   14
Social Accounting Framework   18
Public SCI Benefits   22
Private SCI Benefits   27
SCI Taxes and Contributions   28
SCI Related to Primary Income   29
More on Distinguishing SCI Flows from Other Transfers
   and from Exchange   31
The Representation of Transfers in National Income
   and Products Accounts   37
A Guide to Reading   38

3. Who Receives Secondary Consumer Income and Who Pays for It?

Who Gets the Cash Benefits and What Percentage
  of Income Loss Is Replaced?   40
Who Receives Subsidized Goods and Services?   45
What Part of Each Type of Benefit Goes to the Poor?   52
Who Pays for the SCI Benefits?   56
Who Receives Benefits in Excess of the Taxes
  and Contributions They Pay?   61
A Guide to Reading   65

4. Social Benefits of 1950–1978 Changes in Secondary Consumer Income

The 1950–1978 Changes in the SCI System   69
The Four Explicit Goals of the SCI System   73
Contributions of SCI to Three Other Social Goals   90
Summation and Weighting of Social Benefits   101
A Guide to Reading   106

5. Social Costs of the 1950–1978 Changes in the Secondary Consumer Income System and a Comparison with Social Benefits

Collection, Compliance, and Administrative Costs   109
Loss of Time at Market Work   111
Loss of Productivity per Hour Worked   132
Reallocation of Resources to the Provision
  of SCI Goods and Services   135
Summation and Weighting of Social Costs and
  Their Relationship to Social Benefits   140
A Guide to Reading   146

6. Future Directions for the Secondary Consumer Income System

The Variability of SCI Ratios   147
Projecting Past SCI Trends into the Future   156
The Key Choices Determining the Future Scope
  and Pattern of SCI   159
Where We Stand   169
A Guide to Reading   171

Appendix   174
References   200
Index   217

List of Figures

2.1	Secondary consumer income as part of all transactions.	17
2.2	Secondary consumer income flows among three families via four intermediaries.	33
3.1	Secondary consumer income benefits per person, by pretransfer poverty status, and by age, 1978.	56
3.2	Net secondary consumer income benefits per capita, by pretransfer income level, 1978.	63
5.1	Designs for taxes and benefits, showing relationship to earnings.	117
6.1	Dependency ratio, United States, 1850–2050.	155
6.2	Secondary consumer income ratios, actual, 1890–1978, projected to 2010.	157

List of Tables

1.1	Leading Questions of Economics, by Mood of Inquiry	5
2.1	SCI Benefits by Type and by Intermediary, 1978	15
2.2	Sources of Funds for SCI Benefits, 1978	16
2.3	Selected Tax Savings, by Type, 1978	25
2.4	Direct Interfamily Gifts, by Type and by Age of Recipient, 1978	27
2.5	Income of a Representative Family before and after Interfamily Flows of SCI	30
2.6	SCI Flows (Positive and Negative) by Sector	32
3.1	SCI Cash Benefits and Number of Recipients, Grouped by Risk, 1978	42
3.2	Social Security Benefits for a Worker Retiring at Age 65 in 1978	44
3.3	SCI for Education, by Funding Source, Level of Instruction, and Number of Students, 1978	46
3.4	SCI Benefits for Health Care, and Recipients of Services, by Funding Source, 1978	48
3.5	Number of Persons Covered by Private and Social Health Insurance, 1977	50
3.6	National Health Expenditures, by Type, 1978	51
3.7	Health Care Utilization, by Age Groups, 1978	52
3.8	Hospital and Physician Utilization, Percentages by Age, Sex, and Number of Hospital Episodes, by Funding Source, 1978	53
3.9	SCI Benefits for Food, Housing, and Other Welfare Services, and Number of Recipients, by Funding Source, 1978	54
3.10	Benefits, by Type, with Percentages Received by the Pretransfer Poor and by the Aged, 1978	55
3.11	Funding Sources for SCI Benefits, by Assumed Pattern of Burden, 1978	57
3.12	Effective Rates of Federal, State, and Local Taxes, by Type of Tax and by Population Decile, 1966	58
3.13	SCI Taxes and Contributions Paid by Families, by Poverty Status and by Age, 1978	60
3.14	SCI Benefits Received and Taxes and Contributions Paid, by Pretransfer Poverty Status, and by Age, 1978	62
4.1	SCI Benefits, by Type and Intermediary, 1950–1980	70
4.2	SCI Benefits as Percentage of GNP, 1950–1980	71
4.3	Ratio of 1978 to 1950 SCI Benefits, Sources of SCI Funds, and GNP	72

4.4	Percentage Composition of Government and Private SCI Benefits, by Type, 1950 and 1978	73
4.5	Distribution of Total SCI Benefits among Categories of Population, 1950 and 1978	74
4.6	Beneficiaries of Selected SCI Cash Benefit Programs and Ratios of 1978 to 1950	77
4.7	Enrollment in Educational Institutions, by Level of Instruction and by Type of School, 1949–1950 to Fall 1978	78
4.8	Total Expenditure per Pupil in Average Daily Attendance in Public Elementary and Secondary Schools, 1949–1950 to 1977–1978	79
4.9	The Incidence of Poverty among Persons, 1950–1980, and the Size of the Poverty Income Gap, 1965–1976	83
4.10	Composition of the Poor, 1965 and 1978	84
4.11	Sources of Average Annual Growth of Total Actual National Income, Selected Periods, 1948–1976	95
4.12	Social Benefits Attributable to 1950–1978 Changes in SCI	101
5.1	Civilian Labor Force Participation Rates, Employment and Unemployment Rates, Selected Years, 1950–1978	112
5.2	Civilian Labor Force Participation Rates, Annual Average, by Sex and Age, Selected Years, 1954–1978	113
5.3	Average Weekly Hours of Work, by Selected Categories of Workers, Selected Years, 1950–1978	114
5.4	Distribution of SCI Benefits, by Type, among Categories of Population, 1978	123
5.5	Size of 1978 Full-Time Labor Force if SCI Benefits and Taxes to Pay for Them Were on the Scale of 1950, by Characteristics of Participants	124
5.6	Comparison of Benefit Reductions and Increased Hours Worked in Two Studies	129
5.7	Effects of Noncash SCI Benefits on Allocation of Resources to Selected Goods	138
5.8	Social Costs Attributable to 1950–1978 Changes in SCI	141
5.9	Social Benefits and Social Costs in 1978 Attributable to 1950–1978 Changes in SCI	144
6.1	Components of SCI as Percentage of GNP, Selected Years, 1890–1978	148
6.2	Public Expenditures in Selected OECD Countries on Health, Education, and Income Maintenance, 1975	149
6.3	Selected SCI Benefits in the United States Together with Comparable Items in the Federal Republic of Germany, 1978	150
6.4	Percentage Distribution of the U.S. Population by Age Groups for Selected Years, 1850–2060	154
6.5	OASDI Cost Rates as a Percentage of Taxable Payroll and GNP, 1950–2060	164
A.1	SCI Cash Benefits, Grouped by Risk, 1950–1980	175
A.2	SCI Benefits for Health Care, by Funding Source, 1950–1980	178
A.3	SCI Benefits for Education, by Funding Source, 1950–1980	180
A.4	SCI Benefits for Food, Housing, and Other Welfare Services, by Funding Source, 1950–1980	181
A.5	SCI Benefits, Philanthropy, 1950–1980	182
A.6	SCI Benefits, Interfamily, 1950–1980	185
A.7	SCI Benefits, Selected Tax Savings, 1950–1980	188

A.8	Sources of Funds for SCI Benefits, 1950–1978	192
A.9	SCI Benefits, by Type and Source of Funding, 1978	193
A.10	Funding Sources for SCI Benefits, by Type and Benefit, 1978	194
A.11	SCI Benefits, by Type, with Percentage Received by Pretransfer Poor, 1950	195
A.12	SCI Benefits, by Type and Specific Program, with Percentage Received by Pretransfer Poor and by the Aged, 1978	196

Foreword

It is an honor for me, as Director of the Institute, to write my first foreword for Robert Lampman's major contribution to research on social welfare spending. Robert Lampman has been studying poverty and social welfare spending since the 1950s, was on the staff of the Council of Economic Advisers that developed the War on Poverty proposals, and was instrumental in establishing the Institute for Research on Poverty. Through his writings and through his influence both on a generation of students at the University of Wisconsin and on the staff at the Institute, Lampman, more than any other individual, has guided and influenced poverty research.

What distinguishes Lampman is his persistence in forcing the researcher to confront the difficult basic questions concerning the benefits and costs of social welfare spending. Recently many researchers have placed a premium on finding very precise answers, even if it has meant asking only very narrow questions. Lampman has used those precise findings in this book, but he reminds us that we cannot ignore the more basic questions: What are the goals and purposes of social welfare spending? How are spending flows in the public sector, the private sector, and between families related? What has the rapid growth of social spending accomplished? What have been the unintended consequences? And, given how far we have come, what are future directions for the American welfare state?

Lampman provides a carefully measured analysis to these questions without falling into the rhetorical excesses that characterize both proponents and critics of social welfare spending. For each basic question, Lampman musters the arguments on both sides and weighs what evidence there is. And while he provides enough material to enable his reader to make evaluations, he does not back away from making his own assessments about benefits. For example, he says:

> We have moved from a less to a more insured world. Children born today have greater assurance than did their grandparent against the risks of income loss at each stage of life. They can also count on improved access to such key services as education and health care. (p. 102)

Or about the relationship among benefits and costs:

> To get a strong positive benefit-to-cost ratio, one has to believe that the six nonquantifiable social benefits are sufficiently valuable to more than offset the remaining one percentage point of net quantifiable social costs. . . . I, for one, have no trouble in believing that the reductions in insecurity and income poverty are sufficiently valuable to do that. However, the main point of this exercise is to move you, the reader, to make your own benefit-cost calculation and to come to your own conclusions about whether the nation as a whole is better or worse off as a result of the great rise in [social welfare spending] which occurred in the last three decades. (p. 145)

Social Welfare Spending is thus both the culmination of Lampman's recent research and also the catalyst for you to develop your own answers to the questions raised. This book has been 10 years in the making. Each year, Lampman would examine a fundamental problem, write a paper, circulate it for comments, reflect on the responses, and, in his unique way, raise the next basic question. This volume distills those years of analysis and should have a major impact on students and researchers. I have used the previous papers and this manuscript in my classes and they were well received. Moreover, I can personally recommend the book—Lampman's work has been a major influence on how I conceptualize my own research.

Sheldon Danziger
Director, Institute for Research on Poverty

Acknowledgments

The principal funding for this book was provided by the William F. Vilas Trust Estate. Additional funds were provided by the Graduate School of the University of Wisconsin–Madison and the Richard I. Downing Fellowship in Social Economics at the University of Melbourne. The Institute for Research on Poverty supplied editorial and clerical services.

Time spent at the International Institute of Management in Berlin and at the University of Melbourne enhanced my perspective on comparative social welfare policy. I am indebted to a great many individuals who have given me ideas, encouragement, and criticism. Among those who made specific contributions to the book are the following. In Berlin: Manfred Groser, Benny Hjern, Hans-Jurgen Krupp, F. W. Scharpf, and Günther Schmid. In Melbourne: R. John Harper, Ronald F. Henderson, Duncan Ironmonger, Ian Manning, Andrew Podger, and R. B. Scotton. In the United States: Henry Aaron, Sheldon Danziger, Irwin Garfinkel, W. Lee Hansen, Robert Haveman, Ida Merriam, Eugene Smolensky, and Harold Watts. In addition to the above-named scholars, I want to express my appreciation to all my colleagues at the Institute for Research on Poverty, an organization with which I am proud to have been associated since 1966. The reader will note that this book draws substantially on research done at the Institute.

I also want to acknowledge the quality of work done by Elizabeth Uhr, editor, and Matthew Hendryx, Janet Holtzblatt, Ulrich Lehmann, and Timothy McBride, research assistants, and Marie Goodman, Nancy Rortvedt, and Sue Sticha, typists. I am also grateful to students in several courses who read early drafts of some parts of this book. Their reactions helped me decide what to keep and what to throw away.

I cheerfully accept responsibility for any errors of fact, theory, or judgment that may remain.

CHAPTER 1

Introduction and Overview

Purposes of the Book

This book was inspired and shaped by my encounters with several types of systematic thinking. The first encounter was with teachers at the University of Wisconsin—most notably Elizabeth Brandeis and Edwin E. Witte—who represented social security institutions as the outgrowth of a system of law deeply rooted in custom and tradition, but also as responsive to changes in circumstances. Social security was for them an expansive term that included private charity and self-help by voluntary groups, remedies at common law, and commercial insurance as well as social insurance and public assistance.

The second encounter was with researchers at the National Bureau of Economic Research—particularly, Solomon Fabricant and Raymond Goldsmith—who directed my attention to the discipline of social accounting and its emphasis on a graphic picture of the several parts of an economic system. That discipline has produced a number of loosely related accounting systems. These include (1) the national income and product account and its component sectoral accounts, which are designed to show the employment-generating effect of purchases of goods and services; (2) input–output tables, which detail interindustry flows of goods; (3) flow-of-funds accounts, which emphasize the role of financial intermediaries in moving funds across sectors; (4) balance of payment accounts, which focus attention on movements of goods and money in and out of the country; and (5) national balance sheets, which show assets and liabilities by sector.

The third encounter was with researchers at the Social Security Administration—notably Ida Merriam—who developed a time series of American social welfare expenditures in response to what they thought were unrealistic international comparisons being offered in the 1950s.

They argued that it was important to include state and local government as well as federal expenditures and also to include education, health care, and related social service expenditures in addition to cash benefits. They also argued for the inclusion of certain private expenditures. This series has been continued to date and has had wide usage, but there is not yet a standard method among international agencies, such as the International Labor Organization, the European Economic Community, and the Organisation for Economic Co-operation and Development, for comparing social welfare expenditures.

The fourth encounter was with advocates of the Planning Program Budget System—exemplified by Alice Rivlin and her book *Systematic Thinking for Social Action*—who emphasized the utility of identifying and isolating a social goal and comparing the cost-effectiveness of alternative methods for reaching that goal. This type of systematic thinking was different from and a challenge to the versions of such thinking that I met in the first three encounters.

The fifth encounter was with Kenneth Boulding's vision of a "grants economy," which functions alongside and in a symbiotic way with the "exchange economy." Boulding's book, *The Economy of Love and Fear*, caused me to reconsider what I had learned from the other encounters. In particular, Boulding stressed the motivations for nonexchange transactions, variously referred to as grants or transfers, and the conditions under which they may be constructive or destructive.

These five encounters may be accepted by the reader as a pedigree for this book and an explanation for the selection of questions for discussion. Against this background, the book has three purposes: to apply the discipline of double-entry social accounting to social welfare expenditures, broadly defined, and their sources of funds; to apply benefit-cost analysis to the recent increase in the scale of these expenditures; and to identify the key policy choices that will determine their future pattern.

Every economy has some system for income redistribution, that is, a process whereby the primary distribution of income which arises out of production is modified by an interfamily secondary flow. Considerable interest attaches to the redistributional and reallocational effects of this system, but there is no commonly used accounting framework for identifying and assembling the several parts. It is the first purpose of this book to develop such a framework by defining and portraying, with reference to the United States, what I elect to call a secondary consumer income (SCI) system. The system is defined broadly enough to be useful for historical and comparative research, and to recognize that the several methods of transfer may be substituted for one another. In this mood, I describe the 1950–1978 changes in the scope and composition of the American SCI system.

The second purpose of this book is to compare the social benefits and social costs that may be associated with the 1950–1978 changes in the SCI system. The benefits are defined as extra attainment of such social goals as economic security, reduction of income poverty, and economic growth. The social costs are mainly the additional resources used up for administration and provision of SCI benefits and the induced reduction of hours of work.

The third purpose is to review the explanations that have been given by others for the remarkable growth in the SCI system and to describe the alternative bases for choice with respect to the future directions of this substantial and dynamic system. Throughout the book the reader is urged to consider the rival philosophies that underlie the interfamily givings and takings in which we are all involved. These philosophies or mentalities derive from the four institutional approaches to income redistribution that are followed in the SCI system. The insurance approach calls for an evaluation of transfers and contributions to pay for them in terms of their observance of principles of insurance equity. The public assistance approach evaluates the system in terms of its responsiveness to the needs of the poor. The income tax approach—which embraces the ideals of a progressive tax and a negative income tax—asks whether the SCI system yields net payments to families below a selected break-even income level and imposes net charges on those above that break-even point. The fourth approach starts with efficiency questions and asks whether the social benefits of an SCI program (e.g., an increase of GNP) exceed the social costs of that program (e.g., the resources used up).

It may be helpful to think of the range of activities involved in secondary consumer income as lending itself to a discrete and interrelated set of overarching questions that mark out a subdiscipline or school within economics.[1] The pattern for the economics of SCI is, not unexpectedly, to be found inside the methodological frame of general economics, which stems from a paradigm of society as a complex organism converting natural resources and human energies into outputs for consumption. From this basis, the study divides two ways. On one hand, there are the leading questions of aggregative, allocative, and distributive import: What are the potential and actual levels of produc-

---

[1] This discussion and Table 1.1 are taken from Lampman, "Toward an Economics of Health, Education, and Welfare," *Journal of Human Resources 1* (1966b), 45–53, copyright © Board of Regents of the University of Wisconsin System.

tion? What is produced and how is it produced? Who gets the product? On the other hand, there is descriptive, predictive, and prescriptive inquiry, wherein the questions are respectively: What is? What will or would be? What should be? This two-way division of questions is set out in Table 1.1.

For each leading question there are three moods of inquiry, and for each mood there are three leading questions. For example, beginning with the aggregative question, one can describe what the actual level of production is (question 1-b) and what system is in use for determining that level. Or one can engage in prediction, asking what change in the level of production will follow from specific change in inputs, market arrangements, or government policies. Finally, one may, in a prescriptive mood, assert that certain changes should or should not be made because the predicted results are judged to be good or bad. Prescriptive analysis ties predictive inquiry to a statement of goals or purposes of economic activity. It identifies the benefits from a change, compares the benefits with the costs associated with the change, and renders a judgment concerning the desirability of the change.

Table 1.1, of course, merely presents a set of empty boxes whereby one can identify different schools and subdisciplines in the field of economics. (I will return to the distinction between these two terms later in this chapter.) Thus, Keynesian economics may be classified as emphasizing question 1-b and the predictive and prescriptive moods. Marxian economics emphasizes the predictive proposition that a change in the ownership of the means of production (2-b) would lead to a change in the actual level of production. The emphasis of the SCI subdiscipline is at the point on the grid touching both the allocative and distributive questions, which are numbered 2 and 3 in Table 1.1. It is true that some inquiry relates SCI outlays to the aggregative goals of stability and growth. Such inquiry may seek to quantify social costs in terms of induced loss of production. However, the unique concern of SCI economics is two specialized sets of institutions, one for determining the allocation of resources to, and methods of production of, health care, education, and certain other services, and another, which overlaps the above, for determining the level and direction of SCI cash and in-kind transfers.

The logic of combining health care and schooling is, in part, that they both involve services, including those of professionals, to persons. Moreover, while there is private market activity and family responsibility in both sets of activities, there is more than the usual amount of social interest in the outcome and, hence, extensive public intervention and a degree of compulsion in each of them. Both health care and schooling

TABLE 1.1
Leading Questions of Economics, by Mood of Inquiry

Questions	Mood of inquiry		
	Descriptive	Predictive	Prescriptive
1. Aggregative			
a. Potential level of production			
b. Actual level of production			
2. Allocative			
a. Specific goods and services produced	×	×	×
b. Methods of production			
3. Distributive			
a. Sharing of product via factor payments			
b. Sharing of product via transfer	×	×	×

Note: X indicates points of emphasis of the SCI subdiscipline of economics.

feature extensive public and private transfers of funds to reallocate resources to provide for "social wants" and "merit wants." These transfers redistribute income in kind at the same time that they reallocate resources; hence, they are similar to those SCI programs that redistribute money income. There is also a commonality in the several activities encompassed by SCI economics with respect to the unusual mix of private and public suppliers, the complex structure of demand, and the attention to probabilistic events, uncertain outcomes, and external benefits.

Questions about how performance relates to purposes and priorities move us to the prescriptive mood shown in Table 1.1. It does not always follow that increased outlays for SCI will make people healthier, wealthier, and wiser. Whether outlays will have that effect depends upon the alternative forgone, the quality of the inputs, and the efficiency of the organizations. It is interesting to note that the goals of SCI are now stated more affirmatively than previously. The goals have evolved from mere relief of suffering, rescue from illiteracy, and shielding against poverty, to promotion of positive health and longevity; the cultivation of talent, skill, and new knowledge; and the attainment of income adequacy and security.

SCI economists tend to be placed under the same umbrella because they have more difficulty than economists in more traditional fields in separating allocational efficiency from distributive equity. Benefit-cost analysis in this subdiscipline needs explicitly to integrate efficiency and equity goals. Some of these goals defy quantification.

Up to this point I have referred to SCI economics as a subdiscipline. However, there are some signs that this subdiscipline is the platform for a school. The hallmark of a school in economics is a predictive proposition with strong normative meaning—what can be called a persuasive prediction. SCI expenditures were once looked upon as parasitic, but as having income elasticity of demand of less than unity and, hence, as likely to diminish in relative importance. However, they are now rationalized as productive and as likely to rise in significance as an economy becomes more affluent. The clearest example of this sort of persuasive prediction is Theodore Schultz's hypothesis that extra education outlay is likely to yield an increase in the rate of economic growth (1963). For another example, it is often alleged that a more secure worker will be more productive and more likely to cooperate in the introduction of new technology. On a broader scale, it is claimed that SCI can reduce social tensions and hostilities, and generate more fraternal feelings and national integrity. Another example of a persuasive prediction in support of the SCI system is that it will serve, because of its automatic stabilization properties, to moderate cyclical swings of production and employment.

The goals of the SCI system relate to the secondary distribution of income. The primary distribution arises in the marketplace, but it too is subject to social goals, the most important of which are high employment and positive growth in per capita production. Attainment of these goals, which may be aided by skillful application of fiscal, monetary, and other policies, will ease the problem of reaching the goals of the secondary distribution. Conversely, high unemployment and negative growth will place a heavy burden on SCI.

The goals for the secondary distribution and the two for the primary distribution are reflective of still deeper social goals. These include individual freedom of choice on the part of the consumer and the worker, and equality of opportunity. This complex of goals has some internal conflicts; pursuit of one goal may entail costs in terms of loss with respect to another goal. For example, high offsets to income loss may cause a reduction in labor supply and hence a slowing of economic growth.

Similarly, there are problems in getting an appropriate balance among efforts to achieve each of several goals. Here we confront an economist's paradox. There is such a thing as too much of a desired good, and that can be avoided only by balancing benefits and costs at the margin. For example, suppose we were considering adding $50 billion to SCI. Putting the whole amount into helping people buy education or health care might, at the margin, add less to social utility than putting part of it into reducing (money) income poverty. While there may be wide agreement that the goals enumerated above are the operative goals for policy choice, there is less agreement about the priorities among them. The challenge for SCI reformers is to achieve, by recourse to reason and experience, a desirable balance among the goals of SCI, the primary distribution goals of high employment and positive economic growth, and the broader social goals of choice and equality of opportunity. However, this is not a book of advocacy. That is, it is not a book in which I state a goal and set forth my own opinion about the best policy to follow in pursuit of that goal. Rather, it is a book to explore a particular real-world system that evolves its own goals and its own preferred means for reaching those goals. It is parallel to books that examine the workings of the market system, the military system, the collective bargaining system, the system for public regulation of an industry, the tax system, the health care system, or the education system.

Like other such books, this one explores the historical origins of the system selected for study, in this case, the SCI system. It asks what drives the system from the inside, so to speak, and also what impacts it has on other systems on the outside. It asks what purposes the system serves and what alternative or substitute approaches have been developed to achieve those purposes. It is a theme of this book that every society has its own version of an SCI system with its own emphasis with respect to goals and means to achieve those goals. Moreover, each society may follow its own pattern of experimenting with alternative designs for its system. In line with that thought, this book repeatedly urges the reader to see that one method of intermediating transfers has been or could be substituted for another. For example, social insurance could be substituted for private group insurance or vice versa. At the same time, one form of benefit could be substituted for another. For example, cash could be substituted for food stamps, which in turn could be substituted for gifts of specific food items. A different dimension of substitutability is illustrated by the thought that a given service may be sponsored by alternative providers. That is, child day care may be provided by schools or by other agencies; nursing homes may be thought of as health care or a social service. Moreover, methods of paying for SCI benefits may vary. For example, a payroll tax for social insurance may be substituted for mandated employers' contributions to a private pension plan, or the federal income tax could be drawn upon to replace local property tax revenues in financing public elementary and secondary education.

It is out of long experimentation with such alternatives or substitutes that modern SCI systems of considerable complexity have evolved from simpler ones, which relied primarily on direct interfamily giving for redistribution of cash and education and health care. It is out of awareness of the possibility of substitution that numerous proposals for SCI reforms arise. A good example of this is the proposal to use a variant of the progressive income tax as a substitute for certain public assistance programs. Alertness to substitutability within a complex system helps one to see that a change in one program may have repercussions on another part of the system. For example, changes in the generosity of unemployment insurance will change the number of persons eligible for Medicaid.

In presenting a wide-angle view of my concept of an SCI system, I have relied on the work of many other scholars. However, in certain instances, I have had to go beyond the range of available and trustworthy data and present numbers that only approximate reality. Such approximations are offered, for a few examples, in the discussion of direct interfamily gifts, compliance and administrative costs, and the consumption value of extra leisure time. The presentation of such rough numbers is justifiable only as a way to show the type of information that is needed for a fully rounded evaluation of social policies. I hope that this study will encourage other scholars to develop better estimates to round out this presentation. In the meantime, I depend on you, the reader, to be skeptical about the quality of numbers throughout the book, but I hope you will not miss the main point, which is to learn how one part of the world works and to learn how to make one's own evaluations of the present SCI system and proposals to change it. I am not trying to tell you *what to think*, but rather *how to think*, about social policy questions.

Policy Background

Between 1965 and 1976 social welfare expenditures under public programs managed by federal, state, and local governments combined, took a sudden leap from an amount equal to 11.2% of GNP to 19.3% (Bixby, 1983). In this same period, the U.S. economy experienced "stagflation"—simultaneous slowing of productivity gains, high rates of unemployment, and alarming rates of increase in general prices. Not surprisingly, the thought occurred to many people that perhaps the unprecedented stagflation was due in some part to the explosion of social welfare spending.

Critics widely proclaimed that such government spending was out of control and called for stern measures to prevent continuing escalation of spending for income maintenance, health care, education, and other so-called welfare goods and services. Particularly, the years since 1976 have been marked by a strong political reaction against further rapid increase in governmental spending for these purposes. The administrations of presidents Johnson, Nixon, and Ford led the expansion of social welfare spending, but Carter and Reagan pledged to halt or reverse that trend. The passage of Proposition 13 in California in 1978 signaled a taxpayer revolt against historically high state and local government taxes, the majority of which are devoted to social welfare purposes. These reactions at various governmental levels were undoubtedly at least partly responsible for a leveling off of the public social welfare expenditure ratio, which peaked in 1976 and subsided to 18.2% in 1978.

The United States may be viewed as a laggard in the post-World War II development of democratic welfare states. Even at a ratio of 18%, America is far below the ratios of 30% and more found in a number of West European nations. Nevertheless, at the present time this nation is in the midst of a great debate about the future role of the federal government in social welfare. Political discussion frequently centers on what are called welfare programs, meaning Aid to Families with Dependent Children and a few other public assistance programs, even though such programs comprise a very small part of the 18% ratio referred to above. At other times attention is focused on the large part of that ratio which represents benefits for those who are neither the "truly needy" nor the "deserving poor."

This debate goes beyond economics and into questions of social, political, and moral import which enter into the definition of a good society. Advocates of maintenance or expansion of social welfare programs see them as necessary to national solidarity and community well-being. Some critics on the left see the present ratio as necessary but not sufficient and as merely a whistle-stop on the route to full-blown democratic socialism. Opponents on the right see the programs as destroying creative individualism and self-reliance, and as encouraging irresponsibility, passivity, and other socially undesirable attitudes. Others perceive these programs as imposing social costs by discouraging work and saving. Still others, including some who are not ideologically opposed to the purposes of the programs, base their conclusions on what they regard as the principal lesson of the 1965–1976 period, namely, that the federal government could not achieve, in concert with far-flung state and local governments and private institutions, the complex social goals set out by recent presidents, legislators, and judges. In other words, they conclude, sometimes regretfully, that the limits to social welfare spending are set by inherent limitations of decentralized and democratic government.

Overview

This book aims at providing some perspective on this great national debate. I assert that in order to judge whether public social welfare expenditures are too large or too small, we should see them as part of a larger set of public *and* private expenditures devoted to overlapping or similar purposes. The subject matter might therefore be entitled "social welfare expenditures under public programs and alternatives to them." These alternatives or substitutes include certain elements of what are called tax expenditures or tax savings, which benefit individuals specified by the federal individual income tax law. (For example, the exemption for children may be seen as an alternative to a child allowance.) Another way to achieve some of the purposes of public social welfare expenditures is to encourage private group insurance for pensions and health care for employees and their dependents. A still different institutional framework for achieving these purposes is the private philanthropic organization that accepts voluntary contributions from one family and delivers benefits to another. A final alternative, and a method we have always made use of, is that of direct interfamily giving without intermediation by any private or public institution.

All of these expenditures are involved in a flow of secondary income among consumers, which is distinct from flows between business firms and households. The "takings" of such income by recipient families are made possible by the "givings," in the form of taxes paid and private contributions made by families. I am excluding intrafamily flows between members of the same nuclear family. The terms *transfer* and *secondary* distinguish my subject from that of primary or producer income, which is distributed by the market. Secondary income is by definition income which comes to the recipient as a gift or without a reciprocal exchange of goods or services in the current period. The word *consumer* highlights the distinction between benefits that enhance consumption in the family rather than production in the business sector, and also distinguishes benefits to selected families from benefits that flow to all residents in the form of such public goods as national defense and law and order.

Chapter 2 makes all of these distinctions in defining and describing the American system of SCI as it existed in 1978. In that portrayal, benefits are classified as passing through public or private intermediaries and cross-classified into four types, (1) cash, (2) health care, (3) education, and (4) food, housing, and other welfare services.

SCI benefits amounted to $598 billion in 1978—equal to 27.6% of GNP. This includes social welfare expenditures under public programs, which were equal to 18.2% of GNP in that year, as well as selected tax savings, benefits paid out by private pension and health insurance funds and philanthropic organizations, and direct interfamily gifts.

In 1978, about one-half of the SCI transfers were cash benefits. About one-fifth went to health care, another fifth to education, and one-tenth to food, housing, and other welfare services. About three-fourths of all SCI benefits passed through public as opposed to private intermediaries. About half of the private benefits went through insurance organizations; another substantial part moved directly from one family to another; and a small part moved through philanthropic organizations. About two-thirds of SCI benefits were paid for by taxes, with the remainder paid for by wage diversions, interfamily gifts, and gifts through philanthropic institutions.

Chapter 3 explores two questions, who receives SCI benefits and who pays for them? A substantial part of the population receives cash or in-kind benefits in any single year. However, the benefits are tilted toward those who are old and those who are poor in terms of primary income during the year. Families with children and those who experience illness are also favored. The method of paying for the benefits is roughly proportional to income and does not, by itself, result in much, if any, redistribution of income from rich to poor. The pattern of benefits net of payments for the benefits, however, does result in a transfer from the top half of the income distribution to the lower half in any 1-year period.

Chapters 4 and 5 appraise the social benefits and social costs of the changes that were made in the scale and scope of the SCI system between 1950 and 1978. The social benefits are identified as achievement of such goals as reduction of economic insecurity and income poverty, and several desirable side effects, including a gain in GNP due to a better-educated population. The social costs include using up economic resources—land, labor, and capital—in the direct pursuit of SCI goals, and undesirable effects such as loss of market-work time. The evaluator must assign weights to each of the several types of benefits and costs in order to arrive at his or her own conclusion as to whether the extra social costs of the 1950–1978 change exceed or are exceeded by the extra social benefits of that change.

Similar judgments face us in considering future directions for the SCI system. Chapter 6 identifies some of the reasons scholars have given for the upward trend in SCI spending, and applies some of those reasons to appraising the likelihood of a continuation of that trend. It also offers a range of choices that are open to us at this time.

Chapter 6 stops short of identifying specific alternatives at the particular program level. Judgments about such alternatives often turn on questions of technical efficiency. For example, is one school curriculum better than another in improving students' achievement, or is one mode of providing long-term care better than another at meeting the needs of chronically ill persons? For answers to such important questions, the student will have to look to the literature on the delivery of health care, education, and the several other services involved. The choices emphasized here involve the balance among the SCI intermediaries, namely, governments, private pension and insurance funds, philanthropic organizations, and an imaginary interfamily fund. They also involve the priority to give to selected target groups, such as the aged, children, and the poor; and the emphasis to place on cash versus such in-kind programs as education and health care. There are also important choices to be made about which particular programs—some old and some scarcely off the drawing boards—should grow and which should decline in the years ahead.

A Guide to Reading[2]

Some readers may have difficulty seeing where this book fits in the vast literature on economic and social policy. I see it as suitable for the redistribution section of a course on income distribution, or as supplementary reading for courses in public finance, labor economics, public policy, or social policy, where the emphasis is on issues of income maintenance, antipoverty programs, education, and health care. It is similar

---

[2]Complete references for all works mentioned in the Guides to Reading are provided at the back of the book.

in scope to Lindbeck, *Inequality and redistribution* (1975); Taubman, *Income distribution and redistribution* (1978); Tullock, *Economics of income redistribution* (1982); Wilcox, *Toward social welfare* (1969); and Wilson and Wilson, *The political economy of the welfare state* (1982). It overlaps the subject matter of such textbooks in several fields as Atkinson, *The economics of inequality* (1983); Cohn, *The economics of education* (1979); Browning and Browning, *Public finance and the price system* (1983); P. J. Feldstein, *Health care economics* (1979); Levitan, *Programs in aid of the poor for the 1980s* (1980); and Williams, Turnbull, and Cheit, *Economic and social security* (1982). This book also fishes in the same waters as those on what is variously called social choice, collective choice, and public choice. Examples of such books are Breton, *The economic theory of representative government* (1974); Mueller, *Public choice* (1979); Olson, *The logic of collective action* (1971); Peacock and Rowley, *Welfare economics: A liberal restatement* (1975); and Sen, *Collective choice and social welfare* (1970).

For historical background on issues discussed in this book I recommend Cahnman and Schmitt, *The concept of social policy* (a review of early thought on German welfare statism) (1979); Fraser, *The evolution of the British welfare state* (1973); Mencher, *Poor law to poverty program* (1967); Palmer and Sawhill, *The Reagan experiment* (1982); and Witte, *Social security perspectives* (1962).

Readers who are interested in exploring adversarial writings on welfare state issues will find strong affirmative statements in Ackerman, *Social justice in the liberal state* (1980); Beveridge, *Full employment in a free society* (1944); Meade, *The just economy* (1976); Okun, *Equality and efficiency* (1975); Rawls, *A theory of justice* (1971); Tawney, *Equality* (fourth edition) (1952); and Titmuss, *Commitment to welfare* (1968) and *Essays on the welfare state* (1976). The negative side of the argument is led by Hayek, *The road to serfdom* (1944); de Jouvenel, *The ethics of redistribution* (1951); and Friedman, *Capitalism and freedom* (1962); who emphasize the loss of freedom they see as inherent in such policies. Gilder, *Wealth and poverty* (1981) and Joseph and Sumption, *Equality* (1979), affirm the moral superiority of a relatively untrammeled market economy. Aharoni, *The no-risk society* (1981), and Geiger, *Welfare and efficiency* (1978), are representative of a growing number of writers who raise the alarm about the possibility of heavy efficiency losses from large-scale welfare expenditures. Freeman, *The wayward welfare state* (1981), deplores the failure of some programs to meet their own goals, and the crowding out of national defense spending by an aggressive welfare state lobby.

CHAPTER 2

The System of Interfamily Flows of Secondary Consumer Income

I stated earlier that it is a purpose of this book to develop an accounting framework to reflect the process whereby the primary distribution of income is modified by interfamily secondary flows. Certain secondary income flows are identified as making up what I call a secondary consumer income (SCI) system.

SCI benefits received by families may be money, goods (such as food), or services (such as education and health care). They are paid for by families as taxes or contributions. The interfamily flows may go directly from one nuclear family (which may be a single adult, or one or two adults with or without minor children) to another; or indirectly via a philanthropic organization, a pension fund or insurance company, or a government agency. Tables 2.1 and 2.2 show that the totals of benefits, on one hand, and taxes and contributions to pay for them on the other, amounted to $597.9 billion in 1978.

Let us picture each nuclear family as having primary income, that is, labor income or property income arising out of the market. Further, let us imagine that each such family has a postsecondary consumer income that results from adding to and subtracting from that primary income certain SCI benefits received and contributions made. Some families will gain and others will lose, but the national total of postsecondary consumer income will equal the total of primary income.

SCI as Distinct from Exchange Transactions and as Part of All Transfers

SCI benefits, taxes, and contributions are transfers. The process of transfer is one of giving and taking; the parties are donor and donee

SCI as Part of All Transfers

rather than buyer and seller. Transfer is distinct from exchange. In the latter, each of the two parties is compensated for what it gives up and is thought to be better off after the exchange than before. In a transfer, however, one party is made better off by a sacrifice or uncompensated effort by the other. In that sense, a transfer is a one-way transaction. The sacrifice may be made out of compassion or fear; it may be a gift freely offered or a tribute tendered at the point of a sword. It may be a transfer from the rich to the poor or from the weak to the powerful.

While the flows of SCI that I have selected for study are transfers, they are only a fraction of all transfers, namely, social welfare expenditures under public programs and alternatives to them. This means that

TABLE 2.1

SCI Benefits by Type and by Intermediary, Fiscal Year 1978

Type of benefit	Amount of benefit (billions of dollars)	Benefit as percentage of GNP
Total	597.9	27.6
Government	424.5	19.6
Insurance	73.7	3.4
Philanthropy	13.6	0.6
Interfamily	86.1	4.0
Cash	301.7	13.9
Government	201.4	9.3
Insurance	31.4	1.5
Philanthropy	0	0
Interfamily	68.9	3.2
Health care	120.4	5.6
Government	75.9	3.5
Insurance	42.3	2.0
Philanthropy	2.2	0.1
Interfamily	0	0
Education	113.2	5.2
Government	106.1	4.9
Insurance	0	0
Philanthropy	7.1	0.3
Interfamily	0	0
Food, housing and other welfare services	62.6	2.9
Government	41.1	1.9
Insurance	0	0
Philanthropy	4.3	0.2
Interfamily	17.2	0.8

Source: Tables 4.1 and 4.2.

TABLE 2.2
Sources of Funds for SCI Benefits, Fiscal Year 1978

Source of funds	Amount of benefit (billions of dollars)	Percentage of total
Total	598	100
Taxes paid by families	396	66
Payroll tax	146	24
Local property tax	36	6
State general revenues	92	15
Federal general revenues[a]	122	20
Wage diversion[b]	103	17
Family gifts to philanthropic organizations[c]	14	2
Interfamily gifts	86	14

Source: Appendix Table A.10.
Note: Sums may not add to totals due to rounding.
[a]Includes $33 billion to pay for tax savings shown in Table 2.3.
[b]Includes $31 billion for private employee pensions, $30 billion for public employee pensions, and $42 billion for private group health insurance for public and private employees.
[c]Includes gifts made by private corporations.

our attention is concentrated on the set of arrangements, which are substitutable one for the other, and which overtly alters the primary distribution of income among families after it has been given to us by the market with all its imperfections and governmental interventions.

Some SCI transactions transfer cash to replace or supplement family earnings; others consist of the government or a private agency purchasing consumer goods and services and giving them to particular families. This picture is complicated by the fact that the government purchases things other than consumer goods and services, such as labor and equipment to maintain an army. The benefit of national defense is transferred to the citizenry at large and is not assignable to particular families. National defense is an example of a pure public good because no one can be excluded from its benefit. However, people can be excluded from consuming an SCI good. There is a continuum of degree of excludability of goods that may be purchased by government, and the line dividing purchases of SCI goods from other purchases is a ragged or judgmental one. Some goods that quite clearly fall into the nonexcludable category are law and order, scientific research, environmental improvement, public health, and community development. Goods that are near the dividing line are public playgrounds, art museums, urban transit systems, and mail delivery to residences.

Government also gives money away for reasons other than to replace or supplement family earnings. It may do so to stimulate certain kinds of producer activity—e.g., exploration for oil, or starting small businesses—on the grounds that this will improve the overall productivity of the economy. Government may also give money away to failing business firms with the declared purpose of protecting the jobs of certain workers. These several cases of transfer for the purpose of stimulating producer activity and increasing worker earnings are all excluded from SCI on the logic that government expenditure designed to increase

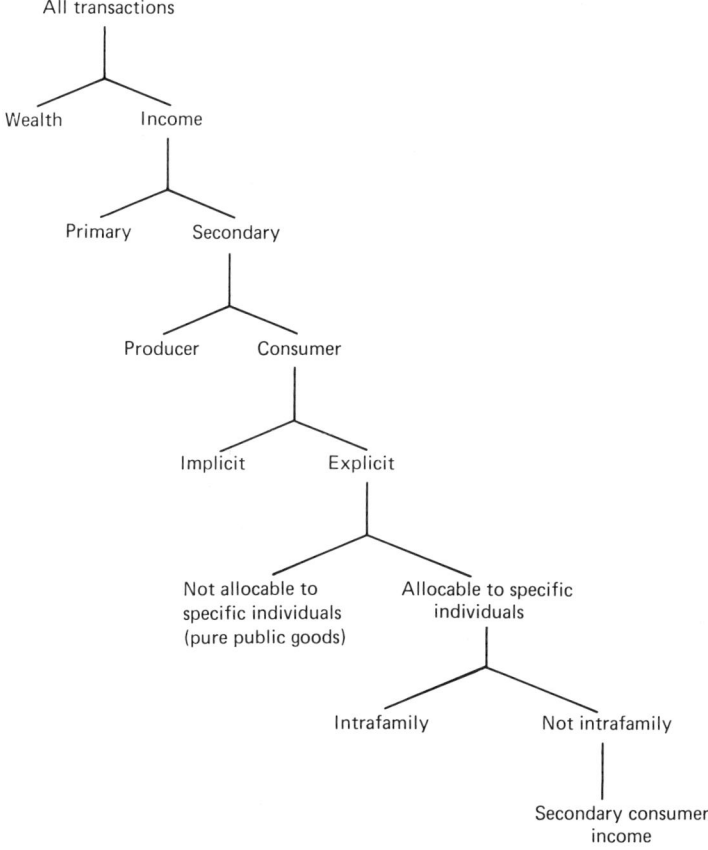

FIGURE 2.1 Secondary consumer income as part of all transactions.

workers' earnings is different from expenditure designed to replace lost earnings with nonearned benefits. The expenditures to increase earnings directly belong more clearly with the family of policies—including monetary and fiscal policies—that seek economic growth and high employment than they do with the family of SCI policies that seek economic security against the failures of growth and employment policies. (See Chapter 4 for a fuller discussion of economic security goals.)

SCI transactions focus our attention on two functions of government; namely, giving money away and making purchases which are then given away. A third function of government is the regulation of markets. This is a nonfiscal function, but it may have indirect effects on consumer incomes. For example, a requirement that all food sold in the United States must be grown by American farmers would have effects on incomes and consumer prices. The effects of regulation on the primary distribution may be defined as implicit grants. These effects are not counted as part of SCI.

It is worth special mention here that I leave out all transfers that occur within the nuclear family. This exclusion is not because intrafamily transfers are unimportant; indeed, the nuclear family is our leading transfer institution, and it certainly merits study as such (Kyrk, 1953). However, I have elected to leave that to another study on the grounds that many policies to effect transfers can be designed and evaluated without examining how incomes are shared within the nuclear family. I also choose to exclude intergenerational bequests on the grounds that they are transfers of a stock of wealth rather than a flow of income. Figure 2.1 offers a decision tree to show how SCI fits into the picture of all transfers.

Social Accounting Framework

The design of any social account calls for numerous distinctions and the drawing of sometimes arbitrary lines (Lampman, 1975b).[1] In the SCI account, interfamily flows must be distinguished from intrafamily ones,

---

[1]The social accounting discipline has produced a number of loosely related accounting systems. The systems most relevant to this study are (1) the national income and product account and its component sectoral accounts, which are designed to show the employment-generating effect of purchases of goods and services; and (2) flow-of-funds accounts, which emphasize the role of financial intermediaries in moving funds across sectors.

wealth from income, transfers from exchange transactions, producer from consumer activity, and primary from secondary income. Social accounting also calls for clear distinctions as to the definition of the income-receiving unit, the number of sectors to have in the system, the income accounting period to use, and whether or not to use double-entry as opposed to single-entry bookkeeping.

The income-receiving unit is defined in a number of ways in the literature on income distribution and consumer expenditure. Sometimes it is the individual earner; sometimes it is the household, which may include all the people living in a housing unit. The economic definition of a family is all persons living together, sharing income, and related by blood, marriage, or adoption. An unrelated individual may be thought of as a one-person family. An economic family may contain more relatives than the nuclear family of parents and their minor children. These may be adult children, parents of a spouse, siblings of a spouse, or other relatives. Such relatives within an economic family may belong to what are designated as subfamilies. However, those same relatives would become separate nuclear families if they moved out of the original nuclear family's home, even though they continued to share income with the original nuclear family. The composition of an economic family is, of course, subject to wide variation.

My interest in income redistribution means that I should rule out the use of both the individual earner and the household as the income-receiving unit. But is it preferable to use the nuclear family or the broader economic family? Use of the broader economic family would fail to account for some transfers between a nuclear family and a related family. Moreover, SCI benefits tend to be targeted to nuclear families (or subfamilies) rather than to broader economic families. For example, the AFDC (Aid to Families with Dependent Children) program does not consider the resources of the applicant's parents in determining the benefit. All this argues for using the nuclear family as the income-receiving unit for this study.

A remaining question is the setting of the age of majority. Should it be 18 or 21 years of age? Many people between 18 and 21 move out of or into their parents' homes, and some divide their time between work and school. In most states, 18 has been established as the age of majority. This has implications for the law of responsibility for the acts of children and parental obligation for their support. Some SCI benefits (e.g., the G.I. Bill) take the form of stipends that are targeted to college students of any age. This move toward cash benefits for college students is pronounced in many nations. I do use 18 as the age of majority and hence identify an unmarried 18-year-old as a separate one-person family whether or not he or she is living in the parental home. Data problems on the income and expenditures of persons aged 18–20 years make the discussion of interfamily direct transfers a particularly rough edge of this study.

My decision is to show one sector for families and one for each of the intermediaries; namely, philanthropic organizations, pension funds and insurance companies, and governments, as well as an imaginary "interfamily fund." The latter is a way to register direct, nonintermediated flows. (In Chapter 3, I will show subsectors of families, namely, the poor and nonpoor, and the aged and nonaged.) One could, of course, design the system to have a different number of sectors. For example, one could show a separate sector for employers (who handle many of the SCI funds) and separate sectors for the federal, state, and local governments.

Most social accounting schemes, including the one I set forth here, use a 1-year accounting period and data problems tend to close off the possibility of using a longer period. The short accounting period tends to bias any view of how much transfer net of contributions really goes on, since the definition of a transfer is a receipt for which no reciprocal payment is made *in the current period.* In reality, people tend to make SCI contributions in years other than those in which they receive benefits. Moreover, it is sometimes difficult to know in what year the benefit is actually realized. Therefore, it would be desirable to use a lifetime income accounting period (Nicholson, 1970; Moss, 1978). Consider the case of tax deferral on a private pension. The amount of net transfer is not knowable until the pension is fully paid out. For another example, one may see social insurance contributors as accumulating social security wealth (i.e., the discounted value of future benefits), at the same time that they are making contributions to the fund (M. Feldstein, 1976). A similar problem arises in the case of health insurance. When is the benefit realized? Is it before or at the time of the receipt of health care services?

The issue of timing is also important with respect to education subsidies. The student beneficiaries are aware that they are making an investment of personal time and effort which is matched in some proportion by governments or private philanthropies. The students are also aware that they will pay back part or all of the public subsidy to the cost of their instruction in the form of tax payments to cover the subsidy for the next generation of students. This suggests that in the long run the net transfer is only to those who do not live long enough or do not earn enough to repay the subsidy. On the other hand, one can see the redistribution in the light of the counterfactual of education in a regime of pure exchange. In such a situation, some students would not go to school simply because they do not own and cannot borrow—given the nature of the capital market—the amount now subsidized. Against this counterfactual, we can say that the greatest gainers are those who would not have gone to school but now do. The investment character of education suggests that outlays for it should be treated as a capital transfer. To do this, the accounts for each sector should be divided into current and capital accounts (Seers & Jolly, 1966; Kendrick, 1972, pp. 128–130). The personal sector's capital account would then show a credit of transfer of capital from government and a debit of accumulation through capital transfer of education. The current account of the personal sector would enter human capital consumption as a deduction from income. Until the substantial revision of national income accounts referred to above is accomplished, there is no option open to us but to carry education along with other transfers in kind as income to the beneficiaries in the year the service is delivered.

The concept of flows of secondary income commits us to double-entry bookkeeping in which total SCI benefits received by families are equal to total SCI taxes and contributions paid by all families. Throughout this book I force an equality between the total of SCI benefits and administrative costs paid out in a year and the SCI taxes and contributions paid in that year. That is, I assume that intermediaries are not accumulating reserves, drawing on reserves, or borrowing. This is not, of course, in strict accord with reality, and can only be justified as a way to simplify the discussion.

I make other simplifying assumptions. Taxes, which are negative transfers from the standpoint of taxpayers, may have their point of impact on the business firm, but I assume that their point of incidence is on the stockholder, the wage earner, or the consumer (all in the family sector). Similarly, I assume that employer contributions to pension funds and health insurance plans are diversions from wages that would otherwise be paid directly to workers. It is consistent with these assumptions that I do not show an employer sector. Also, for the purpose of simplification I do not show any SCI flows between intermediaries. Thus, I do not show payments made by governments to philanthropic organizations, but simply record such payments as flows through the government sector to families

A social accountant should be guided by the uses to be made of the accounts. As I indicated at the outset, this study is motivated by the desire to place the debate over public programs in the broader context of all SCI flows. To do this I want to spread the net widely enough to catch all the flows of SCI that are substitutes for one another at different times and places. In the first instance, this should make it possible to compare the present flows of secondary consumer income in the United States with those that occurred in an earlier time with a somewhat different institutional structure—i.e., when extended family ties were stronger and before group insurance was well developed. Second, it facilitates comparisons of this country with other countries that have modern mixed economies but have different emphasis on the use of the several intermediaries for SCI.[2] It might be that one nation has a higher ratio than another of public social welfare expenditures to GNP, but simultaneously has a lower ratio of SCI to GNP. This could be the case if the first nation has few SCI flows through philanthropic organizations, private pension funds, and insurance companies; and little direct interfamily giving.

Public SCI Benefits

The greater part of SCI benefits are listed in the Social Security Administration's (SSA) compilation of "social welfare expenditures under public programs." Such expenditures are defined as those for cash and services, and administrative costs[3] for all programs operating under public law that are of direct benefit to individuals and families. Included are expenditures for programs providing income maintenance and health benefits through social insurance and public aid, and those providing public support of health, education, housing, and other welfare services. The public expenditures for services are netted of all fees and charges paid by users of the services. The total of such expenditures was $394.4 billion in 1978. I incorporate all of those social welfare expenditures in my list of SCI benefits, with one exception, namely, $4.4 billion for health and education research, which is not allocable to individual beneficiaries. This adjusted amount of $390 billion makes up the larger part of the total of government-mediated SCI shown in Table 2.1.

Should some tax expenditures (or tax savings) associated with the

---

[2]Comparison with nonmarket, socialist economies is difficult. In such an economy, where firms are part of the government, the distinction between a primary and a secondary distribution of income is hard to discover, as is the distinction between a tax and a price, or that between a wage and a subsidy.

[3]Administrative costs are discussed in Chapter 5.

federal individual income tax be added to the list of public SCI benefits?[4] A tax expenditure is a deviation from an idealized income tax, a deviation which introduces a horizontal inequity. This rather slippery concept is expressed by the provisions of the tax law that forgive or reduce tax liabilities for certain categories of people or for people who behave in a certain way. (For a listing of tax expenditures, see the Special Analysis attached to each federal budget since 1976.) It seems clear that Congress can aid a certain family either by paying them a direct subsidy or by reducing their income tax liability by an equivalent amount. This insight, which led to the invention of the negative income tax, points to the idea that tax subsidies fit our definition of SCI benefits as "public social welfare expenditures and alternatives to them." However, before rushing in to add all tax expenditures as SCI benefits, several points must be considered. The first point is that some tax expenditures relate to producer activity rather than consumer activity. The second is that, from a certain point of view, it is a matter of indifference whether one lists tax expenditures as benefits on the income side of the double-entry accounts or as negative taxes on the payment side. A third point is the need to avoid double-counting as SCI both the private benefits induced by certain features of the tax law (for example, private pension benefits) and the tax savings themselves. Indeed, part of the rationale for including some of the private benefits is that they carry a tax subsidy.

The first point suggests that we confine attention to those exclusions, exemptions, deductions, and credits in the tax law which help families to meet the costs of retirement, support of children, education, housing, health care, and other services. The second point urges that most of the consumer tax savings be accounted for on the payments side of the account and as affecting the distribution of the tax burden associated with SCI benefits. The third point indicates that we particularly avoid listing those tax savings on the benefit side of the SCI account that are entangled with existing private benefits. All of this leads to the inclusion of only a few tax savings as SCI benefits. They are tax savings which could be converted into direct government outlays for SCI purposes. In fact, in some nations they have been thus converted. Hence, international comparisons are facilitated by showing them here as benefits. For example, the personal exemptions for children could be convert-

---

[4]State income taxes also have what can be called tax expenditures. Some feature homestead tax credits or "circuit breakers" for property tax relief. These are not taken into account here.

ed into a child allowance paid out of appropriated funds. Similarly, the earned income credit could be converted into a family earnings supplement, and the homeowner tax preference could be reformulated as a housing allowance. The items which I select for inclusion in the list of benefits by type, and their values in 1978, are presented in Table 2.3.

If these tax savings were converted to direct outlays, the budgeted outlays by government would rise and the tax receipts recorded would rise by the same amount. Hence, we force the tax collections up to equal the fictional payment of those benefits. The logic of the statement is illustrated by the case of the earned income credit. At present it is shown as a reduction in tax payable even though some claimants have no tax payable. The entries are made as follows:

Benefit	*Tax*	
	Gross tax payable before credit	$1000
	Earned income credit	−100
	Net tax payable after credit	$900

If this credit were converted to an appropriated benefit, the entries would be as follows:

Benefit	*Tax*	
Earned income supplement $100	Gross tax payable before credit	$1000
	Earned income credit	—
	Net tax payable	$1000

In this case it seems quite clear that it would be understating the scale of SCI if we did not add the tax credit to the list of SCI benefits. The same logic is applicable to the exemptions for children, the additional exemptions for aged and blind persons, the credit for the elderly, the deduction of medical expenses (Steuerle & Hoffman, 1979), and the credit for child care and dependent care.

The tax savings granted to homeowner–occupants are a little more complicated. They arise out of the failure to include gross imputed rent in the calculation of household income and the simultaneous allowance of deductions of mortgage interest and property tax paid. If the economic income from homeownership were treated like other proprietary income, the homeowner would report the gross imputed rent and deduct mortgage interest, property tax, depreciation, maintenance, and

TABLE 2.3

Selected Tax Savings, by Type, 1978

Type of savings	Amount of savings (billions of dollars)
Total	33.0
Cash	14.2
Exemptions for children under 18	11.9
Additional exemptions for aged and blind, and credit for elderly	2.2
Earned income tax credit	0.1
Health care	1.9
Deduction of uninsured medical expenses	1.9
Food, housing, and other welfare services	16.9
Exclusion of net imputed rent and deductibility of mortgage interest and property tax on owner-occupied housing	16.3
Credit for child care and dependent care expenditures	0.6

Source: Appendix Table A.7.

other costs of homeownership. The homeowner's tax base would rise by the amount that gross imputed rent exceeded expenses other than interest and taxes. This increase in the tax base would equal the sum of imputed net rent and the deductions now allowed for interest and taxes (Goode, 1976, pp. 117–125). For example, suppose a taxpayer has $10,000 of wage income and $3000 of gross imputed rent and pays $1000 in mortgage interest, $500 in property tax, and $500 in other expenses. The present tax law treats this person as follows in computing the tax base:

$10,000 wage income
  (3,000 gross imputed rent [excluded])
−1,000 interest (deducted)
− 500 property tax (deducted)
  (500 other expenses of ownership [not deducted])
_____
$8,500 tax base

If imputed rent were treated like other proprietary income, then the tax base for this person would be computed as follows:

```
  $10,000 wage income
  +3,000 gross imputed rent
  −1,000 interest
  −  500 property tax
  −  500 other expenses of ownership
  ─────────────────────────────────
  $11,000 tax base
```

Hence, this homeowner's tax base would rise from $8500 to $11,000 and the tax bill would go up by $2500 times the marginal income tax rate. It is rather hard to imagine that Congress would legislate a conversion of this tax expenditure program into a direct cash benefit called a "homeowner's allowance," but if they were to do so it would involve a change in government accounts similar to that shown above for the earned income credit.

Adding the $33 billion in tax savings that are SCI benefits to the $394.4 billion listed by the SSA, and subtracting the $4.4 billion for health and education research (Bixby, 1981, p. 4 & p. 6, note 19) as well as $1.5 billion paid out as Basic Educational Opportunity Grants (see Appendix Table A.3) gives us total public secondary consumer benefits equal to $424.5 billion (see Table 2.1).

There are other tax expenditures which I have elected not to include in the SCI listing even though they are relevant to this study. The first of these is the tax saving of donors arising out of the deductibility of charitable contributions. (This amounted to $5.4 billion in 1978.) The reason for not including it is that I have included all outlays by philanthropic organizations for social welfare transfer purposes, and it would be double-counting to add this tax saving to the list. It would also be double-counting to add the tax saving associated with the parental exemption for children over age 17, since I show all interfamily contributions to such persons. This tax saving amounted to $0.9 billion in 1978.

The wish to avoid double-counting restrains me from listing tax savings associated with SCI benefits already listed. Most SCI contributions are sheltered from the income tax. Thus, state and local taxes that go to pay for education, Medicaid, and other programs are deductible from the federal income tax base of taxpayers. At the same time, most cash and noncash SCI benefits are excluded from the tax base of the recipients. Employer contributions to private pensions, and interest earned by pension funds (about one-third of private pension benefits are paid out of interest earned) are excluded from employee taxable income. However, pension benefits funded by tax-deferred contributions are taxable at the time of receipt. On the other hand, both health insurance contributions by the employer and health insurance benefits funded thereby are excluded from the employee's tax base. These several tax savings not included in SCI in 1978 amounted to $12 billion for pensions, $6 billion for health insurance, and $8 billion for social insurance and public assistance cash benefits (Budget of the U.S. Government, 1978, Special Analysis, Part F). I refer to these in Chapter 3 in reviewing the distribution of the tax burden.

Private SCI Benefits

To the public SCI benefits discussed above, I add $173.4 billion of expenditures via private group insurance or pension funds; philanthropic organizations such as churches, private schools, and charitable foundations; and direct interfamily gifts of cash, food, and housing (see Table 2.1). These benefits are added in recognition of the fact that they are clear alternatives to or substitutes for public SCI benefits.

Under the heading of group insurance I list benefits paid out by organized private pension plans for private employees and by private health insurance plans for private and public employees. The principal data sources for the insurance benefits are publications of private insurance associations. I make use of estimates by private researchers of outlays by philanthropic organizations for noncash benefits. Notably, no cash benefits are recorded for such organizations.

My own rough estimates, which are based on a number of scholarly studies of direct interfamily gifts in cash and in kind are shown in Table 2.4. These totaled $86.1 billion in 1978. Most transfers are made between

TABLE 2.4

Direct Interfamily Gifts, by Type and by Age of Recipient, 1978
(billions of dollars)

Characteristics of recipients	Cash	Food and housing	Total
Total	68.9	17.2	86.1
Children enrolled in postsecondary school and not at home	7.5	2.8	10.3
Other nonaged	47.5	12.9	60.4
Aged (65+)	13.9	1.5	15.4

Source: Appendix Table A.6.

relatives or between divorced spouses. Some are to adult children 18 years of age and over. Others are to aged parents who may be sharing housing with their adult children. Casual transfers such as birthday gifts, dinner parties, and other erratic and occasional gifts are ignored in these estimates.

I note one special difficulty with respect to the division between public and private benefits. Private health insurance benefits include benefits for public employees, whereas private pensions do not include pension benefits to public employees. The logic of this is that health insurance benefits are mediated by private insurance companies, but employer pension benefits are mediated by government-administered pension funds. My assumption that employee pensions are paid for by wage diversions—i.e., that current wages would be higher in the absence of such pensions—requires that we distinguish the role of government as employer from government as intermediary for SCI benefits going to persons not employed by government. I do not make any change in the SSA's classification, but I refer to this again in discussing SCI taxes and contributions.

SCI Taxes and Contributions

The SSA supplies us with some information about how public social welfare expenditures are funded. They sort out the expenditures paid for by the federal as opposed to state and local governments. They also separate social insurance taxes from other revenues (see Bixby, 1981, Table 1, pp. 4–6). All of this information is useful; however, I do make some adjustments. I reclassify public employee pension and health care benefits from "tax-financed" to "wage-diversion-financed" for the reason indicated above. The total of taxes is forced to exactly equal the total of all public benefits paid out, including the $33.0 billion of tax expenditures, less those assumed to be paid for by public employees via wage diversion. The SSA gives us the number for social insurance payroll taxes. I then supply my own estimates of how the residual of taxes is divided among other federal taxes, state taxes, and local property taxes (Appendix Tables A.9 & A.10). These estimates are based on information about how specific benefits for income maintenance, health, education, and other goods and services are funded by level of government. For example, we know that the local property tax pays for 44% of the cost of public elementary and secondary education; state funds provide 47%, and federal funds the remainder.

A similar procedure is followed with respect to private programs (i.e., an equality is forced between private contributions and the totals of private benefits paid out). In other words, I make the unrealistic assumption that private pension and health care benefits paid out in the year are equalled by the wage diversions by covered employees in that year, and philanthropic benefits paid out are matched by family contributions in that year. My estimated amounts for each type of tax or contribution are shown in Table 2.2, which indicates that 83% of SCI benefits are paid for by taxes and wage diversions.

In Chapter 3, I offer a judgment as to the pattern of the burden of SCI taxes and contributions by income class and by age group. In making that judgment I take account not only of the shifting and incidence of taxes, but also of those tax expenditures that I discussed earlier but declined to list as SCI benefits in order to avoid double-counting.

SCI Related to Primary Income

The complete set of public and private SCI benefits, along with the taxes and contributions to pay for them, make up the SCI system. How that system may affect the income of a particular family is suggested in Table 2.5, which shows that a family's factor income (item 6) is supplemented by benefits and diminished by taxes and contributions to yield an income after flows of secondary consumer income (item 18). The latter, of course, may be more or less than the family's factor income.

The system of SCI flows (items 7 through 16) traverses part but not all of the territory between primary income and final income (item 20). Item 19 refers to other transfers that are not studied here.

Another way to picture how SCI flows are related to the national economy is by use of circular flow analysis. Let us envision an economy without interfamily flows of SCI. It is a two-sector economy of families and business firms. There is a circular flow of income between the two sectors. Families spend all their income on consumption goods produced by the firms, and business firms spend all their receipts on factor payments to families. Income gives rise to expenditure, which in turn generates income. Money flows, in the form of income and consumption expenditures, are matched by flows of factor services and consumer goods.

Now let us add cash transfers to this imaginary economy. Some families share their factor incomes with other families, who then spend their transfer income on consumption. We can represent this as transfer payment and receipt flowing in and out of an imaginary interfamily fund. Also, some families make cash transfers to philanthropic organiza-

TABLE 2.5

Income of a Representative Family before and after Interfamily Flows of SCI

Receipts for supply of factors
   1. Employee compensation (defined to include employer contributions to pension funds and insurance companies)
   2. Rent (including net imputed rent of homeowner-occupants)
   3. Interest
   4. Dividends and undistributed corporate profits
   5. Self-employment income (including home production)
   6. Income before SCI flows (items 1–5)
Receipt of SCI benefits from
   7. Other families
   8. Philanthropic organizations
   9. Insurance companies and pension funds
  10. Governments
  11. Total receipts of SCI benefits (items 7–10)
SCI taxes and contributions paid to
  12. Other families
  13. Philanthropic organizations
  14. Insurance companies and pension funds (wage diversions for item 1)
  15. Governments (for SCI only)
  16. Total SCI taxes and contributions paid (items 12–15)

Summaries
  17. Net SCI benefits (item 11 less item 16)
  18. Income after SCI flows (item 6 plus item 17)
  19. Net other transfers to and from families (not part of SCI)
  20. Income after SCI flows and after other transfers (item 18 plus item 19)

Note: This table does not reflect the possibility that employers and governments may make contributions to other intermediaries.

tions, which distribute them to other families,[5] and some families make payments to insurance and pension funds, which distribute them to other families. Further, families pay taxes to the government, which distributes the tax proceeds in the form of cash benefits to families. Note that there are no compensating flows of goods and services associated with these cash flows. Factor income and consumption expenditures are unchanged. In accounting terms this means that cash transfers are part of the flow of funds; they do not use resources and are not reflected in the national product account.

Now let us assume that government uses its transfer receipts to make purchases of social welfare goods and distributes them to families.

---

[5]In fact, as I show in Table 2.1, philanthropic organizations do not pay SCI benefits in cash.

(The same analysis applies if nongovernment intermediaries make transfers of goods.) In this case private consumption expenditures are reduced by the amount of SCI taxes, but family income now includes the receipts of the SCI goods. Resources have been reallocated from private consumption goods to SCI goods. If the latter are goods that would have been purchased if families had been given cash transfers, then the reallocation may not be very significant. However, if they are very different from the purchases families would have made, then there will be a significant reallocation. In any event, factor payments and total production are unchanged.

Several important points are communicated by the foregoing discussion. SCI transfers made in total equal the total received. The total of income after transfers equals the total of income before transfers. Cash transfers will not, unless we assume that they affect personal saving, change the total of private consumer expenditure. However, the transfer of goods, as opposed to money, substitutes collective purchase of social welfare goods for individual purchase. These transfers of cash and goods may be simple and direct (i.e., from one family to another), or they may be complex and involve one or more intermediaries. Each sector and each intermediary makes and receives transfers. Hence, transfers may be designated as positive or negative. From the standpoint of the family sector, a tax is a negative transfer; and a contribution received by a philanthropic organization is a positive transfer.

Following these insights, Table 2.6 shows contributions flowing out from the nuclear families (column 1). Note that these contributions are by definition limited to those destined for SCI benefits. For example, the only taxes entered at line 4 are those to pay for social welfare expenditures under public programs (SSA definition). For another example, the benefits to families from insurance and pension funds (line 7) include only those payments identified above as private SCI benefits.

Figure 2.2 shows how SCI flows may move from a set of three families through our four intermediaries and back to the same set of three families.

More on Distinguishing SCI Flows from Other Transfers and from Exchange[6]

In the first section of this chapter I discussed the relationship between SCI flows and the broad range of transfers. I stated that SCI

---

[6]The reader may skip the remainder of this chapter without loss of continuity.

TABLE 2.6
SCI Flows (Positive and Negative) by Sector

Transfer item	Nuclear families (1)	Interfamily transfer fund (2)	Philanthropic organizations (3)	Insurance and pension funds (4)	Government (5)
Nuclear families					
1. Contributions to interfamily transfer fund	−	+			
2. Contributions to philanthropic organizations	−		+		
3. Contributions to insurance and pensions	−			+	
4. SCI taxes paid	−				+
Interfamily fund					
5. Benefits to families	+	−			
Philanthropic organizations					
6. Benefits to families	+		−		
Insurance and pension funds					
7. Benefits to families	+			−	
Government					
8. Benefits to families	+				−
Balancing					
9. Receipt of SCI benefits less payment of SCI contributions and less taxes		0			

More on Distinguishing SCI Flows 33

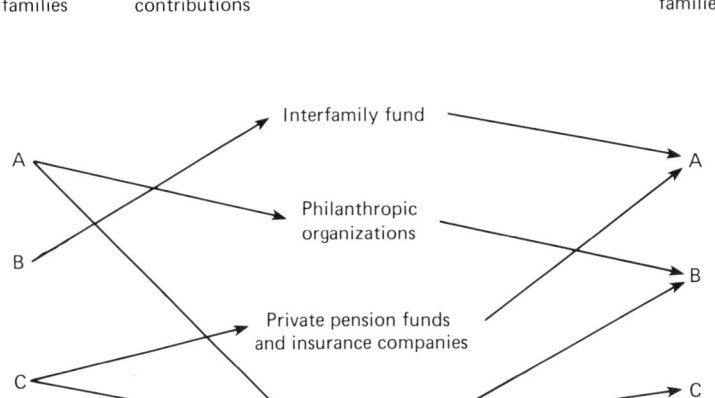

FIGURE 2.2 Secondary consumer income flows among three families via four intermediaries.

transfers are selected out of all transfers for the purpose of clarifying the policy debate about the size and scope of public social welfare expenditure. The selection is admittedly a matter of judgment, as is the definition of the term transfer (see Figure 2.1).

Some readers might prefer to discuss public social welfare expenditures in a broader context of welfare state policies, including those designed to change the primary distribution of income, such as public service employment, employee ownership of business, employee codetermination of business policy, tariff and quota protection of domestic industry, regulation of business location, regulation of minimum wages and occupational wage differentials, licensure and other restrictions on entry into various occupations, antidiscrimination policies with respect to employment, and antitrust policies with respect to business.

It is true that these policies and others do involve explicit or implicit transfers, but I have excluded discussion of them from this book. Some readers, no doubt, look favorably on some or all of these policies. Others are predisposed to oppose many of them on the grounds that they represent steps away from the ideal of a fully competitive economy and give rise to illegitimate or monopoly rents, which are sometimes equated with the term transfer. This predisposition leads to the classification by some commentators of the income of suppliers of goods and services to governments (e.g., defense contractors) as rent or transfer (Buchanan, Tollison & Tullock, 1981). Still others contrast the existing primary distribution with the counterfactual of a socialized economy and classify all property income going to private owners as transfers or unearned income. Many nonsocialist writers classify property income going to passive, nonmanagerial owners as transfers on the grounds that current changes in the output of a corporation often are not related to current changes in the amount of land and capital goods employed nor to changes in the level of interest and dividends paid out. Capital gains and losses are generally treated by social accountants as transfers either of income or wealth (Budd, Radner, & Whitehead, in press; Eisner, in press).

Social accounting texts provide us with the other interesting examples of what may be regarded as transfers on the supply side (Yanovsky, 1965; Ruggles & Ruggles, 1970; Kendrick, 1972). An employer may pay a beginning worker a wage in excess of his or her current product, and at the same time impart valuable training to that employee. Employees may make transfers to a business firm by working for less than current product. Workers make a transfer to the business sector by bearing the opportunity cost of being frictionally unemployed and thereby contributing to the overall efficiency of the economy. Similarly, families make a transfer to business by meeting the costs of rearing children to working age.

So, I anticipate that readers of several predispositions will be disappointed in the narrow slice of transfers selected for discussion and the emphasis on secondary consumer income as opposed to secondary producer income. Even readers who are content to consider separately the consumer side of the transfer field may complain that I have left out many such transfers. Theft, which is a form of transfer, is excluded, as are gambling winnings and losses. Other examples of secondary consumer income not discussed in this book are the following. A physician may charge some clients less than the going rate for his or her services, with the difference being a transfer. A public utility may collect less than cost from some of its customers. A business provides households, via its advertising budget, free radio and television programming on commercial stations. A business makes available the services of executives, while they are on the company payroll, to a philanthropic agency.

The borderline between public social welfare expenditures and other public expenditures is also, as I noted earlier, rather arbitrary. We are at that borderline when we confront the distinction between a government job created for a hard-to-employ person (now excluded from the public expenditures for social welfare on the grounds that work is exchanged for the benefit) and a government training program (now included).

Another interesting borderline case has to do with private nongroup insurance for annuities and health care. From one point of view, pure insurance, purged of savings, is a simple purchase of financial service, namely, 1 year's worth of protection against a defined risk. The transaction is completed in the year of purchase and any payment received should be ignored in the income accounts. From another point of view, however, such insurance can be viewed as a mechanism for transfer among families. In any year, some families pay premiums in excess of benefits received and others receive benefits in excess of premiums. We can assume that private nongroup insurance observes the principle of insurance that requires each risk class to pay its combined costs and hence that there is redistribution or transfer only within risk classes. (In some private group insurance and in most social insurance, such insurance equity is not observed and there is redistribution across risk classes.) Benefits paid out by private, nongroup insurance against death or disability of a family breadwinner and health care cost amounted to about $9 billion in 1978. I decided not to include those benefits in my SCI list, but it was a borderline decision. I include social insurance and group private insurance, but exclude nongroup private insurance.

These examples suggest that transfer is omnipresent. It pervades the private sector as well as the public sector of the economy. It enters into the primary distribution of income as well as the secondary distribution. I have elected to exclude most transfers from the interfamily flow of SCI. The SCI system is thus only part of a much broader system of public and private transfers. The latter system coexists with a system of exchange. The two systems interact in determining answers to the leading questions that face every economy, namely what is to be produced, how will it be produced, who will get the product, and what will be the level of productive activity.

It can be argued that social insurance benefits are not transfers but are, rather, a part of an exchange transaction. The argument is in two parts: (1) Is the employer making a transfer? and (2) Are certain employees making transfers to other employees? My answer to the first question is, probably not; and the answer to the second is, probably yes. But let us review the argument. What courts and legislators have done in developing social insurance, it is argued, is to revise the labor contract. This revision states that any contract must contain the implicit clause that the employers will pay for certain periods of nonwork. The employers must think of employee compensation in two parts, one being the wage for work performed and the other being insurance to provide income when certain events prevent the employee from working. The employers are free to pay the same amount of total compensation under the two-part arrangement that they paid in wages alone under the prior unrevised contract.

According to this line of thought, social insurance is part of the primary distribution and, hence, not a transfer from employers. Employers calculate the insurance charge as part of their labor cost. The employees consider the probabilistic insurance benefit as part of their compensation for work. The revised labor contract is a version of a lifetime contract of the kind that prevailed in precapitalist Europe and that is found in contemporary Japan. Most labor contracts envision frequent departures from the equating of wages and current marginal product, with payment for periods of training, vacation, and declining productivity after a certain age, but with variations up and down netting out to a close relationship between total compensation and worker contribution to production over the lifetime. Perhaps the only contract in which compensation is free of such deviations from marginal product is that of the piece-rate worker whose tenure is momentary—the potato picker who is hired for the day and paid at the end of each row, for example.

In support of the argument that social insurance is part of the exchange process, one should note that contracts are shaped by law in a number of other ways. A contract is, by definition, an agreement that is enforceable by law. To be enforceable, agreements must conform to such standards as limits on specific performance, which protect against involuntary servitude, safety standards, and protection of minors. In this sense, we have never had full freedom of contract.

However, a labor contract that promises payment for nonwork cannot be said to be free of transfer. Transfer is defined as a one-way transaction in which one party is made better off by an uncompensated or sacrificial effort by another. One can add precision to that definition by limiting the time period for observation to, for instance, 1 year. Many, if not most, labor contracts have some element of transfer in them, if not from employer to employee, then from employee to employee.

One other point should be made in discussing the revision of the labor contract occasioned by insurance to provide income during periods of nonwork. I mentioned above that the employer is free to pay the same amount of total compensation under the two-part arrangement as was paid in wages alone under the prior nonrevised contract. If, in fact, total compensation did not rise, we could say that the incidence of the change of contract was borne by employees. Hence, it is misleading to refer to employers as the donors, and better to think of them as the intermediaries in a scheme that diverts funds from all employees to those few who suffer disability or unemployment. The law or a collective bargaining agreement may determine who will play the role of intermediary, but economic factors will determine who is the donor.

The Representation of Transfers in National Income and Products Accounts

The system of SCI flows that I have sketched out does not match the representation of transfers in the national accounts. The national income and product accounts, and the sectoral income and outlay accounts that appear in the *Economic Report of the President,* and the *Survey of Current Business,* do not display a full picture of the role that transfers play in the economy. The statement of national product, of course, shows no trace of transfers; it shows only the purchase of final product by sectors. One can loosely translate that purchasing as consumption by households, investment by business, and public use by government. The parallel national income account, however, does reveal certain transfers as an important component of charges against the GNP. Those transfer items that involve the business sector as a payer or receiver include the following nonfactor charges: indirect business taxes, subsidies to business, current losses by government enterprises, and business transfer payments to households (which comprise write-offs of consumer bad debts and contributions to philanthropic organizations). Business transfers also are shown in three factor-cost items: corporate profit taxes, employer contributions for social insurance, and similar contributions for private insurances. The latter two are carried under the heading of "other labor income" or "supplements to wages and salaries."

To find other transfer items one must look to secondary flows recorded in the sectoral accounts, but not in the U.S. national income and product account. These are nonbusiness items and include personal tax and nontax payments, personal contributions for social insurance (but not those for private insurance), and government transfer payments to persons via social insurance and public assistance. Pensions and health insurance benefits paid to persons by private intermediaries do not appear. Net interest paid by government and interest paid by consumers are shown. Net interest paid by government is considered a transfer, since it is largely a payment for services on a debt incurred in the past and hence has no counterpart in current product. Consumer interest is justified as other than primary income because no imputation to product is made by accountants for the services of lenders. Both of these items seem to defy the ordinary definition of transfer, since the recipients have supplied a reciprocal service in the current period.

My SCI accounts include some of the tax and government transfer payment items found in the national income account. They also include some items not found in that account, namely, direct interfamily transfers, certain private insurance transfers, and certain government transfers in kind. Further, I break down the household account to show an imaginary interfamily transfer fund sector, an insurance and pension fund sector, and a philanthropic organizations sector.

The national accounts classify certain items I have identified as SCI items—government-purchased education and health care are examples—as purchases rather than as transfers. I discussed earlier the rationale for including some but not all government purchases in the SCI list of benefits. In other cases, certain SCI items are classified in the national income accounts as factor income. This is true of employer contributions to social insurance and private group insurance plans, which are classified as "other labor income." This is not inconsistent with my view that the employer is diverting part of the employee's wages to an intermediary for transfer purposes. However, the sector accounts are not symmetrical in their treatment of social insurance and private insurance. Government transfers to persons are shown; private transfers are not. Personal contributions to social insurance are recorded; those to private insurance are not. Benefits received from social insurance are recorded; those from private insurance are not. In this book I show the employer contribution along with the employee contribution to both social and private group insurance as diversion of wages to a transfer intermediary and I show benefits received from both social and private group insurance as SCI benefits. The case for this symmetrical treatment is supported by the fact that most group insurance is governed by benefit formulas that deny a close association between benefit and contribution, that is, they are redistributive among covered workers. In certain cases, however, as in defined-contribution pensions payable in a lump sum, the benefits amount to a return of principal plus interest, and the only transfer is the tax saving due to income tax deferral.

A Guide to Reading

Those readers who are intrigued by social accounting issues raised in this chapter are encouraged to investigate Merriam and Skolnik, *Social welfare expenditures under public programs in the U.S., 1929–66* (1968);

Moon (ed.), *Social accounting for transfers* (in press); Morgan, David, Brazer, and Cohen, *Income and welfare in the U.S.* (1962); and U.S. Treasury, *Report of the commission on private philanthropy and public needs* (1977a) (a six-volume collection of papers known as the *Filer report*).

Much of the current interest of economists in transfers, gifts, and grants may have been sparked by the conference sponsored by the National Bureau of Economic Research, which gave rise to a volume edited by Dickinson in 1962. Other writings along these lines include Boulding, *The economy of love and fear* (1973); Collard, *Altruism and economy* (1978); Ireland and Johnson, *The economics of charity* (1970); Macauley and Berkowitz (eds.), *Altruism and helping behavior* (1970) (by social psychologists); Matthews and Stafford, *The grants economy and collective consumption* (1982); and Phelps, *Altruism, morality, and economic theory* (1975).

CHAPTER 3

Who Receives Secondary Consumer Income and Who Pays for It?

The previous chapter sketched out the broad outlines of secondary consumer income flows. The benefits and contributions are partly public and partly private, partly compulsory and partly voluntary. About half are in cash and about half are in kind. Some of the transfers are made directly from one nuclear family to another, but most pass through a philanthropic organization, a pension fund, an insurance company, or a government agency. The broad types of the private as well as public SCI benefits are cash on one hand and the subsidy of education, health care, food, housing, and other welfare services on the other. These benefits are paid for by taxes, wage diversions, contributions to philanthropies, and direct interfamily contributions.

This chapter continues the description of the SCI system as it existed in 1978. It responds to four questions: (1) Who gets the cash benefits? (2) Who receives subsidized goods and services? (3) What part of each type of benefits go to the poor? and (4) Who pays for the SCI benefits? Necessarily, my answers are rough and incomplete. They assume a 1-year income period. However, Chapter 4 offers some speculations of how the answers might differ if a longer income period were assumed.

Who Gets the Cash Benefits and What Percentage of Income Loss Is Replaced?

Retired persons receive about one-half of all cash benefits (see Table 3.1). Most of the remaining one-half goes to disabled persons, families with children present that have lost a breadwinner, and to unemployed persons. Relatively small amounts are received by intact families with children present.

The most frequently received of the cash benefits is the tax saving associated with the exemption for children under 18, which is the American substitute for a child allowance. This benefit reached 34.2 million taxpayers for 71 million children (see Table 3.1). Other benefits that were received by large numbers of people were Old Age Insurance (OAI) benefits, received by 21.0 million; tax savings for the aged and blind, received by 12.7 million; and Aid to Families with Dependent Children (AFDC), received by 10.6 million mothers and children. Table 3.1 does not provide an exact count of the number of people who received cash SCI benefits because some of the people listed undoubtedly received more than one cash benefit. However, close inspection of the table suggests that close to half of the population must have received at least one cash benefit in 1977, with at least 25 million getting a retirement benefit, at least 5 million getting a disability benefit, at least 11 million getting a benefit for loss of family breadwinner, at least 4 million getting an unemployment benefit (see lines 26–28, Table 3.1), and 37 million getting one of the other benefits. These groups tend to be mutually exclusive.

In 1978, 42% of all households received a cash transfer from 1 or more of 10 government programs (Danziger & Plotnick, in press). Let me underscore this fact. Almost half of all households received a cash benefit from at least 1 of the 10 selected government transfer programs. Among households headed by a person 65 or older, 96% received such a transfer in that year. The reader should note that these data are for households while some data in the preceding paragraph are for persons.

Most cash benefits are designed to replace income lost for reasons presumed to be beyond the control of individuals. (This concept is discussed in Chapter 4). People get old and cannot work, they get disabled or die prematurely, they suffer involuntary unemployment. The amount of income loss that is offset depends on the provisions of particular programs with respect to coverage, eligibility for benefits, and the formula for reckoning the actual benefit. Social insurance, for example, may extend coverage to employees in either many or only a few industries; eligibility can depend on a short or a long period in covered employment; and benefits for eligible workers can be either closely or loosely related to the contributions made by those workers.

The American system for offsetting income loss features programs of social insurance, public assistance, private group insurance managed by employers, and direct interfamily transfer. In some cases, decisions are made and carried out by the federal government; in other cases, the key features are settled by state or local governments with or without matching payments by the federal government. At the same time, indi-

TABLE 3.1

SCI Cash Benefits and Number of Recipients, Grouped by Risk, 1978

Type of benefit	Amount of benefit (billions of dollars)	Number of recipients[a] (millions)
1. Total	301.7	—
2. Retirement	157.7	—
3. Old Age Insurance	58.7	21.0
4. Survivors' Insurance (aged only)	13.3	4.6
5. Supplemental Security Income (aged)	2.6	2.0
6. Public employee retirement	29.9	3.9
7. Railroad Retirement	4.0	0.6
8. Veterans' pensions	1.7	3.8
9. Additional income tax exemptions for aged and blind, and credit for elderly (tax savings)	2.2	—
10. Exemption for aged	—	10.5
11. Exemption for blind	—	2.2
12. Credit for elderly	—	0.8[b]
13. Private pensions[c]	31.4	9.1[d]
14. Interfamily (aged)[c]	13.9	n.a.
15. Disability	32.4	—
16. Disability insurance	12.8	4.9
17. Supplemental Security Income (blind and disabled)	4.6	2.2
18. State and railroad temporary disability insurance	1.1	0.2
19. Workers' compensation	5.9	1.3
20. Veterans' compensation	8.0	3.3
21. Loss of family breadwinner	20.5	—
22. Survivors' Insurance (children present)	7.4	2.9
23. Aid to Families with Dependent Children	12.5	10.6
24. Veterans' life insurance	0.6	5.0[e]
25. Unemployment	24.1	—
26. Unemployment Insurance and Employment Service[f]	12.7	2.0[g]
27. General Assistance	1.5	0.8
28. Other public aid[h]	9.9[i]	2.5

vidual employers and unions have considerable latitude concerning the type of private benefit plans they will carry out. And, of course, interfamily transfers, while mandated in such cases as divorce and separa-

Who Gets the Cash Benefits? 43

TABLE 3.1 (Continued)

Type of benefit	Amount of benefit (billions of dollars)	Number of recipients[a] (millions)
29. Other	67.0	—
30. Exemptions for children under 18 (tax savings)	11.9	34.2[b]
31. Earned income tax credit (tax savings)	0.1	5.0[b]
32. Interfamily (nonaged)[i]	55.0	n.a.

Sources: Benefits are from Appendix Table A.1. Number of recipients are from the following sources: Lines 3, 4, 16, and 22 are from Board of Trustees, Federal OASDI Trust Funds (1982), pp. 84–85. Lines 5, 6, 7, 15, 17–20, 23, and 26–27 are from *Social Security Bulletin, Annual Statistical Supplement* (1980), Tables 13, 150, 174–177. Line 8, federal total of 3.2 million (1.0 million receiving veterans' compensation and 2.2 million receiving veterans' pensions) is from the *Budget of the United States Government, Appendix* (1980), pp. 795–797, and state total of 0.6 million compiled from Institute for Socioeconomic Studies (1978b) by adding totals for all states shown in the book. Lines 10–12, 30, and 31 are from U.S. Department of the Treasury, *Statistics of Income* (1978), p. 125. Line 13 is from Munnell (1982). Line 21 is from Institute for Socioeconomic Studies (1978a), pp. 20, 122. Lines 24 and 28 are from Institute for Socioeconomic Studies (1978b).

Note: Dash = number cannot be calculated; n.a. = data not available.
[a]Monthly unless otherwise indicated.
[b]Number of tax returns.
[c]Includes benefits for disability, loss of breadwinner, and unemployment.
[d]Annual.
[e]Number of persons covered.
[f]Includes Railroad Unemployment Insurance.
[g]Weekly.
[h]Work relief, other emergency aid, surplus food for the needy, repatriate and refugee assistance, temporary and emergency assistance, and work experience training programs under the Economic Opportunity Act and Comprehensive Employment Training Act.
[i]Includes items mentioned in footnote c plus support for college students. The latter amounted to $7.5 billion.

tion, are generally voluntary and related to the availability of other transfers from government or employer programs.

These decisions by numerous actors have resulted in an uneven pattern of benefits. Some income losses suffered by some groups are more completely offset than others, and losses of some people are not offset at all. Income loss associated with old age and retirement is without doubt more completely offset than any other income loss. This has been accomplished by extending coverage to virtually all workers. In 1978, about 90% of all workers were covered by OAI in social security, and most of the remaining 10% were covered by government employee

TABLE 3.2

Social Security Benefits for a Worker Retiring at Age 65 in 1978

Prior year's earnings ($)	Amount of benefit (per year in $)		Benefits as a percentage of prior year's earnings	
	Single worker	Worker with spouse	Single worker	Worker with spouse
Low: 4600	2880	4320	63	94
Average: 9779	4595	6893	47	70
High: 16,500	5727	8591	35	52

Source: Advisory Council on Social Security (1978), p. 3.

or private pension plans. OAI makes eligibility for a retirement benefit at age 65 dependent upon a modest record of covered employment (40 quarters for permanent eligibility) and a benefit formula that is designed to replace about half of lost earnings for a person who has worked steadily until age 65 at the average wage. The formula also has a tilt in it that yields higher replacement rates for those with lower than median wages, and lower replacement rates for those with above median wages (Leimer, 1979; Schulz, Leavitt, & Kelly, 1979; A. Fox, 1982). The picture is further complicated by the existence of dependent benefits in OAI for spouses and others (see Table 3.2).

The variation in OAI replacement rates should be seen in relationship to Supplemental Security Income (SSI) and private pensions. At present, about 10% of aged persons draw an SSI pension that is related not to wages earned but to a means-tested version of need. Veterans' pensions are also available on the basis of need. On the other hand, another 25% of the aged draw, in addition to OAI benefits, a benefit from a public or private employee pension. This combination produces a replacement for many higher-wage workers of 50% or more. The pattern of replacement rates means that something close to one-half of the aggregate income loss of all persons due to retirement is being offset by the three-part approach to retirement security.

By way of contrast, less than one-fourth of the total income loss due to unemployment is presently offset. The eligibility for and the benefit levels of unemployment insurance (UI) are set by the several states, but on average about 70% of workers are in covered employment. However, eligibility is restricted to those with a certain pattern of recent and covered employment. The incidence of unemployment is higher among those who are not eligible for UI. Hence, only 40% of those counted as unemployed are eligible. The benefit formula tends to pay a typical worker about 50% of wages for a maximum of 26 weeks. In this case, as with OAI, the nontaxability of benefits means that the replacement rate is higher if calculated against disposable rather than pretax income. This is offset, however, by the fact that unemployed workers may lose, in addition to their wages, valuable fringe benefits, such as private health insurance, which are not counted as income. (So may OASDI beneficiaries.)

The aggregate income loss due to disability is probably the least offset of the several types of loss. Since 1955, the disability provisions of OASDI have paid benefits to covered workers who suffer a permanent and total disability. These benefits are calculated on a sliding scale like that used for OAI. SSI again pays a needs-based benefit for disabled persons, including nonworkers. However, there is no federal insurance program for permanent and partial disability nor for temporary disability. Four states do pay benefits for the latter risk since it relates to nonoccupational illness or injury, and all states do pay income-loss benefits under workers' compensation programs.

The loss of income due to premature death of a family breadwinner or due to family separation or divorce is offset by survivors' insurance in OASDI and/or by AFDC. The former pays benefits to surviving spouses with minor children or spouses aged 60 or older. AFDC provides means-tested benefits to mothers with dependent children. In recent decades, the eligibility conditions have eased so that about 75% of female-headed families with children are now eligible for AFDC. At the same time, state legislatures have set per capita benefit levels for this program well below those of SSI. Participation (or take-up) rates of those eligible for benefits have risen substantially, but are thought to be less than those for the social insurance programs. These relatively low rates are generally explained by lack of information or by low benefits for those near the break-even level of income or by the stigma associated with the receipt of public assistance.

Who Receives Subsidized Goods and Services?

While 50.5% of SCI benefits are in the form of cash, the remaining 49.5% goes to helping people buy certain goods or services that are considered to merit subsidy. These include education, health care, and a disparate array of other goods and services, which range from housing and food to family counseling, child day care, legal assistance, and job training. In 1978, about 19% of all SCI benefits went to education, 20% went to health care, and only 10% went for other goods and services (Table 4.4).

In 1978 59.2 million students—over one-fourth of the total population—were enrolled in all levels of instruction from kindergarten through higher education (see Table 3.3). The total cost of instruction was 6.0% of GNP, about 90% of which was financed out of SCI funds. The remainder was paid by students and their parents in the form of tuition and fees. Virtually every child under age 14 was in a public or private school; 94% of those aged 14–17 were in school, and 39% of those aged 18–24 were in school. Eleven percent of elementary and secondary students and 24% of students in higher education attended private schools.

Some students in higher education receive not only subsidized tuition but also a cash benefit designed to cover part of their living costs while in school. Veterans' education benefits and Basic Educational Opportunity Grants (now called Pell grants) paid stipends to several million students (see Table 3.3). Further, many students received benefits in

TABLE 3.3

SCI for Education, by Funding Source, Level of Instruction, Number of Students, 1978

Funding source and level of instruction	Amount of benefit (billions of dollars)	Number of students (millions)
1. Total	113.2	59.2
2. Government (lines 3–7)	106.1	51.6[a]
3. Elementary and secondary	73.2	42.8
4. Higher	21.9	7.7
5. Vocational and adult	6.1	1.1
6. Veterans' education benefits	3.4	2.3
7. Basic Education Opportunity Grants	1.5	2.0
8. Philanthropy (lines 9 + 10)	7.1	7.6
9. Elementary and secondary	2.6	5.1
10. Higher	4.5	2.5

Sources: For benefit totals, see Appendix Tables A.3 and A.5. Figures for the number of students, lines 3–5, 9, and 10, are from Digest of Educational Statistics (1980). Line 6 is from the *Budget of the U.S. Government, Appendix* (1980), p. 799. Line 7 is from Institute for Socioeconomic Studies (1978a), p. 174.

[a] Does not include lines 6 and 7 because they are already counted.

terms of a lower than market rate of interest on Guaranteed Student Loans and National Defense Student Loans. The volume of such loans was $2.7 billion in 1978 (Hauptman, 1982). I have not included such interest subsidies in any of the SCI tables. In 1978 social security survivors' benefits provided a kind of scholarship to students up to age 22. (This benefit, which was phased out after 1981, is included in cash benefits in Table 3.1.) Cash scholarships from philanthropic organizations are shown in Table 3.3 under the heading of philanthropy. Interfamily gifts to students are shown in Table 2.4 as worth $10.3 billion.

Public and private SCI funds pay 64% of the nation's bill for health care (compare Tables 3.4 & 3.6). The benefits for health care and the number of recipients of these benefits are presented in Table 3.4. The remaining 36% is purchased "out-of-pocket" by consumers. A larger proportion of health care than of education is purchased directly by the consumer. Over three-fourths of all Americans have some coverage under private or social health insurance (see Table 3.5). That insurance has emphasized payment for care in the hospital, but has been slow to extend coverage for out-of-hospital expense. Yet, as can be seen from Table 3.6, the amount spent on hospital care is less than half of the amount spent on personal health care. Similarly, many employees can claim reimbursement via workers' compensation for medical expenses related to an industrial accident, but not for an accident unrelated to work. Some people have multiple coverage for a particular medical expense; some have no coverage at all. Some insurance programs set maximum payments. Unemployment often occasions the loss of private health insurance. The nonsystematic nature of the public and private transfer arrangements leads to rather strange patterns of out-of-pocket expenditures for health care across income, occupational, and age classes. This is, of course, one of the reasons why there is considerable support for the adoption of a single, overarching national health insurance plan.

Health care benefits may be thought of in two ways. One is in terms of insurance protection. The other is in terms of health care actually consumed in the year. Utilization of health care varies by age and sex, as illustrated in Tables 3.7 and 3.8.

The amount of hospital care used by the aged far exceeded their proportion in the U.S. population. Those 65 and over, 10.7% of the population in 1978, used 29.7% of the hospital days provided in that year (see Table 3.8). The group aged 45–64 also used proportionally more than their share. Though only 20.3% of the population, they used 30.3% of the hospital days in 1978. The young, on the other hand, used

TABLE 3.4
SCI Benefits for Health Care, and Recipients of Services, by Funding Source, 1978

Type of benefit	Amount of benefit (billions of dollars)	Number of recipients (millions)
1. Total	120.4	—
2. Government	75.9	—
3. Medicare	25.2	—
4. Hospital insurance	—	6.0
5. Supplementary medical insurance	—	15.0
6. Medicaid	20.4	22.9
7. Hospital and medical care[a]	10.7	n.a.
8. Veterans' health and medical programs	4.9	3.0
9. Workers' compensation (health care only)	3.8	0.2
10. Vocational rehabilitation (health care only)	0.3	0.1
11. State temporary disability insurance (health care only)	0.1	n.a.
12. Maternal and child health	0.7	n.a.

13. School health	0.4	n.a.
14. Other public health activities	5.0	11.0
15. Construction of medical facilities	2.5	n.a.
16. Income tax deductions of medical expenses (tax savings)	1.9	16.3[b]
17. Private	44.5	—
18. Group insurance[c]	42.3	n.a.[d]
19. Philanthropy	2.2	n.a.

Sources: For benefit totals, see Appendix Table A.2. Figures for the number of recipients, lines 4, 5, 10, and 14, are from Institute for Socioeconomic Studies (1978a), pp. 63, 64, 196, and 198. Line 6 is from *Social Security Bulletin, Annual Statistical Supplement* (1980), Table 13. Lines 8, 9, and 11 (column 1) are from *Budget of the U.S. Government, Appendix* (1980), pp. 801–804 for federal totals, and Institute for Socioeconomic Studies (1978b) for state totals (compiled by adding totals for all states shown in the book).

Note: Dash = number cannot be calculated; n.a. = data not available.

[a] This amount is funded about 50%–50% by the federal government and state and local governments. Of the federal money, $3.6 billion goes to care for military personnel and their dependents, and the remainder goes to civilian programs. Of the state and local money, the bulk goes to mental hospitals.

[b] Number of tax returns.

[c] Includes insurance for public employees.

[d] For coverage, see Table 3.5.

TABLE 3.5

Number of Persons Covered by Private and Social Health Insurance, 1977

Insurance program	Persons covered (millions)	Percentage of U.S. population covered
Private[a]		
Hospital	164.2	76.8
Physicians' services		
Surgical	162.2	75.8
In-hospital	155.5	72.7
X-ray and laboratory	150.9	70.6
Office and home visits	124.1	58.6
Dental care	46.6	21.8
Prescribed drugs	150.2	70.2
Private-duty nursing	147.3	68.9
Visiting nurse service	145.9	68.2
Nursing-home care	70.4	32.9
Social[b]		
Medicare		
Hospital insurance	24.0	
Supplementary medical insurance	23.5	
Workers' compensation	78.1	

Sources: Private numbers are from *Social Security Bulletin* (Sept. 1978), p. 4. Social numbers are from *Social Security Bulletin, Annual Statistical Supplement* (1981), Tables 4 and 134.

[a]The number of persons covered includes those covered by one or more than one private policy.

[b]Not corrected for coverage under more than one social program. No data are available for the number of people who hold both public insurance coverage and private insurance coverage.

less than their proportional share. Those under 17 (27.6% of the population in 1978) used only 9.4% of the hospital days in that year. The 42.4% who were under 25 used only 18.5% of the hospital days provided. Women used 54.9% of the total number of hospital days.

Almost 90% of the population did not go to a hospital in 1978. Table 3.8 shows that 0.5% of the population used 16.9% of the hospital care in the United States in 1978 (the 0.5% who went to the hospital three times or more); 1.9% used 42% of the hospital care, and 10.5% used all the hospital care in 1978.

Beyond education and health care, the SCI system directs another 3% of GNP to the purchase of food, housing, and "other welfare services." Three-fourths of this amount is for food and housing and the remainder is for such personal services as counseling, job training, adoption and foster care, child day care, and legal services (see Table 3.9).

The leading public program to subsidize housing is the set of tax savings extended to owner-occupied housing in the federal income tax. As I mentioned in Chapter 2, these savings arise out of excluding gross imputed rent from the tax base while allowing the deduction of property tax and mortgage interest. The tax saving to a homeowner will, of course, increase with the homeowner's taxable income. There are no comparable tax savings for the minority of families who rent housing. The greatest part of these tax savings goes to those in the upper half of the income distribution.

The public program that does the most to help people buy food is the Food Stamp program, which is fully funded by the federal government out of general revenues (MacDonald, 1977). About half of the transfer of food and housing is from one nuclear family directly to another via a sharing of living quarters or kitchens.

TABLE 3.6
National Health Expenditures, by Type, 1978

Type of health care expense	Expenditures (billions of dollars)	Percentage of GNP
Total	189.3	8.7
Health services and supplies	179.5	8.3
Personal health care	166.7	7.7
Hospital care	75.7	3.5
Physicians' services	35.8	1.7
Dentists' services	11.8	0.5
Other professional services	4.1	0.2
Drugs and medical sundries	15.4	0.7
Eyeglasses and appliances	4.1	0.2
Nursing-home care	15.2	0.7
Other health services	4.5	0.2
Program administration and net cost of insurance	7.5	0.3
Government public health activities	5.3	0.2
Research and construction of medical facilities	9.8	0.5
Research	4.4	0.2
Construction	5.3	0.2

Source: Gibson and Waldo (1982), Table 1, p. 20.
Note: Fiscal year GNP as in Table 4.2. Round errors are carried over from Gibson and Waldo.

TABLE 3.7
Health Care Utilization, by Age Groups, 1978

	All ages	Under 17	17–24	25–44	45–64	65 and Over
Total population (millions)	213.8	59.0	31.7	56.9	43.4	22.8
Hospital utilization						
Number of hospital days per person	1.0	0.3	.6	.8	1.5	2.8
Number of hospital days per person with one episode or more	9.7	6.4	5.8	7.3	12.3	15.6
Number of persons, by number of episodes (millions)						
0 episodes	191.5	55.9	28.4	50.5	38.1	18.7
1 episode	18.3	2.7	2.9	5.5	4.1	3.0
2 episodes	3.0	0.3	0.3	0.7	0.9	0.8
3+ episodes	1.0	0.1	0.1	0.2	0.3	0.3
Physicians' visits						
Number of persons visiting physicians[a] (millions)	161.1	44.8	23.5	42.4	32.3	18.2
Number of visits per person	4.8	4.1	4.3	4.7	5.3	6.3
Dental visits						
Number of persons visiting dentists[a] (millions)	106.6	29.9	17.5	30.7	21.2	7.3
Number of visits per person	1.6	1.6	1.5	1.7	1.7	1.2

Source: U.S. Department of Health, Education, and Welfare (1978), pp. 25–34.

[a]Derived from response to question about interval since last visit. All those who responded that they had last visited a physician (or dentist) a year or more earlier were not counted.

What Part of Each Type of Benefit Goes to the Poor?

Many of the SCI cash benefits and those directed to the subsidy of selected goods and services go to nonpoor as well as poor persons. Some insight may be gained into the priority given to reducing income poverty by determining the extent to which each of the transfer programs pays out its benefits to people who may be classified as having pretransfer (or primary) income below the poverty lines (Lampman, 1966a, 1970, 1974).

What Part of Each Type of Benefit Goes to the Poor?   53

In 1978 about one-third of all SCI benefits went to the 20% of the population who were poor before receiving any transfers. The poor group's share of cash benefits was 41%; of education benefits only 17%; of health care benefits, 32%; and of food, housing, and other welfare services, 30% (see Table 3.10).

If the $598 billion in SCI benefits had been distributed evenly among the total population of 219 million, then each person would have received $2730, or each of the 76 million households would have received $7867. In fact, the pretransfer poor, who were 44 million in number, received $4534 per person, while the 175 million nonpoor persons received $2277 per person. The top panel of Figure 3.1 shows the profound bias of the SCI system in favor of the aged, with the aged poor receiving 1.4 times as many benefits per person as do the nonaged poor. This pro-aged bias is even more pronounced among the nonpoor, with the aged receiving almost seven times as much per person as do the nonaged. The bottom panel of Figure 3.1 illustrates the pro-aged bias another way. SCI benefits average $8067 for the aged and $2073 for the nonaged. It is noteworthy that the aged, nonpoor group receives

TABLE 3.8

Hospital and Physician Utilization, Percentages by Age, Sex, and Number of Hospital Episodes, 1978

	Percentage of total U.S. population	Percentage of hospital days	Percentage of physicians' visits
By age			
Under 17	27.6	9.4	23.8
17–24	14.8	9.1	13.3
25–44	26.6	21.5	26.2
45–64	20.3	30.3	22.6
65 & over	10.7	29.7	14.1
By sex			
Male	48.3	45.1	41.0
Female	51.7	54.9	59.0
By hospital episode			
3+ episodes	0.5	16.9	n.a.
2 episodes	1.4	25.2	n.a.
1 episode	8.6	58.0	n.a.
0 episodes	89.6	0	n.a.

Source: Calculated from data presented in U.S. Department of Health, Education, and Welfare (1978), pp. 25–34.

Note: n.a. = not applicable.

TABLE 3.9

SCI Benefits for Food, Housing, and Other Welfare Services, and Number of Recipients, by Funding Source, 1978

Type of benefit	Amount of benefit (billions of dollars)	Number of annual recipients (millions)
1. Total	62.6	—
2. Public	41.1	—
3. Food Stamps	5.1	17.1 (monthly)
4. Child nutrition	3.6	31.1
5. Public housing	3.6	0.1
6. Other housing	1.6	1.3
7. Income tax savings on owner-occupied housing	16.3	17.7 (tax returns)
8. Veterans' welfare services	0.8	0.7
9. Public assistance social services	2.8	14.0
10. Vocational rehabilitation (excluding medical)	1.0	0.3
11. Institutional care	0.4	0.6
12. Child welfare	0.8	0.1
13. Income tax savings on child care and dependent care expense	0.6	2.9 (tax returns)
14. Special OEO and ACTION programs	0.9	0.6
15. Social welfare not elsewhere classified[a]	3.6	0.8
16. Private	21.5	—
17. Philanthropy	4.3	n.a.
18. Interfamily for food and housing	17.2	n.a.

Sources: For benefit totals, see Appendix Table A.4. Number of recipients, line 3, is from *Social Security Bulletin, Annual Statistical Supplement* (1980), Table 13. Lines 4, 6, 8, and 10–12 are from Institute for Socioeconomic Studies (1978b) for state total (compiled by adding totals for all states shown in the book) and Institute for Socioeconomic Studies (1978a) for federal totals. Line 5 is from *Statistical Abstract of the United States* (1981), Table 1418. Lines 7 and 13 are from U.S. Department of the Treasury (IRS) (1978). Lines 9 and 14 are from the *Budget of the U.S. Government, Appendix* (1980), pp. 492, 1050.

Note: Dash = number cannot be calculated; n.a. = data not available.

[a] Indian welfare and guidance, activities related to aging and juvenile delinquency, and certain manpower and human development activities. State and local expenditures include amounts for antipoverty and manpower programs, day care, child placement and adoption services, foster care, legal assistance, care of transients, and other unspecified welfare services.

$12,167 worth of benefits per person, which is more than any other group receives. This means that the SCI system is pro-rich for the aged and pro-poor for the nonaged.

TABLE 3.10

SCI Benefits, by Type, with Percentages Received by the Pretransfer Poor and by the Aged, 1978

Type of benefit	Amount of benefit (billions of dollars) (1)	Percentage to pretransfer poor (2)	Amount to pretransfer poor (billions of dollars) (3)	Amount to aged (billions of dollars) (4)	Amount to aged pretransfer poor (billions of dollars) (5)
Total	597.9	33	200.5	193.6	84.1
Cash benefits	301.7	41	123.6	138.1	59.4
Education	113.2	17	19.8	0	0
Health care	120.4	32	38.2	44.6	21.5
Food, housing, and other welfare services	62.6	30	18.9	10.9	3.2

Source: Appendix Table A.12.

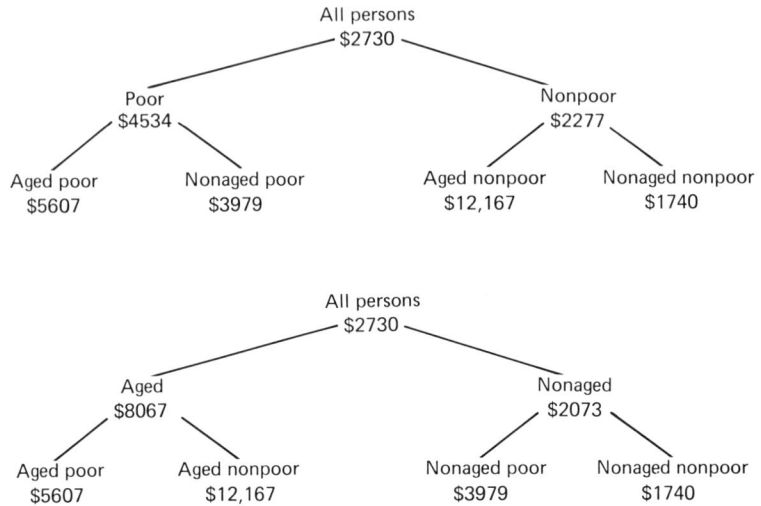

FIGURE 3.1 Secondary consumer income benefits per person, by pretransfer poverty status, and by age, 1978 (from Table 3.14, column 4). Note: The number of persons in each of the groups is as follows: All persons, 219 million; aged, 24 million; nonaged, 195 million; poor, 44 million; nonpoor, 175 million; aged poor, 15 million; nonaged poor, 29 million; aged nonpoor, 9 million; nonaged nonpoor, 166 million.

The income poverty lines set in 1964 were drawn in terms of "total money income." Hence, only cash transfers (as opposed to in-kind transfers) can contribute to reductions of income poverty as it was defined in 1964. Government cash transfers in 1978 changed the number counted as pretransfer poor—20% of the population—into a much smaller number of posttransfer poor—11% of the population. If in-kind government transfers of food stamps, public housing, and health care are counted, "adjusted income poverty" afflicted only 6.1% of the population in 1978. (See Chapter 4 for further discussion of this point.)

Who Pays for the SCI Benefits?

SCI benefits in 1978 were equal to about 27.6% of GNP. About two-thirds of the bill for these benefits was met by taxes and the remainder was funded by wage diversions (17%), interfamily contributions (14%), and philanthropy (2%). These sources are listed in Table 3.11, together with my conclusion (top line) that the burden of funding the SCI system is regressive. This means that those with low incomes in any one year pay a larger share of their incomes in SCI taxes and contributions than do those with higher incomes.

How the burden of taxes is distributed is not easy to determine. It depends on assumptions about the income base and the elasticities of demand and supply in both factor and product markets. It also depends on whether a short or a long period is assumed for adjustment to changes in taxes and whether partial or general equilibrium analysis is used. Pechman and Okner (1974) present a range of estimates using the most to least progressive incidence assumptions. They use what they call adjusted family income, which includes factor income and government cash transfers, as the income base. Their two extreme estimates are reproduced in Table 3.12. By following one set of assumptions, the overall tax system appears to be progressive, with most of the progression in the first, second, and tenth deciles. By following the other set of assumptions, the pattern appears to be proportional. The main differences are in the corporation income tax and the property tax. Payroll taxes also show a difference with respect to the first two deciles, but in both cases the highest rates are found in the middle deciles.

By taking a position between the two extremes offered by Pechman and Okner, I offer the conclusions shown in Table 3.11. Payroll taxes are at least mildly regressive; federal general revenues are clearly pro-

TABLE 3.11
Funding Sources for SCI Benefits, by Assumed Pattern of Burden, 1978

Funding source	Amount (billions of dollars)	Pattern of burden on factor income plus SCI cash benefits
Total	598	Regressive
Payroll taxes	146	Regressive
Federal general revenue	122	Progressive
Wage diversion[a]	103	Proportional
State general revenue	92	Regressive
Interfamily	86	Proportional
Local property tax	36	Proportional
Philanthropy	14	Proportional

Source: Column 1 from Table 2.2.
Note: Sums may not add to totals due to rounding.
[a] Includes $31 billion for private pensions, $30 billion for public employee pensions, and $42 billion for private health insurance for public and private employees.

TABLE 3.12

Effective Rates of Federal, State, and Local Taxes, by Type of Tax, Variants 1c and 3b, and by Population Decile, 1966

Population decile	Individual income tax (%)	Corporation income tax (%)	Property tax (%)	Sales and excise taxes (%)	Payroll taxes (%)	Personal property and motor vehicle taxes (%)	Total taxes (%)
Variant 1c							
First[a]	1.1	1.7	2.1	8.9	2.6	0.4	16.8
Second	2.3	2.1	2.6	7.8	3.8	0.4	18.9
Third	4.0	2.2	2.6	7.1	5.4	0.4	21.7
Fourth	5.4	1.9	2.1	6.7	6.1	0.4	22.6
Fifth	6.3	1.7	1.8	6.4	6.3	0.3	22.8
Sixth	7.0	1.5	1.6	6.1	6.2	0.3	22.7
Seventh	7.5	1.6	1.7	5.7	5.8	0.3	22.7
Eighth	8.3	1.8	1.8	5.5	5.4	0.3	23.1
Ninth	8.8	2.2	2.2	5.0	4.8	0.3	23.3
Tenth	11.4	8.1	5.1	3.2	2.2	0.2	30.1
All deciles[b]	8.5	3.9	3.0	5.1	4.4	0.3	25.2
Variant 3b							
First[a]	1.2	6.1	6.4	8.9	4.5	0.4	27.5
Second	2.0	5.4	5.1	7.5	4.5	0.4	24.8
Third	3.9	5.0	4.6	6.8	5.4	0.4	26.0
Fourth	5.1	4.4	3.8	6.5	5.7	0.3	25.9
Fifth	6.0	4.1	3.3	6.2	5.8	0.3	25.8
Sixth	6.7	3.9	3.2	5.9	5.6	0.3	25.6
Seventh	7.3	3.7	3.2	5.6	5.4	0.3	25.5
Eighth	8.0	3.7	3.2	5.3	5.0	0.3	25.5
Ninth	8.4	3.9	3.2	4.9	4.5	0.3	25.1
Tenth	11.9	5.2	2.9	3.3	2.5	0.2	25.9
All deciles[b]	8.4	4.4	3.4	5.0	4.4	0.3	25.9

Source: Pechman and Okner (1974), Table 4.9, p. 61. Published by permission of the Brookings Institution.

Note: Variant 1c is based on the most progressive assumptions, and variant 3b on the least progressive assumptions.

[a] Includes only units in the sixth to tenth percentiles.
[b] Includes negative incomes not shown separately.

gressive; state general revenues, which rely heavily on sales and excise taxes, are regressive; and the local property tax is proportional. Payroll taxes are generally considered to be regressive with respect to factor income because they exempt property income, they cover only the fraction of earnings up to a stated maximum, and they do not adjust the tax for family size nor for expenses of earning income (Brittain, 1972). Contributions to employee pensions usually do not have maximums, but otherwise are similar in form to a payroll tax. It should be noted that the 50% of workers covered by private pensions tends to be in the upper half of the earnings distribution. For that reason I classify wage diversions as proportional.

Several studies have found that philanthropic contributions and interfamily contributions are roughly proportional to family income (Morgan et al., 1962). By adding all the nontax sources of funds into Table 3.11, I show that of the total of $598 billion taxes and contributions, $122 billion was paid in a progressive fashion and $238 billion in a regressive pattern; the remainder were proportional. Since the regressive pattern dominates the progressive, it seems reasonable to conclude that the burden of SCI taxes and contributions is regressive against factor income and SCI cash benefits as a base.

It is important to keep in mind that certain features of the federal individual income tax that relate to SCI have the effect of reducing the progressivity of that tax. These are the income tax savings from exclusion of employer-paid health insurance, the deferral of tax on private pensions, and the deductibility of state and local taxes and charitable contributions. (Tax savings rise with the marginal tax rate of the individual and, in 1978, could have amounted to as much as 70% of the amount excluded from or deducted from the tax base.) The deferral of taxes on employer contributions to, and interest earnings of, private pensions means an extra tax saving if the taxpayer falls into a lower tax bracket after retirement than before. The reader will recall that in Chapter 2 I included some other income tax savings in the list of SCI benefits. These are the savings arising out of exemptions for children, aged, and blind persons; the earned income credit; the credit for child and dependent care; the deduction of extraordinary uninsured medical expenses; and the tax preferences for homeowner occupancy. Hence, it would be double-counting to include them here.

With the aid of some heroic assumptions, some rough calculations can be made as to how the SCI burden is divided between the pretransfer poor and nonpoor groups. Consider just the pretransfer poor, who received $124 billion in cash benefits (Table 3.10). About half of this amount went to the aged poor and half to the nonaged. This amount,

TABLE 3.13

SCI Taxes and Contributions Paid by Families, by Poverty Status and by Age, 1978
(billions of dollars)

Tax or contribution	Total amount paid (1)	Paid by pretransfer poor		Paid by pretransfer nonpoor	
		Aged (2)	Nonaged (3)	Aged (4)	Nonaged (5)
Total	598	14	24	23	537
Payroll taxes	146	0	5	0	140
Federal taxes	122	0	2	6	115
Wage diversions	103	0	2	1	100
State taxes	92	5	5	5	75
Interfamily contributions	86	1	4	5	76
Property taxes	36	7	5	4	21
Philanthropic contributions	14	1	1	2	10

Sources: Column 1 is from Table 2.2. Estimates for other columns by author as discussed in the text.

together with their $34 billion (2% of the total) of factor income, totals $158 billion of posttransfer money income, which gives some indication of their ability to pay taxes. Let us assume that the 15 million aged poor receive about half of the total of $34 billion of factor income and the 29 million nonaged poor receive the other half.

We know that the aged poor are unlikely to be paying payroll or federal income taxes, or making wage diversions to health insurance or pension funds. On the other hand, they are likely to pay relatively heavy sales and property taxes. The nonaged poor are more generally liable to pay more payroll than income taxes. Transfer income is not part of the tax base of payroll and income taxes except that the income tax does apply to the employer-funded share of employee pensions. Transfer income is 60% of the total income of the posttransfer poor. The nonworking poor do bear a share of the burden of property and sales taxes, however, and the so-called working poor are subject to sales, property, and payroll taxes. However, the federal income tax, via personal exemptions and the low-income allowance, or minimum standard deduction, protects most workers with earnings below the poverty line. Moreover, the earned income tax credit in effect refunds much of the OASDHI payroll tax paid by low-income workers with children.

Table 3.13 shows the results of my rough calculations and the conclusion that pretransfer poor families paid $38 billion of the total of $598 billion of SCI taxes and contributions. The remaining $560 billion is paid by the nonpoor.

Who Receives Benefits in Excess of the Taxes and Contributions They Pay?

In any 1 year, all the giving and taking carried out by the SCI system results in a divergence between primary income and income plus and minus SCI for most families. This means that the size distributions of the two types of income will be quite different from each other. The degree to which they are different is a measure of the redistribution among income size classes that results from SCI if we assume that primary income is unaffected by the redistribution.

We can combine information about SCI taxes and contributions with information about benefits to show in Table 3.14 that the pretransfer poor receive on average $4534 worth of benefits and pay an average amount of $864. The pretransfer nonpoor paid more in SCI taxes and contributions ($3198) than they received in benefits ($2277). The pretransfer poor have an average net gain of $3670 and the nonpoor have an average net loss of $921. These crude averages are not descriptive of the experience of most families. One may speculate that the relationship between receipts and outpayments changes gradually as income rises and that at an income level near the median, the receipts equal the outpayments. Figure 3.2 offers a rough picture of this relationship.

In speculating about the slope of the net benefits or CC line, it is of interest to consider how earnings-conditioned benefits affect the picture. Some benefits, for example, AFDC benefits, are designed to fall by a certain amount with each additional dollar of earnings. The rate of fall, which is often set at 50 cents or more per extra dollar of earnings, is known as a benefit-reduction rate. This rate and the marginal tax rate determine the break-even point, which is shown in Figure 3.2 where the CC line crosses the 45° line. The average tax and contribution rate for SCI is about 30% of income. However, as noted, this will vary by type of income and, hence, by work status. The combined marginal rates in payroll taxes, wage diversions for private pensions and health insurance, and state and federal income taxes, can run well over 30% on extra earnings. This, together with benefit-reduction rates, means that the net wage for additional work, or for an additional worker in the family, may

TABLE 3.14
SCI Benefits Received and Taxes and Contributions Paid, by Pretransfer Poverty Status and by Age, 1978

Characteristics of population	No. of persons (millions) (1)	Total SCI benefits (billions of dollars) (2)	Total SCI taxes and contributions (billions of dollars) (3)	SCI benefits (per capita) (4)	SCI taxes and contributions (per capita) (5)	Net benefits (per capita) (6)
Total population	219	597.9	597.9	2730	2730	0
Pretransfer poor						
All ages	44	199.5	38.0	4534	864	3670
Aged	15	84.1	14.0	5607	933	4674
Nonaged	29	115.4	24.0	3979	828	3151
Pretransfer nonpoor						
All ages	175	398.4	559.7	2277	3198	−921
Aged	9	109.5	22.7	12167	2522	9645
Nonaged	166	288.9	537.0	1740	3235	−1495

Sources: Column 1 is from Table 4.11. Column 2 is from Table 3.11. Column 3 is from Table 3.14. Column 4 = column 2 ÷ column 1. Column 5 = column 3 ÷ column 1. Column 6 = column 4 − column 5.

Note: There are two difficulties in calculating these numbers. One is that the numbers of pretransfer poor are literally "pre government transfer and pretax" poor and therefore "post private pension and direct interfamily transfer" poor. This means I have understated the numbers of pre-SCI poor and therefore overstated the per capita benefits of the pre-SCI poor aged. A second difficulty is that I have assumed that all retirement benefits go to people who are 65 years of age and over. To the extent that such benefits go to persons under age 65 I have overstated the per capita benefits of the aged and understated the benefits to the nonaged.

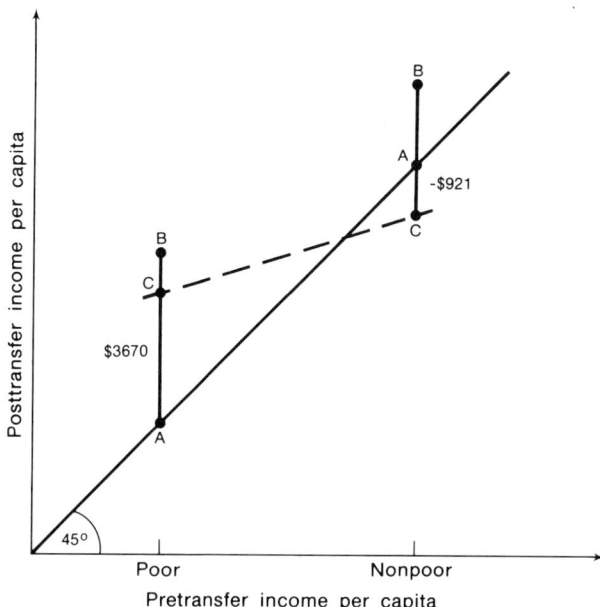

FIGURE 3.2 Net secondary consumer income benefits per capita, by pretransfer income level, 1978. AB = SCI benefits received ($4534 poor, $2277 nonpoor); BC = SCI taxes and contributions paid ($864 poor, $3198 nonpoor); AC = SCI benefits net of SCI taxes and contributions (from Table 3.14; columns 4, 5, and 6. Figure by University of Wisconsin Cartographic Laboratory.)

be perceived as being substantially below the gross wage rate (and hence below the labor cost to the employer).

I commented earlier on the pro-aged bias of the SCI system. Table 3.14 shows what look like two systems—one for those under 65 and one for the aged. The 24 million aged persons received about one-third of all the benefits and paid less than one-tenth of the taxes and contributions. The nonaged, nonpoor group received the least benefits per capita but paid nine-tenths of the SCI bill. This means the nonaged net benefit line lies below that for the total population. This feature of the SCI system means that two kinds of income redistribution are going on simultaneously. One is from the nonaged nonpoor to the poor, and the other is also from the nonaged nonpoor, but goes to the aged nonpoor (Moon, 1977).

There is a substantial literature on the redistribution of income other than that between the poor and nonpoor. Two types of recent study are relevant here. One is directed to the question of how the income share of the lowest fifth of households, ranked by primary income, is altered by taxes and government transfers. The other looks to the shares of all five quintiles and seeks a summary measure of the difference in overall inequality before and after redistribution. Research into these questions is plagued not only by the limits on available data, but also by the lack of agreement on the appropriate definitions of income, income-receiving unit (family or individual), time period (1 year or lifetime), and on whether to rank units before or after adjustments are made for taxes and transfers. Further, there is an almost insurmountable difficulty in identifying the pretax, pretransfer distribution of income. The standard method of finding this is to start with the posttransfer income of each unit and add and subtract from that the taxes paid and the transfers received by that unit. But this method overlooks the very real possibility that people may have modified their efforts to gain labor or property income because of the existence of taxes and transfers. Also, people may over time take more leisure or rearrange their living and income-sharing arrangements in response to increased taxes and transfers.

The best studies of how transfers modify the income share of the lowest fifth of income receivers are those by Browning and Johnson (1979) and Hoagland (1982). Both of these studies cover cash and in-kind (food, housing, and medical care) transfers as well as taxes. However, they do not cover private SCI benefits or contributions. This means that the scope of these studies is less than that of my study of SCI. Both cover persons who live as unrelated individuals as well as those in multiperson families. Browning and Johnson do not rerank units when shifting from pre- to posttransfer inequality, but Hoagland does rerank units. Browning and Johnson find that the income share of the lowest fifth of income receivers is increased from 1.6% before tax and transfer to 6.2% after tax and transfer. Hoagland finds a somewhat larger shift, from .6% to 6.5%. It seems unlikely that these findings would be greatly altered by adopting the broader definitions of contributions and benefits that I have incorporated in my definition of the SCI system.

Danziger, Haveman, and Plotnick (1981) review eleven recent studies of the effect of transfers across the entire income distribution. The effect on inequality is measured by the change in the Gini coefficient. They note that while the papers vary in data, methods, and concepts, the estimated effect of transfers is strikingly similar—"a 15% reduction in the Gini due to cash transfers and a further 4% decline due to in-kind transfers" (p. 1012). They find that the impact of benefits is large relative to that of taxes. The inequality in per capita or per equivalent adult income is less than in household income.

There are, of course, other ways of thinking of redistribution than in terms of the size distribution of income. For example, there are the intergroup differences in mean or median income for young and old, whites and blacks, farm and nonfarm residents, men and women. There is great policy interest in how SCI programs may affect those differences. I have already noted how SCI alters the relative income position of the aged compared to the nonaged. Chapter 4 looks at some other intergroup differences in the context of the goal to reduce income inequalities.

A Guide to Reading

SCI benefits can be classified by the type of benefit or by the target groups to which they are directed. Some suggestions for further reading following that pattern of classification are offered below, along with suggestions on taxes and contributions, and redistribution by income class.

Income Maintenance

Ball. 1978. *Social security, today and tomorrow.*
Hamermesh. 1977. *Jobless pay and the economy.*
Hartman. 1983. *Pay and pensions for federal workers.*
Johnson, Curington, and Cullinan. 1979. Income security for the disabled.
Munnell. 1982. *The economics of private pensions.*
Root. 1982. *Fringe benefits: Social insurance in the steel industry.*
Skidmore (ed.). 1981. *Social security financing.*
Smith and Lilienfeld. 1971. *The social security disability program: An evaluation study.*
Stein. 1979. *Social security and the private pension system.*
Wilson (ed.). 1974. *Pensions: Inflation and growth.*

Health Care

Campbell. 1973. *Economics of health and public policy.*
Davis and Schoen. 1978. *Health and the war on poverty.*
Gibson and Waldo. 1982. National health expenditures, 1981.
Gornick. 1976. Ten years of medicare: Impact on the covered population.
Newhouse. 1978. *The economics of medical care.*
Pauly. 1971. *Medical care at public expense.*
Sloan, Cromwell, and Mitchell. 1978. *Private physicians and public programs.*

Education and Training

Blaug. 1970. *An introduction to the economics of education.*
Carnegie Council on Policy Studies in Higher Education. 1975. *The federal role in postsecondary education.*
Haveman (ed.). 1977. *A decade of federal antipoverty programs.* (See Chapter 4 on job training and education.)
Owen. 1974. *School inequality and the welfare state.*
Schultz (ed.). 1972. *Investment in education: The equity-efficiency quandary.*
Stiglitz. 1974. The demand for education in public and private school systems.
Zymelman. 1976. *The economic evaluation of vocational training programs.*

Food, Housing, and Other Welfare Services

Kamerman and Kohn. 1979. *The day-care debate.*
Krashinsky. 1978. *The cost of day care in public programs.*
Levitan and Alderman. 1975. *Child care and ABC's too.*
Neenan. 1981. *Urban public economics.* (Housing)
Olsen. 1982. The role of government in the housing sector.
Young and Nelson (eds.). 1973. *Public policy for day care of young children.*

The Aged and Disabled

Burkhauser and Haveman. 1982. *Disability and work.*
Moon. 1977. *The measurement of economic welfare: Its application to the aged poor.*
Schulz. 1980. *The economics of aging.*
Worrall. 1978. A benefit-cost analysis of the vocational rehabilitation program.

Students

Crew and Young. 1977. *Paying by degrees.*
Woodall. 1978. *Review of student support schemes in selected OECD countries.*

Veterans

Levitan and Cleary. 1973. *Old wars remain unfinished: The veterans benefit system.*
Levitan and Zickler. 1973. *Swords into plowshares: Our GI bill.*
Sapolsky. 1977. America's socialized medicine: The allocation of resources within the veterans' health care system.

The Poor

Danziger and Plotnick. In press. Has the war on poverty been won?
Haveman (ed.). 1977. *A decade of federal antipoverty programs.* (See Chapter 7 on legal services.)

Hoagland. 1982. The effectiveness of current transfer programs in reducing income poverty.
Lampman. 1971. *Ends and means of reducing income poverty.* (Especially Chapter 6.)
Plotnick and Skidmore. 1975. *Progress against poverty.*

Redistribution across Income Classes

Brittain. 1972. *The payroll tax for Social Security.*
Browning and Johnson. 1979. Taxes, transfers, and income inequality.
Krenzle. 1982. Post-fisc distribution of income: Measuring progressivity with application to the U.S.
Okner. 1979. Distributional aspects of tax reform during the past fifteen years.
Reynolds and Smolensky. 1977. *Public expenditures, taxes, and the distribution of income.*
Ruggles and O'Higgins. 1981. The distribution of public expenditures among households in the U.S.
Sawyer. 1976. *Income distribution in OECD countries.*
Taussig and Danziger. 1976. *Conference on the trend in income inequality in the U.S.*

CHAPTER 4

Social Benefits of 1950–1978 Changes in Secondary Consumer Income

Chapter 3 described the pattern of who pays and who benefits under the 1978 SCI system. Chapters 4 and 5 address a different question, namely, what social benefits and social costs flow from the expansion of the system? This question transcends the sharing of benefits and burdens among individuals or groups and asks whether the national enterprise as a whole is better or worse off as a result of the change. Did the increase in the scope of the SCI system cause the nation's well-being to rise faster or slower than it would have if the increase had not occurred?

Policy analysis and evaluation has become an accepted discipline for guiding policymakers in deciding on the social value of any particular program (Rivlin, 1971; Levitan & Wurzburg, 1979; Gramlich, 1981). This methodology dictates that the first step in evaluating any program is to identify its goal. The second is to measure the degree to which that goal is achieved; the third is to add any side effects of the program which may be said to contribute to the achievement of other social goals. Some sort of weighting of the relative importance of the several types of goals may be applied. The sum total of the properly weighted social benefits should then be compared with the total of weighted social costs engendered by the program.

I propose to follow these precepts of evaluation, but rather than evaluate a single program, I shall do what might be called a global evaluation of the 1978 complex of SCI flows against the counterfactual of the 1950 complex of such flows. The reader may well ask why the 1950 system is taken as the counterfactual. The more common choice of counterfactual is the present economy with no social interventions, that is, to assume that all the SCI programs are eliminated. From a historical point of view, that counterfactual is so unrealistic as to be almost meaningless. It is a theme of this book that every society has an SCI system and that much of the change that goes on is shifting use of the several intermediaries and of the specific types of benefits. The year 1950 was selected because in that year the reconversion from the wartime economy had been completed and the social legislation of the 1930s was being ratified, so to speak, by the Eisenhower administration. The great explosion of social welfare programs of the 1965–1975 years was still ahead. The year 1978 is representative of the new plateau of SCI ratio. The 1950–1978 span covers the experience of only one generation, but that seems to be an appropriate length of time.

In this chapter, I first describe what changes occurred. Then I identify and discuss the four explicit goals of the SCI system, give a rough judgment of the degree to which those goals have been attained, and indicate the importance of several side benefits of the SCI system. This chapter also gives attention to four competing schools of thought that guide social philosophers in assigning weights to the several goals and to alternative ways of paying for and delivering SCI benefits. Chapter 5 is devoted first to social costs and second to pointing the reader to the judgments that need to be made in deciding whether or not the benefits of expanding the SCI system exceeded the social costs.

The 1950–1978 Changes in the SCI System

Table 4.1 shows the growth in SCI benefits for selected years from 1950 to 1980. In the past three decades SCI and the taxes and contributions to pay for it, increased faster than GNP (see Table 4.2). The ratio of SCI to GNP increased from 17.2% in 1950 to 27.6% in 1978.

The several panels of Table 4.3 and also Tables 4.4 and 4.5 are designed to show which items in the SCI accounts changed the most in the 1950–1978 period. The most striking changes include the following:
- Health care benefits increased at a faster rate than any other broad type of benefit. (See Table 4.3, panel B, and Table 4.4.)
- Noncash benefits grew faster than cash benefits. (See Table 4.3, panel B, and Table 4.4.)
- Benefits intermediated by insurance companies and governments grew faster than those intermediated by philanthropic

TABLE 4.1
SCI Benefits, by Type and Intermediary, 1950–1980 (billions of dollars)

Type of benefit	1950	1955	1960	1965	1970	1975	1978	1980
Total	49.4	68.6	100.6	139.4	238.4	440.4	597.9	755.6
Government	32.4	44.3	67.2	92.4	164.3	316.9	424.5	532.0
Insurance	1.9	4.1	8.0	13.8	26.2	48.9	73.7	98.3
Philanthropy	1.7	2.5	3.3	4.6	6.6	10.1	13.6	17.3
Interfamily	13.4	17.7	22.1	28.6	41.3	64.5	86.1	108.0
Cash	26.8	38.4	56.4	73.9	116.2	219.1	301.7	389.9
Government	16.9	24.1	36.4	46.3	72.1	146.9	201.4	252.2
Insurance	1.0	1.9	3.5	6.0	11.7	21.6	31.4	51.3
Philanthropy	0	0	0	0	0	0	0	0
Interfamily	8.9	12.4	16.5	21.6	32.4	50.6	68.9	86.4
Health care	4.5	7.3	11.8	18.1	40.9	80.5	120.4	148.1
Government	3.3	4.7	6.8	9.5	25.4	51.6	75.9	98.2
Insurance	0.9	2.2	4.5	7.8	14.5	27.3	42.3	47.0
Philanthropy	0.3	0.4	0.5	0.8	1.0	1.6	2.2	2.9
Interfamily	0	0	0	0	0	0	0	0
Education	10.1	13.0	19.7	30.5	55.2	90.9	113.2	134.4
Government	9.4	11.8	18.0	28.1	51.6	85.4	106.1	125.2
Insurance	0	0	0	0	0	0	0	0
Philanthropy	0.7	1.2	1.7	2.4	3.6	5.5	7.1	9.2
Interfamily	0	0	0	0	0	0	0	0
Food, housing, and other welfare services	8.0	9.9	12.7	16.9	26.1	49.9	62.6	83.2
Government	2.8	3.7	6.0	8.5	15.2	33.0	41.1	56.4
Insurance	0	0	0	0	0	0	0	0
Philanthropy	0.7	0.9	1.1	1.4	2.0	3.0	4.3	5.2
Interfamily	4.5	5.3	5.6	7.0	8.9	13.9	17.2	21.6

Sources: Derived from Appendix Tables A.1, A.2, A.3, A.4, A.5, A.6, and A.7.

organizations and those handled by direct interfamily gifts. (See Table 4.3, panel C, and Table 4.4.)
- Benefits targeted to the aged, disabled, and female heads of households with children grew far faster than those targeted to all others. (See Table 4.3, panel D, and Table 4.5.)
- Funds raised by payroll taxation and wage diversion rose at a faster rate than funds from any other source. (See Table 4.3, panel E.)
- Federal government expenditures grew faster than those of state and local governments. (Not shown in any table.)

TABLE 4.2
SCI Benefits as Percentage of GNP, 1950–1980

Type of benefit	1950	1955	1960	1965	1970	1975	1978	1980
Fiscal Year GNP (billions)	$286.5	$400.0	$506.5	$691.1	$992.7	$1549.2	$2163.9	$2633.1
Total	17.2%	17.2%	19.9%	20.2%	24.0%	28.4%	27.6%	28.7%
Government	11.3	11.1	13.3	13.4	16.6	20.5	19.6	20.2
Insurance	0.7	1.0	1.6	2.0	2.6	3.2	3.4	3.7
Philanthropy	0.6	0.6	0.7	0.7	0.7	0.7	0.6	0.7
Interfamily	4.7	4.4	4.4	4.1	4.2	4.2	4.0	4.1
Cash	9.4	9.6	11.1	10.7	11.7	14.1	13.9	14.8
Government	5.9	6.0	7.2	6.7	7.3	9.5	9.3	9.6
Insurance	0.3	0.5	0.7	0.9	1.2	1.4	1.5	1.9
Philanthropy	0	0	0	0	0	0	0	0
Interfamily	3.1	3.1	3.3	3.1	3.3	3.3	3.2	3.3
Health care	1.6	1.8	2.3	2.6	4.1	5.2	5.6	5.6
Government	1.2	1.2	1.3	1.4	2.6	3.3	3.5	3.7
Insurance	0.3	0.6	0.9	1.1	1.5	1.8	2.0	1.8
Philanthropy	0.1	0.1	0.1	0.1	0.1	0.1	0.1	0.1
Interfamily	0	0	0	0	0	0	0	0
Education	3.5	3.3	3.9	4.4	5.6	5.9	5.2	5.1
Government	3.3	3.0	3.6	4.1	5.2	5.5	4.9	4.8
Insurance	0	0	0	0	0	0	0	0
Philanthropy	0.2	0.3	0.3	0.3	0.4	0.4	0.3	0.3
Interfamily	0	0	0	0	0	0	0	0
Food, housing, and other welfare services	2.8	2.5	2.5	2.4	2.6	3.2	2.9	3.2
Government	1.0	0.9	1.2	1.2	1.5	2.1	1.9	2.1
Insurance	0	0	0	0	0	0	0	0
Philanthropy	0.2	0.2	0.2	0.2	0.2	0.2	0.2	0.2
Interfamily	1.6	1.3	1.1	1.0	0.9	0.9	0.8	0.8

Sources: Table 4.1, converted to percentages using fiscal year GNP from Bixby (1983), p. 15, Table 3.

TABLE 4.3

Ratio of 1978 to 1950 SCI Benefits, Sources of SCI Funds, and GNP

Item	1950 ($billions)	1978 ($billions)	Ratio of 1978 to 1950
A. Total SCI benefits			
	49.4	597.9	12.1
B. SCI benefits, by type			
Cash	26.8	301.7	11.3
Health care	4.5	120.4	26.8
Education	10.1	113.2	11.2
Food, housing, and other welfare services	8.0	62.6	7.8
C. SCI benefits, by intermediary			
Government	32.4	424.5	13.1
Insurance	1.9	73.7	38.8
Philanthropy	1.7	13.6	8.0
Interfamily	13.4	86.1	6.4
D. SCI benefits, by population category			
Age 62 and older	10.9	227.2	20.8
Disabled, under age 62	2.5	59.8	23.9
Female family head, with children	2.0	47.8	23.9
All others	34.0	263.1	7.7
E. Sources of SCI funds, by type			
Taxes, total	31	396	12.8
Payroll	4	146	36.5
Property	3	36	12.0
State general revenue	7	92	13.1
Federal general revenue	17	122	7.2
Wage diversion	3	103	34.3
Philanthropy	2	14	7.0
Interfamily	13	86	6.6
F. SCI benefits as percentage of GNP			
GNP	286.5	2163.9	7.6
Total SCI/GNP (percentage)	17.2	27.6	1.6

Sources: Panels A, B, and C are from Table 4.1. Panel D is derived from Table 4.5. Panel E is from Appendix Table A.8. Panel F is from Table 4.2.

Note: Sums may not add to totals due to rounding.

TABLE 4.4
Percentage Composition of Government and Private SCI Benefits, by Type, 1950 and 1978

Type of benefit	1950			1978		
	Government	Private	Combined	Government	Private	Combined
Cash	52	58	54	47	58	50
Health care	10	7	9	18	26	20
Education	29	4	20	25	4	19
Food, housing, and other welfare services	9	31	16	10	12	10

Source: Table 4.1.
Note: Private SCI includes insurance, philanthropy, and interfamily.

The Four Explicit Goals of the SCI System

I assert that the four explicit goals[1] of the SCI system are (1) reduction of insecurity with respect to income loss, and (2) with respect to irregular and extraordinary expenditures, (3) reduction of income poverty, and (4) fair sharing of SCI burdens.[2] I discuss each of these goals in turn, giving attention to how they have evolved over time.

Reducing Insecurity with Respect to Income Loss

About half of SCI benefits arise out of concern for losses of income associated with old age, disability, unemployment, and loss of a family

---

[1] I call these the explicit goals because it has been my experience that the sponsors of public and private SCI programs state that these are the goals they seek. Moreover, these same sponsors often deny that what I call the side effects, such as reducing income inequality, are the goals of their proposals. Scholars, rather than political activists, are quick to identify these side effects as the possible consequences of SCI programs. However, the reader should know that there is a continuing controversy about what goals underlie collective choices in this realm.

[2] See Goodin (1982, pp. 150–151), who discusses the definition of the "ideal type" of welfare state. He quotes Asa Briggs as saying, in 1961, that the traditional concerns of such a state are the first three of the goals I have listed. Goodin notes two other features of welfare states. One is that only a limited range of goods and services are involved. The second is that the welfare state adjusts final distributions rather than basic resources or the relations of production. It refuses to undertake any redistribution of formal titles to the means of production. He notes that "statutory guarantees of a certain future stream of income might, in effect, if not in name, produce much the same result. But backhandedness in this regard is itself a hallmark of the welfare state" (p. 151).

TABLE 4.5

Distribution of Total SCI Benefits among Categories of Population, 1950 and 1978

Characteristics of recipients	Percentage of benefits		Benefits received as percentage of GNP	
	1950 (1)	1978 (2)	1950 (3)	1978 (4)
Aged 62 and older	22	38	3.8	10.5
Disabled, under age 62	5	10	0.9	2.8
Female family heads with children	4	8	0.7	2.2
All others	69	44	11.9	12.1
Totals (percentages)	100	100	17.2	27.6

Sources: Column 1 is calculated by same method as Table 5.4, column 2. Column 2 is from Table 5.4, column 2. Column 3 = column 1 × 17.2% (from Table 4.2, recorded on bottom line of column 3). Column 4 = column 2 × 27.6% (from Table 4.2, recorded on bottom line of column 4).

breadwinner. These income losses are presumed to flow from events beyond the control of the beneficiaries. The preferred method for offsetting such loss is social insurance, which features contributions by employers, and, in some cases, by workers, and which pays benefits without a means test. The fact that income falls below its customary or expected level, even though the one afflicted is not reduced thereby to poverty, is deemed a sufficient basis for social intervention. This concept was enacted into legislation after long development in the English and American law of torts. A tort is defined as "a wrongful act for which a civil action will lie except one involving a breach of contract." This branch of the common law is concerned with assigning liability for damages. A general principle of such law is that the costs of an accident should lie where they fall unless it can be proved that a second party, for example, the employer of an injured worker, caused the accident out of malice or negligence. This may be called the doctrine of individual fault.[3] Following this doctrine, the courts, in a series of cases, established a heavy burden of proof for the injured worker. The latter had to prove that the employer had failed to provide both a safe place to work and safe equipment, and that no fellow-servant had caused the accident.

---

[3]This doctrine was, of course, compatible with the idea of explicit, freely negotiated labor contracts, and quite at odds with the precapitalistic idea of paternalistic employers bearing responsibility for maintaining the status of their employees.

Further, workers had to prove that they had not willingly assumed the risk of the work and had not, by their own negligence, contributed to the causes of the accident.

For a time, it was the general practice that only if workers could overcome each of these employer defenses could they recover compensation for damages suffered. But there were exceptions. For example, it was determined early on that in certain highly dangerous occupations, such as transporting explosives, the employer defenses did not apply.[4] Later the courts and legislatures began to moderate the employer defenses in all cases, making it easier for workers to prove that employers had not provided a reasonably safe place to work, and allowing workers to recover partial damages even though they were contributorily negligent. Gradually, the courts moved to the doctrine of social fault, which assigned the costs of an industrial accident to the party best able to pay for and best able to prevent the accident. This meant that the burden of proof was shifted from workers to employers. It also meant that employers had to bear a greater financial risk of large damage claims. Beginning in 1911, state legislatures enacted this doctrine as workmen's compensation (now called workers' compensation) laws, which required employers to insure against this risk and which introduced a formula for determining (and limiting the maximum) benefits for specific injuries and fatalities. These laws marked the advent of social insurance in the United States.

This doctrine of social fault, which implies that dangerous employments and goods produced by dangerous methods should "pay for the blood of the worker," was relatively easy for legislators to apply to the loss of income due to involuntary unemployment of experienced workers. Unemployment insurance, in a manner parallel to workers' compensation, is based on the theory that employers are able in some instances to regularize and spread employment and thereby reduce unemployment.[5] Lacking that ability, they may build insurance premiums into the costs of doing business and pass that cost on to consumers or back to all employees. In any case, the cost or the damage of unemployment is no longer limited to the minority who are unemployed.[6]

Insurance against income loss due to retirement and to disability

---

[4]One noted legal scholar, Roscoe Pound, stated that this case about explosives signaled "the end of capitalism" by denying freedom of contract.

[5]Experience rating in unemployment insurance and merit rating in workers' compensation are meant to reward the employer who manages to reduce the frequency of unemployment or accidents.

[6]Note that the common law has parallel principles in the laws of contracts and property to cover consumers and property owners who suffer damages. Hence, a consumer may

not related to work is generally rationalized on grounds other than social fault. While some might argue that forced retirement is like involuntary unemployment in that it is within the power of the employer to avoid it, few would claim that nonoccupational accidents and illnesses are due to bad planning by the employer. Insurance against such income loss is advocated as a straightforward collective purchase and rationalized on grounds of convenience. Unlike most commercial insurance, social insurance has formulas for contributions and benefits that depart from the principles of insurance equity.

The recent growth in the number of people drawing cash benefits is indicated by Table 4.6.

Reducing Insecurity with Respect to Irregular and Extraordinary Expenditures

Education

A second explicit goal of the SCI system is to help people buy certain goods and services. A leading example under this heading is public and philanthropic spending for education, which amounted to 5% of GNP in 1978. Free public education at elementary and secondary levels is provided as a civil right (Tobin, 1970) and funded partly out of local property tax revenues. Parents are compelled to send their children of specific ages to school and must meet certain noninstructional costs of school attendance, including the forgone earnings of children, out of their own pockets. Families who send their minor children to private elementary and secondary schools typically pay fees that are lower than full cost, with the balance coming from school endowments, philanthropic organizations, or, in special cases, governments.

Tuition subsidies are also found in private schools of higher education and to a greater degree in public colleges and universities, where in-state students are charged a fee or tuition that is one-third of full instructional costs or less. Higher education, more clearly than primary and secondary education, is funded on a matching basis, with the students or their families expected to bear the students' living costs. These family-

---

be able to recover from the seller for damages arising out of an accident in using a purchased good or service. And property owners may be able to collect for damages on the ground that their property rights have been damaged by the act of another. It is also of interest in this connection that some states have legislation requiring all automobile owners to carry liability insurance. Others appropriate public monies to compensate victims of certain crimes. The latter measure would seem to be based on a doctrine of social fault for crime.

TABLE 4.6

Beneficiaries of Selected SCI Cash Benefit Programs and Ratios of 1978 to 1950

Type of benefit	Number of beneficiaries (millions)		Ratio of 1978 to 1950
	1950	1978	
Retirement			
OASDHI	1.9	21.8	11.5
Railroad Retirement	0.2	0.6	3.0
Federal employee retirement	0.2	1.9	9.5
State and local retirement	0.2	2.0	10.0
SSI (aged only)	2.8	2.0	0.7
Disability			
OASDHI	—	4.9	
Veterans' programs	2.3	3.3	1.4
Federal retirement	0.1	0.5	5.0
State and local retirement	0.3	0.2	6.7
SSI (blind and disabled)	0.2	2.2	11.0
Loss of family breadwinner			
AFDC	2.2	10.6	4.8
OASDI (Survivors' Insurance)	1.1	7.6	6.9
Unemployment			
Unemployment Insurance	1.4	2.0	1.4
General Assistance	0.9	0.8	0.9

Source: *Social Security Bulletin, Annual Statistical Supplement* (1980), Tables 13, 150, and 174–177.

Note: dash = program did not exist.

to-student gifts are identified in Chapter 2 as interfamily direct transfers. More than half the total cost of higher education is composed of earnings forgone by students (Schultz, 1963). That is, the total cost includes such direct costs as teachers' salaries, laboratory supplies, and also the earnings the students might have received had they worked full-time and not gone to school.

The total resources allocated to 12, 16, or more years of education adds up to a substantial investment in each student. The cost of education to the family is subsidized in recognition of the difficulties most families have in planning for—or borrowing for—the costs of schooling, and also in the faith that there are external benefits to be captured.

America led the world in providing mass education. It did so in pursuit of equality of opportunity and as a necessary step in developing a well-informed citizenry that would be capable of participative self-

TABLE 4.7

Enrollment in Educational Institutions, by Level of Instruction and by Type of School, 1949–1950 to Fall 1978
(millions of students)

Type of education	1949–1950	1959–1960	Fall 1969	Fall 1978
All levels (elementary, secondary, higher)	31.3	45.2	58.6	59.2
Elementary and secondary	28.7	42.0	51.4	47.9
Kindergarten–grade 8	22.2	32.4	37.0	32.2
Grades 9–12 and postgraduate	6.5	9.6	14.4	15.7
Higher education	2.7	3.2	7.1	11.3
Elementary and secondary				
Kindergarten	1.2	2.3	2.8	2.9
Public	1.0	1.9	2.6	2.7
Nonpublic	0.1	0.4	0.2	0.2
Grades 1–8	21.0	30.1	34.2	29.4
Public	18.4	25.7	30.0	25.8
Nonpublic	2.6	4.3	4.0	3.4
Grades 9–12 and postgraduate	6.5	9.6	14.4	15.7
Public	5.7	8.5	13.0	14.2
Nonpublic	0.7	1.0	1.3	1.4
Higher education				
Resident degree-credit enrollment	2.7	3.2	7.1	11.3
Publicly controlled	1.4	1.8	5.1	8.8
Privately controlled	1.3	1.4	2.0	2.5

Source: *Digest of Educational Statistics* (1981), Table 3, p. 8.
Note: Sums may not add up to totals due to rounding.

government. It saw education as a way to improve the quality of life for succeeding generations. A shared educational experience based upon a common language was seen as an integrating force—one that would moderate the class, religious, and ethnic differences within the community. So education has been seen both as consumption and as investment in the human resources of the nation. Education was deemed an object meriting transfer, not only from the parents of those currently in school, but from all members of the community. While social insurance may be seen as a device for sharing adversity, the public school is an institution for sharing hope for the future.

It is of historical interest that philanthropic organizations—most of them religious—led the way in developing schools in this country, but by the middle of the nineteenth century most state governments had established high priorities—indeed, most enshrined them in their constitutions—for public education. The great "high school revolution" occurred in the early decades of this century and attendance at the college level exploded after World War II (see Table 4.7).

Between 1950 and 1978 the percentage of persons aged 14–17 who were in school rose from 77 to 94; and the percentage of those aged 18–24 who were in school went up from 26 to 39. (These numbers are not shown in any table.) The absolute number in high school more than doubled, and enrollments in college about quadrupled (see Table 4.7). In constant 1978 dollars, $605 were spent in 1950 for each student in average daily attendance in public elementary and secondary schools. In 1978, the amount was $2021 (Table 4.8).

The changes in enrollments summarized above have been accompanied by several trends in funding sources. One is a decline in the relative importance of privately controlled schools. In 1978 10% of elementary and secondary students and 22% of higher-education students were in private schools. In 1950, these percentages were 12 and 48 (Table 4.7). A second trend is away from local funding of public schools. In the 1970s, the state share of the funds for elementary and secondary schools went up from 40 to 44% (*Digest of Educational Statistics*, 1981). This can be seen as an effort to equalize expenditure per pupil within states. Federal outlays for such schools went up from almost nothing to 9% of the total in the late 1960s and have stayed there ever since. A third interesting trend is that toward providing stipends for students in higher education. The first step in this direction was the so-called G.I. Bill for veterans of World War II. Social security survivors' benefits were extended to students from age 18 up to age 22 in 1965 and withdrawn in 1981. The

TABLE 4.8

Total Expenditure per Pupil in Average Daily Attendance in Public Elementary and Secondary Schools, 1949–1950 to 1977–1978

School year	Expenditure per pupil in unadjusted dollars	Expenditure per pupil in 1978–1979 dollars[a]
1949–1950	259	605
1959–1960	472	874
1969–1970	955	1480
1977–1978	2002	2021

Source: *Digest of Educational Statistics* (1981), Table 71, p. 82.

Note: Expenditure includes current expenditures for day schools, capital outlay, and interest on school debt.

[a]Based on the Consumer Price Index.

Basic Educational Opportunity Grant program was introduced in 1972. (Interest rate subsidies on loans to students are not accounted for here.) Such stipends are evidence that the demand for higher education as well as the supply of it are increased by SCI outlays. However, it should be noted that such stipends may substitute for interfamily cash or in-kind gifts to college students. The latter are also part of the SCI system.

Health Care

Transfers for health care have increased more rapidly than those for any other broad category of SCI. This increase has been led by private health insurance, Medicare (a social insurance program for people over age 65 and for some others), and Medicaid (a public assistance program for the medically indigent of all ages). Both Medicare and Medicaid were introduced in 1965. These "fast-growers" have supplemented the more traditional programs of workers' compensation, veterans' health care, public health programs, and private philanthropy. (See Appendix Table A.2 for more details.)

The growth of the present patchwork of private and public transfers over the past 30 years has improved access to and utilization of health care services. Between 1950 and the present, the number of physicians per 100,000 people rose from 149 to 204. Differences in utilization of health care between whites and blacks and between poor and nonpoor have been narrowed.

Over the decades important changes have been made in the disposition of health care resources. Hospital bed statistics reveal the sweeping nature of some changes. The total number of beds declined from 1.5 million in 1950 to 1.4 million in 1978. Not long ago a third of such beds were occupied by mental patients. Now only a sixth are. Today there are almost as many beds in nursing homes as in hospitals; 30 years ago the ratio was one to four. Structural change is also reflected in the increasing use of the hospital emergency clinic as the entry point for patients seeking primary care. It may be unnecessary to point out that many services, such as open heart surgery, kidney dialysis, chemotherapy, and artificial joints, are new to the scene. Such technological changes are no doubt important in explaining the rapid growth of health care spending, which in 1978 amounted to almost 9% of GNP.

However, most analysts ascribe an important part of the increase in utilization and price of health care to the advent of third-party financing into a field where the traditional method of payment has been fee-for-service to decentralized suppliers (P. Feldstein, 1979). Under American health insurance, consumers may choose among physicians, and physicians are free to determine the pattern of care and to charge "reasonable" and "customary" fees. This particular pattern stands in sharp contrast with that in education, where third-party financing is also practiced, but where the school board determines the pattern of instruction and sets the financial terms in advance.

We appear to be moving toward the view that health care, like education, should be available as a civil right. Government expenditures for this purpose, which amounted to 3.5% of GNP in 1978, were 40% of total health care outlays. However, in recent years, group health insurance directly paid for by employers has been an increasingly popular method for financing health care. This form of collective purchase amounts to 2.0% of GNP and reaches the great majority of American families. This voluntary insurance has not grown in response to any findings by the courts that employers should bear the social fault for damages sustained by employees with respect to nonoccupational illness. Rather, it seems to have been a response to a demand by employees and their unions—encouraged by a tax policy decision that health care benefits are not taxable to either the employer or the employee—for paternalistic group purchase by the employer. The cost of insurance is built into the compensation contract. (In the same spirit, some companies have undertaken group purchase of insurance against the need for legal services by employees.) It is notable that this form of insurance yields a distribution of benefits that diverges from the distribution of wages. For example, employees with dependents gain at the expense of those with no dependents. In that sense, there is a redistribution of income among employees.

Food, Housing, and Other Welfare Services

SCI for miscellaneous benefits, including food and housing, has not kept up with the growth of all SCI and in 1978 stood at 10% of the total. Public transfers are far greater than private transfers in this category, but it should be noted that private purchases dominate in-kind transfers with respect to most of the specific items. This is true for such examples as food, housing, child day care, and legal services. By way of contrast, transfers dominate private purchases of education and health care.

Most, but not all, of these benefits are administered through a public assistance framework (i.e., through means testing), and some are tied in with receipt of cash assistance benefits. Indeed, one may think of food stamps and public housing subsidies, both of which are income-tested, as close substitutes for cash benefits under income maintenance programs, since they free family money income for other uses. There has been a strong movement in recent years to separate the administration of social services from that of public assistance, and such a separation has come about with respect to family counseling and some other services.

Such in-kind transfers as food stamps and public housing are less responsive to the needs or wants of the recipients than are cash benefits (Olsen, 1971; Thurow, 1974; Smolensky et al., 1977). Nonetheless, there have been recent movements to develop some new benefits of this type, e.g., the Low-Income Energy Assistance program of 1978, and to target them on the poor by means of income-testing.

Some of the social services in this broad category of SCI might be seen as auxiliary to or substitutes for education or health care services. Thus, child day care and job training overlap the work of the school, and institutional care overlaps that of the medical establishment. Still other social services look back to an earlier day when it was assumed that poverty arose out of moral fault and that the remedy was to inspire the victims to "do right."

Reducing Income Poverty

The third immediate goal of SCI is to reduce income poverty (Lampman, 1971, 1974). This goal encourages a tilt of SCI in the direction of those people with limited means. President Johnson in 1964 set forth a nationwide poverty standard in terms of posttransfer money income, namely, $3000 per year in 1962 dollars ($8000 in 1978 dollars) for a family of four. In 1978, 11.4% of the population fell below that standard. On the other hand, 20.2% of the population had a pretransfer money income below the poverty line. The distance between the 20.2% in pretransfer poverty and the 11.4% in posttransfer poverty reflects the contribution of social insurance and public assistance in reducing income poverty. The greater part of the contribution is made by social insurance.

If we redefine income poverty in terms of money income plus the bonus value of food stamps, public housing, and the insurance value of health care benefits, then it appears that the percentage of the population in poverty in 1978 was about 6% (M. Anderson, 1978; Paglin, 1980; Hoagland, 1982; Smeeding, 1982).

Table 4.9 shows that the pretransfer poverty rate did not fall consistently over the 1965–1976 period, but remained near 20% of the population. This would appear to reflect the slow growth of the economy during the 1970s and the accelerating divorce rate. On the other hand, it may be due to disincentives to earn primary incomes set up by the

TABLE 4.9

The Incidence of Poverty among Persons 1950–1980, and the Size of the Poverty Income Gap, 1965–1976

Year	Income Concept			
	Pretransfer income	Prewelfare income	Posttransfer income	Adjusted income[a]
	Incidence of poverty (percentages)			
1950	n.a.	n.a.	32.0	n.a.
1960	n.a.	n.a.	22.0	n.a.
1965	21.3	16.3	15.6	12.1
1968	18.2	13.6	12.8	10.1
1970	18.8	n.a.	12.6	9.4
1972	19.2	13.1	11.9	6.2
1974	20.3	13.1	11.6	7.8
1976	21.0	13.1	11.8	6.5
1978	20.2	12.6	11.4	6.1
1980	21.9	14.2	13.0	6.1
	Poverty gap (billions of 1974 dollars)			
1965	34.6	20.2	16.3	12.8
1970	36.8	20.2	14.6	9.3
1976	48.4	23.1	15.2	9.2

Source: For 1950 and 1960, data are from Lampman (1971), p. 57. For 1965–1980, data are from Danziger and Plotnick (in press).
Note: n.a. = data not available.
[a] Adjusted income is all money income plus in-kind transfers of food stamps, public housing, and health care.

increased levels of SCI benefits and taxes. However, the increase in cash transfers is associated with a reduction in posttransfer poverty from 15.6% to 11.4%. At the same time, the poverty-income gap (i.e., the difference between actual income and the poverty line for all poor persons), rose in pretransfer terms but fell slightly in posttransfer terms (see the bottom panel in Table 4.9). The adjusted income column includes in-kind government transfers of food stamps, public housing, and health care. These transfers brought "adjusted income poverty" down to 6.1% in 1978.

Table 4.10 uses the same income concepts, but illuminates the changing composition of the population and of the part of the population in poverty. The bottom two rows show that the aged and female

TABLE 4.10
Composition of the Poor, 1965 and 1978

Income concept	Percentage of all poor living in households headed by					Total no. of persons in all categories (millions)
	Nonaged white men	Nonaged nonwhite men	Nonaged white women	Nonaged nonwhite women	Aged[a]	
Pretransfer income						
1965	34.3	14.2	11.2	9.6	30.3	40.8
1978	26.9	6.6	17.1	13.8	35.7	43.5
Prewelfare income						
1965	39.0	17.6	11.6	11.9	19.9	31.2
1978	30.3	8.8	23.1	20.7	17.0	27.2
Posttransfer income						
1965	39.6	17.9	11.2	11.7	19.6	29.9
1978	31.5	8.9	23.1	20.8	15.8	24.5
Adjusted income						
1968[b]	37.9	15.1	16.9	14.1	16.0	19.8
1978	47.5	9.7	26.1	14.2	2.5	9.0
Composition of the total population						
1965	71.9	8.1	6.2	2.8	11.1	191.3
1978	65.3	7.6	9.9	4.4	12.8	215.6

Source: Danziger and Plotnick (in press).
[a] All households headed by persons over 65 years of age (heads of both sexes and races).
[b] Data not available for 1965.

heads of households grew in relative importance in the total population between 1965 and 1978. The top two rows show that these two groups also grew in relative importance within the pretransfer poor population. The remaining rows show that the aged poor fell in relative importance with respect to each concept of posttransfer income, but that female-headed households grew in relative importance. This indicates that government transfer programs have in recent years been made increasingly supportive of the aged poor.

The traditional method, among all transfer methods, for reducing poverty has been public assistance, that is, means-tested benefits funded out of general revenues for special groups of the poor. (I am excluding from this discussion all policies aimed at getting more primary income into the hands of the poor.) Some of these benefits are in cash and some, for example, food stamps and Medicaid, are in kind. Most of such benefits go to the categories of the aged, blind, disabled, and families headed by women with children. The poor who are traditionally regarded as undeserving are the so-called working poor, namely, the intact families with income below the poverty level headed by able-bodied, nonaged men as well as nonaged, unrelated individuals. They have often been considered to have the potential means to provide for themselves, and hence have been denied eligibility for the more generous forms of categorical aid.

Public assistance is the bottom level of transfer. If social insurance and all forms of private transfer are inadequate, then and only then may one turn to public assistance. The latter is informed by the theory that government should not make "being on welfare" comfortable as a way of life lest it induce a great mass of people to abandon the work effort and saving whereby a nation may progress. It is consistent with this theory to treat nonworkers as social deviates who are to be stigmatized, denied citizenship rights, and reformed by a battery of welfare services. This strategy for reducing poverty was first enunciated in the poor laws of Elizabethan England, which compromised the feudal concept of status with the open-market concept of free contract (Poynter, 1969). The status concept is expressed in the emphasis in public assistance on local (parish) jurisdiction and family responsibility. The free contract concept is implicit in the emphasis on the employability of the individual in the national labor market.

Recent developments in public assistance illustrate a move away from key tenets of the old poor law. The Food Stamp program, since the amendments of the 1970s, is essentially a national, as opposed to a local, program and has no categorical limits on eligibility. SSI, again a nationwide program that absorbed earlier programs in support of the aged, blind, and disabled, explicitly rejects both the lien law (under which all assets of the beneficiary are pledged to the state to repay, at time of death, all benefits received) and relative responsibility (under which adult children are deemed financially responsible for their aged parents).

Sharing Private Contributions and Tax Burdens Fairly

The fourth explicit goal of the SCI system is fair sharing of the voluntary and compulsory contributions that are used to pay for the benefits. People have subjective standards that guide their direct interfamily giving to relatives and others and their giving to philanthropic organizations. In some cases, such standards are written down as policy for mandated private contributions. For instance, the courts determine what is a fair amount of child support to be paid by a divorced parent. The Pell Grant program spells out what is the "expected parental contribution" to a college student.

Similarly, the community has notions of the appropriate responsibility of employers toward the transfer benefits of their employees. As I noted above, the courts and legislatures determined that employers had a responsibility to pay much of the cost of industrial accidents. Beyond this, it strikes many people as reasonable that the employer, in what is a throwback to the paternalistic role of the medieval master, should help employees buy such essentials as health insurance, life insurance, and retirement annuities. At the same time, however, there is general agreement that employees should make compulsory payments in the form of payroll taxes for certain social insurance programs, thereby establishing what is often called a contractual right to future benefits.

The individual income tax appears to be a preferred tax for financing SCI. (It is surpassed only by the payroll tax for this purpose; see Table 2.2). It expresses—albeit imperfectly—the ideal of horizontal and vertical equity, wherein equals are to be treated equally, and those with higher income status face higher tax rates. It also touches on the goals of SCI expenditures as I have discussed them above. That is, it helps to offset income loss by giving tax preference to casualty losses and retirement income; it helps people buy selected goods and services by allowing deductibility of extraordinary medical expenses and of private health insurance premiums and by subsidizing home ownership and child day care; and it helps to reduce posttax income poverty by means of the personal exemption, the minimum standard deduction, and the earned income refundable credit for low-income families with children (see Appendix Table A.7).

The overall American tax system reflects the notions that taxes should relate to benefits received, the autonomy of local governments, convenience of the taxpayer, and ability to pay. History suggests that we want—or are willing to accept—a set of combined tax rates that are roughly proportional to income throughout most of the posttransfer income range. Note that most transfer receipts are not subject to income or payroll taxes. Progressivity affects only the top 5% or so of income receivers, according to the consensus view of tax incidence (see Table 3.12). Although the level of taxes is higher than it was, the pattern across income ranges has changed very little in the last several decades.

The pattern of SCI taxes and contributions appears to have become more regressive since 1950. Table 4.3 shows that payroll taxation and wage diversion have increased faster than other sources of revenue, and have substituted particularly for federal general revenues, philanthropy, and interfamily giving. It is notable that the payroll tax (a regressive tax) increased in relative importance, and federal general revenues (progressive taxes) decreased in relative importance.

Chapter 3 suggests that upper income classes pay more than they get back in SCI benefits in any single year. But that is not a full statement of the redistribution across income classes because it fails to take account of (1) the lifetime pattern of receipt of SCI benefits, (2) the sliding of benefits to secondary beneficiaries, and (3) donor benefits. These are discussed in turn.

If we could move from a 1-year income period to a lifetime income period, much of the interclass redistribution would seem to disappear. It is plain that some SCI benefits tend to go to people during the relatively low-income years of a lifetime (e.g., years of unemployment and retirement). Hence, it follows that the total benefits received over a lifetime will be more nearly uniform across income groups, as a share of total lifetime income, than 1 year's benefits as a share of 1 year's income.

It also is plain that some other SCI benefits, while not always coinciding with abnormally low-income years, tend to be paid out in a short period of high consumer need. This is true of benefits for schooling and for health care. Taxes and contributions paid over a lifetime for such services may equal benefits received for many families at each lifetime income level. (Interesting exceptions arise when new programs—e.g., OAI in 1935—are introduced.) Similarly, both the progressivity and regressivity of taxes will appear to be less when the income period is lengthened. It needs to be added that the underlying primary income distribution, and every person's ranking within it, will be different when we move from 1-year to lifetime incomes.

A special problem in identifying redistributive effects arises with what may be called "secondary beneficiaries." Consider the case of a disabled person who receives a government cash benefit. This will be recorded in an income survey as transfer income going to an otherwise destitute person. However, it might be that in the absence of the government program, a rich relative would have made a cash transfer to the disabled person. Against such a counterfactual, one may say that the rich relative is the one whose income has been increased. The income-redistribution effect of the increase in government benefits is considerably biased by the failure of most data sources to account for the "slide" of benefits to such secondary beneficiaries (Lampman & Smeeding, 1983). The lesson here is that the beneficiaries and eventual payers of the bill for a social welfare transfer program are not always fully identified in the legislation.

The same lesson can be learned from consideration of how a transfer may be valued by a donee, a donor, and a third party. In a voluntary exchange, it is usually assumed that the buyer and the seller are getting their money's worth, so to speak, and that the optimal quantity of the good is being produced. This assumption is less valid with respect to donor and donee who are parties to a transfer. Consider the donee. Donees may find that donors have surrounded the gift with conditions that severely limit its value to them. For example, the donors may give certain food items that are deemed inedible by the donees, or they may give educational benefits on which the donees place a low value.

Now consider the donors. They may regard the transfer as a contract to purchase certain behavior from the donees—which may be to provide adequate nutrition for the donees' children or to send them to school—and to the extent that the donees fulfill the contract the donors are satisfied. Alternatively, the donors may consider a transfer as having a reciprocal character. For example, individuals may contribute to the support of their aged parents in the belief that their children will do the same for them when they are old. Or, persons may contribute to the financing of a school in recognition of the fact that in the past they or their children had received a transfer of education benefits from that school. These several cases of donor benefit seem to contest whether there is a meaningful difference between exchange and transfer.

For another case, imagine a donor who gets satisfaction out of seeing the donee enjoy the gift. Parents may increase their own utility more by seeing their children wearing new clothes than they would by extra purchases for themselves. This is a case of interpersonal utility and it seems to dictate that some of the benefits of the transfer should be allocated to the donors. However, the story may not stop there, since third parties may also gain utility from seeing the children wearing new clothes. It is this insight that has led some theorists to identify a transfer as a public good, that is, a good defined as nonrivalrous and nonexclusive in consumption (Hochman & Rodgers, 1969).

There is also a public-good quality to private outlays that have significant production externalities. The control of communicable disease is a good example. Education is also often identified as a good with positive externalities. Financial aid to the poor may also have externalities. (Note that production externalities, which relate to reductions in the "cost of doing business" for third parties, are distinguishable from the direct interpersonal satisfactions of, for example, "seeing the child wear new clothes," which I call "interpersonal utility.")

Simply indicating that there are secondary beneficiary effects, donor benefits, and externalities does not establish that the upper income classes are getting a good deal out of the SCI system. That redistributive question is entangled with another question, one of efficiency import, namely, are the donors making transfers in the quantity that they really want? The answer to that question is that we cannot be sure that either voluntary private giving or coerced public giving will yield the level of transfer that is efficient in the sense that it expresses the specific wants of all donors. It is doubtful that voluntary contributions will yield the level of expenditures that people really want, since many will wait to see how much others will contribute. At the same time, those who do contribute may feel that they have contributed more than their fair share and may, therefore, reduce their contributions the next year. This is known as the free-rider phenomenon, which can be overcome by coercion. But there is a special problem in evaluating the outcome of a public choice. Is there any way of knowing whether coercion results in the purchase of the quantity of a public good which people would voluntarily buy—the quantity which equates marginal benefit and marginal cost—if there were no free-rider problem? This inscrutable question confronts us not only for national defense, but also for public outlays on law and order, environmental improvement, basic research, and, arguably, income transfers to selected classes of citizens.

In the case of externalities, the national benefit is alleged to exceed the sum of the benefits to the direct purchasers. This constitutes an argument for public expenditures to increase the outlay on items with such benefits in the hope of equating marginal social benefits with marginal social costs.

Some of these benefits are external to the direct beneficiaries and, as in the case of a more healthy and better-educated population, take the intangible form of a better society in which to live. Some other social benefits associated with SCI are best classified as donor benefits, which may arise out of "redistribution as a public good." By the resolution of the free-rider problem with respect to charity, SCI may reflect an efficiency gain from the donor point of view, just as there may be an efficiency gain from the taxpayer point of view in the coercive decision on a national defense budget. However, as Musgrave and Musgrave (1980, p. 103) put it: "It is difficult to say to what extent the actual budgetary process of redistribution should be viewed in terms of voluntary giving and the social goods approach, or the extent to which it should be viewed as a process by which a majority succeeds in transferring income from an unwilling minority."

Contributions of SCI to Three Other Social Goals

The recent expansion of the SCI system may have yielded social benefits by attaining to a higher degree the four explicit goals of the system. It may also have had side effects that might be counted as social benefits. The side effects that claim attention are (1) reductions of income inequalities, (2) contributions to economic growth and stability, and (3) improvement of the social and political environment.

Reductions of Income Inequalities

Some writers assert that the underlying goals—and hence an important basis for evaluation—of SCI are related to inequalities among persons. Consider first intergroup inequalities. The most dramatic effect of the SCI system is to modify the inequalities between the aged and nonaged. The aged are the greatest net gainers, averaging about four times as much per person as the nonaged in net benefits (Figure 3.1). Similarly, but to a lesser degree, SCI reduces the income difference between black and white persons, residents of North and South, intact and broken families, disabled and nondisabled, families with and without children, and large and small families. Some of these differences are thought to be related to inequality of opportunity. Most of these differences have been moderated though not eliminated in recent decades, in part owing to the expansion of SCI benefits. Thus, incomes of farm residents now average about 90% of nonfarm residents' income, and the North-South difference is less than it once was. For example, Mississippi's per capita income rose at 1.25 times the national average between 1950 and 1978. In 1950, the per capita income of the poorest region (the East South Central region) was only 51% that of the richest region. By

1978 it was 71%. During the 1950–1978 period, black family incomes rose from 54 to 59% of white family incomes, and blacks' share of total income increased from 7 to 8%. The median income of Hispanic families probably also rose in relation to the national median and now stands at 68% of the latter. (Only recent data are available.) The median educational difference between whites and blacks narrowed from 2.7 years to less than 1 year. At the same time, at least up to 1978, it seems that the income advantage associated with additional schooling remained unchanged—men having 4 years of college earned about twice as much as those with only 8 years of schooling. (For a discussion of recent changes, see R. B. Freeman, 1982.) One important group income difference that has not been reduced is that between men and women. Incomes of women working full time, year around were 64% those of men in 1950 and 57% in 1978.[7]

Another basis for evaluation is change in the size distribution of the postsecondary income distribution. Although there is a clear pattern in the SCI of taking from the rich and not so rich and giving to the poor in any single year, the postsecondary income distribution shows little change in inequality over time. Some studies (see the review of such studies by Taussig and Danziger, 1976) have found that when in-kind transfer and the value of leisure are included, and when an adjustment is made for family size, there has been a trend toward less inequality in recent years. Other studies, notably that of Reynolds and Smolensky (1977), find a trend toward greater inequality in the primary distribution. They also find that greater transfers have been needed each year to prevent a rise in the Gini coefficient of the distribution of final income.

I do not fully understand why the rise in SCI has not been more clearly reflected in a change in the measured distribution of final income. One reason is that there may be a time trend in the quantity of new transfers that slide over to the secondary beneficiaries identified in the previous section. Another is offsetting changes in the distribution of primary income, some of which may have been induced by changes in SCI. The latter may include lessened work effort (discussed in Chapter 5); changes in household size, composition, and location; and the shifting of benefits to suppliers, all of which are discussed below.

SCI benefits can have indirect effects on the size distribution of

---

[7]The numbers in this paragraph are from publications of the U.S. Department of Commerce, Bureau of the Census, including the U.S. Department of Commerce (Bureau of the Census), 1980c; *Statistical Abstract of the United States*, various years; and *Historical Statistics of the United States, Colonial Times to 1970*, 1976. These income changes are discussed in Danziger and Lampman (1978).

income and on intergroup differences in incomes by influencing decisions about family size and composition and also about location of residence (My discussion of these points draws heavily from Danziger, Haveman, & Plotnick, 1980.) Any transfer program can influence in two ways decisions about living arrangements or whether to divorce or remarry. Programs that increase the income available to the whole living unit may reduce personal tensions created by economic problems and promote greater family stability. For example, UI benefits or food stamps alleviate financial pressure that otherwise might rupture a marriage. Second, some programs extend actual or potential benefits only to some members of the household. This independent source of income, or the prospect of such support, exerts an "independence effect" that allows the actual or potential recipients to live separately from the rest of the family. For example, elderly persons or couples may choose to live alone instead of with their children if their social security benefit (plus other income) is sufficient. Unmarried youths' UI may permit them to remain independent of their parents during a period of joblessness. Similarly, the AFDC benefit that a woman with children may potentially receive may lead her to separate from her husband, and convert the potential benefit into an actual one. Once divorced, a woman with children may be less likely to remarry because of AFDC's independence effect (Bradbury, 1978; MacDonald & Sawhill, 1978). It is important to remember that the AFDC program and survivor benefits in OASDI were designed in 1935 to encourage women to keep their children rather than give them up for adoption.

Another demographic issue concerns the pronatalist or antinatalist effects of income transfer programs. To the extent that such programs are conditioned by family size or require the presence of children in the home in order for the family to remain eligible for benefits, they could lead people to believe they can afford the expense of having an extra child and thereby increase birth rates. Because many of the income support programs have these family-size characteristics, there has been a good deal of speculation about their pronatalist incentives and effects, but the empirical evidence suggests that these are not large.

In short, transfer policy can change the financial benefits and costs to those contemplating household composition changes, and, by doing so, encourage certain types of living arrangements or family sizes rather than others. Naturally, decisions on these personal matters are motivated by far more than financial incentives, but it is equally true that economic variables can have an identifiable impact of their own.

Certain transfer benefits, notably social security and other retirement pensions, are not dependent on where one lives. The sharp rise in payments from these programs has permitted many older people to move to geographic areas—including areas outside the United States—that they find more desirable. Population shifts toward the Sunbelt and rural recreation areas are partly due to this separation of income from locale.

Transfer benefits that vary from state to state or nation to nation may also affect migration decisions. It is often suggested that states or nations with relatively large welfare benefits attract some low-income persons for this reason. Greater benefits offer the prospect of increased income to persons wishing to live off of welfare. And for those intending to work, larger benefits will provide a better cushion in the event of ill health or unemployment.

Another reason why the final income distribution has not changed over time is that transfers may be shifted from the party who actually pays or receives them. Taxes, which are negative transfers from the standpoint of taxpayers, may have their point of impact on the business firm but their point of incidence on the wage earner or the consumer. This shift in the burden of tax is conventionally described in partial equilibrium analysis as resulting from a shift in the supply of or demand for a particular consumer good or factor in production. A subsidy to a particular good or factor is a negative tax and may also be shifted via a price change from the business sector to the household sector. In some instances, the deductive analysis of the burden of a tax or the benefit of a subsidy can be highly complex, with the perceived result turning on whether partial or general equilibrium analysis is employed and on what properties are assumed for the relevant demand or supply functions. Predictions of outcomes of a particular shift derived from such deductive analysis cannot be easily checked by any empirical information. Hence, most scholars tend to be cautious in making statements about who actually bears a tax or who benefits from a subsidy. To cite one example, suppose a government undertakes to pay to hospitals one-half of the hospital charges contracted for by consumers. Presumably, this means an addition to the quantity of hospital care that will be supplied at each price. Depending upon the elasticities of demand and supply, the price per unit of hospital care may rise by almost the full amount of the subsidy and the quantity of care delivered may increase very little. If that is the case, one may assert that the benefit of the subsidy goes chiefly to the suppliers of hospital care. However, the outcome in this case will depend on the number of consumers to be subsidized. If only aged or poor consumers are eligible for the subsidy, presumably the rise in the price of hospital care will be less. However, those ineligible for the subsidy will bear both the tax to pay for the smaller total subsidy and the higher price. Hence, the distribution of costs and benefits will be different in the two cases (Browning & Browning, 1983).

Similar shifting is observed with a general subsidy to wages paid by private employers, which may lead to a substitution of labor for capital, a higher total wage payment to workers, a lower payment to the suppliers of capital, and less productivity per worker employed. The effects may be different if the wage subsidy is targeted to, for example, handicapped or disadvantaged workers (Golladay & Haveman, 1977).

There are, then, several plausible explanations for the fact that inequality in the posttax posttransfer size distribution of income failed to decline between 1950 and 1978.

Contributions to Economic Growth and Stability

From a national planner's point of view, education can be viewed as an object of investment like highways or irrigation projects. Outlays for education are good investments if they yield a rate of return, in terms of extra national product, equal to or greater than that from other investments. This comparison should be made at the margin. For example, the return from educating a million more children should be compared with the return from building an extra thousand miles of highway. In this connection, it is also reasonable to compare the national stock of human capital with the stock of nonhuman or tangible capital.

Denison (1979) attributes 11% of the 1948–1973 growth of national income to the increase in educational attainment of those in the labor force, that is, .41 of a percentage point out of total growth of 3.65 percentage points per year (see Table 4.11). For 1973–1976, he assigns .67 points, or more than 100% of measured growth in national income, to education. Let us assume that 11% of the actual 1950–1978 growth is attributable to the increase in education. National income in 1950 was $662 billion in 1978 dollars (adjusted by the GNP price deflator). The comparable figure for 1978 was $1724 billion, which means that growth equalled $1062 billion over the period. Eleven percent of $1062 billion is $117 billion, which represents the contribution of extra education to the 1978 national income. Not all of this extra national income can be claimed for the increase in SCI outlay for education, since only part of the costs of education are covered by SCI. The $117 billion was 5.4% of the 1978 GNP. A plausible figure for the effect of SCI is in the range of 4% of GNP.

We can check that number by reference to changes in the stock of human capital. Eisner and others (1981, Tables 14 and 15) estimate the dollar value of the nation's stock of human capital for benchmark years

TABLE 4.11

Sources of Average Annual Growth of Total Actual National Income,
Selected Periods, 1948–1976
(contributions to growth rates in percentage points)

Item	1948–1973	1973–1976
National income	3.65	0.58
Total factor input	2.13	1.23
Labor	1.42	0.77
Employment	1.22	0.66
Hours	−0.24	−0.46
Age-sex composition	−0.14	−0.19
Education	0.41	0.67
Unallocated	0.17	0.09
Capital	0.71	0.46
Land	0	0
Output per unit of input	1.52	−0.65
Advances in knowledge and n.e.c.[a]	1.10	−0.58
Improved resource allocation	0.29	−0.01
Legal and human environment	−0.04	−0.34
Dwellings occupancy ratio	−0.01	0.02
Economies of scale	0.32	0.19
Irregular factors	−0.14	0.07

Source: Denison (1979), Table 8.1, p. 104.
[a] n.e.c. = not elsewhere classified.

since 1945. That stock for 1976 was $6.3 trillion, which was almost equal to the stock of tangible capital of $6.9 trillion. They define human capital as (1) the investment cost of providing and acquiring education and training, broadly defined, and (2) one-half the cost of health care. Investments are depreciated in accord with assumed service lives (e.g., for most education the service life is 50 years). The Eisner numbers for current and 1978 prices are shown below. I made the conversion to 1978 prices by use of the GNP price deflator.

Human capital (billions of dollars)	1945	1950	1955	1960	1965	1970	1976
Current prices	430	654	919	1290	1837	3075	6305
1978 prices	1706	1832	2444	2823	3719	5066	7092

The growth in the stock of human capital in 1978 prices from 1950 to 1976 was $5260 billion. If we can say that half of that increase occurred because of the rise in SCI expenditures for education, and if the net rate of return to human capital is 5%, then we can say that $2630 billion times .05—or $132 billion—is the amount by which the 1978 GNP was increased owing to the rise in SCI for education. The $132 billion is 6.1% of the 1978 GNP. I take this as confirmation that the 4% derived from Denison is not too high and I will, therefore, carry the latter number forward as a social benefit of the extra SCI outlays in education.[8]

SCI benefits other than those for education may also make contributions to economic growth. Better nutrition, health care, and housing may elevate motivation and energy levels. Allowing nonemployed persons to conduct more effective searches for new positions—as UI and some other cash benefit programs do—may yield a more productive match between workers and jobs. Further, private employee benefits may reduce labor turnover and enhance loyalty to the firm. The growth of SCI may be seen as a necessary accommodation to the process of economic growth.

As Abramovitz (1981) puts it:

> The pace of growth in a country depends not only on its access to new technology, but on its ability to make and absorb the social adjustments required to exploit new products and processes. . . . The process includes the displacement and redistribution of populations among regions and from farm to city. It demands the abandonment of old industries and occupations. . . . [It implies] a great change in the structure of families and in their roles in caring for children, the sick, and the old. Because the required adaptations can and do alter the positions, prospects, and power of established groups, conflict and resistance are intrinsic to the growth process. To resolve such conflict and resistance in a way which preserves a large consensus for growth, yet does not impose a cost which retards growth unduly, a mechanism of conflict resolution is needed. The national sovereign state necessarily becomes the arbiter of group conflict and the mitigator of those negative effects of economic change which would otherwise induce resistance to growth. The enlargement of the government's economic role, including its support of income minima, health care, social insurance, and the other elements of the welfare state, was therefore—at least up to a point—not just a question of reducing irregularities of outcome and opportunity, though that is how people usually think of it. It was and is—up to a point—a part of the productivity growth process itself. (p. 2)

The argument that the SCI system helps to stabilize the national economy stems from the Keynesian idea that the federal government budget should be in deficit during a recession and in surplus in a boom.

---

[8]Because we are dealing with the return on an investment, this item is not strictly compatible with the 1-year accounting period assumed for the other items in Tables 4.12 and 5.9. The 5% rate of return used is net of the opporunity cost of capital. Cohn (1979, pp. 115–116) reports social internal rates of return to secondary schooling of 10.7% in 1970 and to college education of 8.5–10.5% in 1973. Hence, I take 10% as the gross return to education and subtract an assumed opportunity cost of capital of 5% to get a net rate of return of 5%.

Increasing governmental spending and cutting taxes are ways to offset the contractions of private spending that characterize a recession. When private spending rises too fast, the appropriate fiscal response is to increase tax collection and to reduce government spending and thereby to restrain inflation. Such a countercyclical policy may be managed by timely changes in tax laws and appropriations or it may be left to automatic changes. The progressive income tax is an automatic stabilizer, since revenue from it increases faster than personal income does and vice versa. UI, with its fixed formula of entitlement for benefits and a set tax rate per employee, yields a rise in spending and a fall in tax collections when a tax recession hits. Hence, UI reserves are drawn down in recession and built up in a boom. The same pattern is found in OAI (Vroman, 1969; Snyder, 1970).

The idea that SCI serves as a stabilizing force was severely challenged when stagflation made its unwelcome appearance. Countercyclical fiscal policy is premised on the "normal" business cycle of alternating overemployment and underemployment with inflation threatening only in the boom. In the late 1960s the rate of price increase was about 5% per year, but in the 1970s it averaged almost 10% in the presence of high unemployment. The Consumer Price Index, based on 1967 at 100, rose to 272 in 1981.

One may think of inflation as a rival of the SCI system. Both of them involve redistribution of income and wealth, though inflation's pattern of redistribution is quite different from that of SCI. Inflation alters income relationships between debtors and creditors, old and young, rich and poor, homeowners and renters. It upsets the value of insurance policies and pensions. Inflation (like depression) is to the SCI system what witchcraft is to scientific medicine.

Since the unsatisfactory record on price increases occurred simultaneously with the rapid rise in SCI expenditures in 1965–1975, it is widely believed that the SCI increase was in some part responsible for the price increases. Some of the arguments supporting that belief are the same as those to be reviewed in the Chapter 5 discussion of productivity decline, namely, those having to do with intensity of work effort, saving, and capital formation. However, some arguments have to do with deficit financing and upward pressure on wage costs.

Inflations are often classified as those caused by "demand-pull" and those due to "cost-push." Demand-pull can cause inflation when spending rises faster than the supply of goods. If the government runs a deficit and thereby increases total demand at a time when the economy is already producing at capacity, inflation is likely to follow. But what does the 1965–1975 increase in the SCI ratio have to do with this? It is true that the federal budget was in deficit in all but 1 of those years—1969. But it is also true that production was well below capacity levels in the 1970–1975 period (i.e., unemployment was high and rising). Inflation and high unemployment were occurring at the same time—a novel experience. Taxes could have been raised or expenditures could have been cut to prevent the deficits, but to do so would have invited increases in already high unemployment. (Nothing I have said here is meant to condone the gross error of "double-indexing" social security benefits in 1972.)

Cost-push inflation is not caused by fiscal policy but rather by rises in the cost of raw materials or labor or other inputs to production. The most dramatic case of this was the instance of oil in 1973. Some critics point to the success of organized public employees—including teachers and nurses—in raising wages during this period as a cost-push factor. Indexing the social security tax base in 1972 (effective in 1974) is viewed by some as having been a cost-push inflationary step. In this book I assume that the social security payroll tax is borne by employees, but some critics argue that the 1974 and 1977 tax increases were passed along by employers as price increases to the consumer.

I pointed out earlier that SCI has properties of automatic stabilization which are thought capable of restraining the swings of a normal business cycle. But what automatic or discretionary responses by SCI are appropriate in a period of stagflation? How do people's expectations of future inflation alter the picture? There is no consensus on the answers to these questions. It is not likely that the policy dilemma presented by stagflation would have been much different if the increase in SCI had not occurred. It is not clear that SCI caused the great inflation of the 1970s, nor that change in it could prevent any future inflation.

Improvement of the Social and Political Environment

Advocates of a substantial scale for public SCI programs often argue that lessened inequality of opportunity and more economic security would reduce social tensions and interclass hostilities. They feel that a better-educated and healthier population would not only be economically more productive but would be better citizens. According to this line of argument, the personal alienation bred by the exchange system needs to be ameliorated by the integrative forces of a transfer system in order to have a balanced and healthy society (Tawney, 1952; Boulding, 1973). The competition of the market divides people into winners and losers; the SCI system brings all people into cooperative relationships in community enterprises in pursuit of shared human values.

One of these human values is freedom, about which there is considerable controversy in the welfare state literature. Tawney asserted that "freedom for the pike is death for the minnow." Some of John Dewey's disciples adopt his concept of "positive freedom," that is, the freedom to enjoy traditional social and political liberties, a freedom that is effectively denied to some by the market distribution of income and property. According to this concept, freedom is equivalent to effective power to do specific things (MacCallum, 1967). Attention is thus diverted to the distribution of specific freedoms among persons and to the relative importance of the several types of freedom. It is not enough to establish that some people suffer certain interference by the introduction of an SCI program; one must also investigate the possibility that some other persons (or even the same persons) may have acquired, by virtue of the new program, some new freedoms or capacities that they did not have before. With such an approach, one can entertain the possibility that the sum of liberty in a community may be fixed and only the distribution of it may be altered by institutional change, or that the quality of liberty may be maximized if the more important liberties are secured through the sacrifice of the less important ones. Followers of this approach (e.g., Rawls, 1971) give examples of specific positive freedoms, such as the freedom to go to college, which come up in the discussion of the four goals of SCI having to do with security, poverty, and fair sharing. To a large extent, I have already included the "positive freedoms" as social benefits of SCI and it would be double-counting to add them here. However, an understanding of the positive freedom argument is helpful in evaluating not only the claim of loss of freedoms, but also the claim of loss of market efficiency (discussed in Chapter 5) as social costs of the SCI system.

Classic liberals deny that a large-scale SCI system promotes the survival of democratic capitalism and, in particular, argue that it strikes at its central value, namely, freedom. Hayek and his followers set up the discussion in terms of freedom *from* certain interferences by government, or what can be called "negative freedom." Classic liberals use the laissez-faire state as the counterfactual to the welfare state and presume that private property does not itself constitute a barrier to freedom.

The SCI system is largely built on sharing of income and collective purchase. By contrast with the market's emphasis on free choice for the individual worker and consumer, SCI stresses centralization of decision-making in the hands of a paternalistic and coercive authority (Hayek,

1960; Friedman, 1962; Friedman & Friedman, 1980). Even if the majority of beneficiaries and contributors concur in decisions for a particular program, it is likely that some minority will stay in the program only if they are forced to do so. Not only are contributors to public and many private SCI programs forced to pay, the beneficiaries are often compelled to abide by rules for specific behavior if they intend to receive benefits. Parents are forced to send their children to a school that meets state standards; an aged person cannot receive OAI benefits if earnings exceed a certain level; a worker cannot agree to forgo future social insurance or private pension benefits and accept a correspondingly lower wage and benefit package. (In the latter case, we see the same restriction on freedom of contract as that in the minimum wage law.) Almost all SCI benefits have strings attached to them which, in some sense, restrict freedom of choice and, hence, can be said to limit opportunity to do something else. For example, an employee who is forced to divert some wages to a company pension fund may feel denied the opportunity to invest those funds in a more promising venture.

It seems to be a fact of life that public SCI programs, and some private ones as well, spawn a large number of rules and regulations, some of which are intended to protect against abuse by administrators as well as by beneficiaries. Moreover, many decisions tend to be made not by legislators but by remote, specialized bureaucrats and technical experts, all of whose decisions are open to review by the courts. Some critics see the need for voice by the beneficiaries (e.g., by "welfare rights organizations" or groups of students or hospital patients [Jackson & Johnson, 1974]). Others emphasize "exit" as a means of protest against arbitrary administration (Hirschman, 1970, 1982). Alternative schools and competing health insurance plans allow dissenters to "vote with their feet" (Harris & Seldon, 1979). Still others argue for consumer cooperatives and self-help groups as alternatives to government provision of housing, child day care, and other services (Gershuny, 1978). In this connection, a case can be made for local autonomy in the provision of SCI benefits, thus allowing those who favor one scope and scale of such benefits to congregate within a particular jurisdiction. However, local autonomy flies in the face of another principle, namely, the right of all citizens to equal protection of the laws and equal opportunities within a state.

What Hayek called "the road to serfdom" was the trend toward greater generosity of SCI benefits leading to more centralization and nationwide uniformity of administration. The more remote and less adaptable to local circumstances the administration becomes, the greater the dissent, protest, and attempts to avoid and evade the rules and regulations. This in turn calls forth successively tougher administrators, who are willing to use stronger and stronger methods to enforce the laws. One need not agree with Hayek's apocalytic bottom line to see that there is some merit in the point that there tends to be some trade-off between SCI—particularly some forms of SCI—and freedom. Like "security," the value of "freedom"—both positive and negative—is intangible and defies quantification.

Summation and Weighting of Social Benefits

In line with an evaluation procedure, I offer a summary that identifies four explicit goals of the SCI system along with three other social goals (see Table 4.12). I have sought to compare the degree of goal attainment in 1978 with the degree of goal attainment that might have been achieved with an SCI system on the order of that which was obtained in 1950. The right hand column shows my personal judgment as to whether or not there has been increased achievement—and therefore a social benefit—with respect to each goal.

Two explicit goals of the SCI are to reduce insecurity with respect to income loss and with respect to irregular and extraordinary expenditures. The SCI system appears to have made progress on these goals in

TABLE 4.12
Social Benefits Attributable to 1950–1978 Changes in SCI

Item	Degree of increased achievement of goal
1. Reduction of insecurity with respect to income loss	+
2. Reduction of insecurity with respect to irregular and extraordinary purchases	+
3. Reduction of income poverty	+
4. Fair sharing of SCI taxes and contributions	0
5. Reduction of income inequality	+
6a. Production increases due to improved education, health, and economic security of the workforce	$+^a$
6b. Production increases from more effective automatic stabilization	0
7. Improvement of the social and political environment	+ or −

[a] About a 4% increase in 1978 GNP due to increased SCI outlays for education (as discussed in text).

the sense that a larger number of people are drawing benefits and the typical benefit covers a larger share of the income loss or of the cost of the specified good. This means that we have moved from a less to a more insured world. Children born today have greater assurance than did their grandparents against the risks of income loss at each stage of life. They can also count on improved access to such key services as education and health care. Rawls (1971) would have us evaluate this increased insurance—or entitlement or endowment—from behind the veil of ignorance of whether we will be born to rich or poor parents, or of whether we will have good or bad health.

Two other explicit goals are to reduce income poverty and to achieve fair sharing of the taxes and contributions that go to pay for each year's SCI benefits. The ratio of SCI benefits going to the poor has risen from 28% in 1950 to 33% in 1978 (compare Appendix Tables A.11 and A.12) while the percentage of the total population in pretransfer poverty has fallen slightly. Posttransfer poverty has, thus, been substantially reduced. However, there have been changes in the pattern of SCI taxes and contributions toward more regressivity. Those funding sources for SCI classified as regressive in Table 3.11 have grown faster than total SCI (see panels A and E in Table 4.3). I put down a + for item 3 and a 0 for item 4.

I enter a weak + for reduction of income inequality. Since the increased outlays for education have contributed to higher labor productivity, we can enter a positive score for item 6a—production increases due to improved education, health, and economic security of the workforce—even though the SCI contribution to economic stabilization is not clear (item 6b). A "not clear" is the verdict on whether the social and political environment has improved, item 7, partly because of the overlap of this goal with the four explicit goals of SCI.

My judgments of the degree to which these goals have been achieved are simply that—judgments based on fragmentary evidence. Evaluation of the SCI system is more art than science, and I invite the reader to substitute his or her own judgments for those in Table 4.12.

The next step in evaluating the social benefits of the expansion of the SCI system is to rank the seven goals in terms of relative importance. Here again the judgment of the individual evaluator is needed. This section is devoted to a discussion of how people are predisposed to rank one goal over another.

In the foregoing discussion of the explicit goals of American SCI, each of the four goals is associated with a preferred method for pursuing it. Reducing insecurity with respect to income loss is associated with social insurance; helping people to meet irregular and extraordinary need is associated with the public school and voluntary health insurance; reducing poverty with public assistance; and fair sharing of contributions with wage diversion and the income tax. One can continue this linking of ends with means by noting that there are philosophies or mentalities that are built around certain approaches to SCI. These overlap some of the goals and preferred means identified above. They include the mentalities of offset of losses, efficient social investment, minimum provision, and horizontal and vertical equity. It would seem that individual analysts and policymakers are often conditioned to approach any SCI question with the priorities and techniques associated with one or another of the preferred means. Thus, those who are devoted to the insurance method emphasize offset of losses; those who have a background in economics or business planning emphasize social investment; those who start with management experience in public assistance stress poverty reduction through the provision of aid to the needy; and those who are trained in income tax theory place highest priority on achieving horizontal and vertical equity. During the 1964–1972 debate on welfare reform, I came to realize that both advocacy of and opposition to the negative income tax as a substitute for existing cash and in-kind programs often stemmed from those who hold fast to one or another of these four approaches. I review some of this conflict in Lampman (1977a).

The mentality of offsetting loss is tied to the maintenance of whatever status a person has had. Those who see SCI in these terms are not easily attracted to the goal of raising the share of income going to all in the lowest income group. For them, justice is identified with preventing loss of rank. They tend to build on the notion of employer responsibility—a medieval concept, but one restated in the modern law of torts.

Those who focus on efficient social investments see transfer as means to increase the national income. Justice or equity is not the aim so much as achieving a high rate of return on the outlay for, say, education. For them the decision on whether to make an educational investment would take into account all costs—private and social—and all benefits—direct and indirect. Such a decision would be affirmative only if the benefits, given a rate of return, exceeded the costs.

Those with a minimum-provision mentality emphasize the targeting of SCI benefits on those who need them the most and who are least able to solve their personal problems. According to this mentality, intervention is most appropriate in crisis situations and for the purpose of meeting emergency need. Those conditioned to this view are not sensitive to the fine-graded needs of those not in crisis.

Those trained in income tax theory and design emphasize horizontal and vertical equity. They tend to have trouble with those who emphasize offset of loss, or efficient social investment, or minimum provision. According to the horizontal and vertical equity mentality, equity means treating equally all those who are similarly stationed (i.e., who have the same income and family size), and narrowing inequality among all families ranked in a superior to inferior relationship with respect to income. This mentality comes into direct conflict with the other views when it is proposed that a negative income tax (NIT) should replace some or all public SCI benefits. The advocate of the negative income tax tends to view with horror the categorical exclusions, the abrupt withdrawal of benefits, the high benefit-reduction rates, and the capricious changes of rank order of families that are brought about by many existing SCI programs. On the other hand, some opponents of the NIT charge that the income tax mentality has less motive power than do the other mentalities to reach out to genuine human needs. They also claim that the income tax goal of narrowing income inequality is vague, formless, and alarming.

Economists try to sort out these conflicts among viewpoints by identifying the acceptable purposes of governmental intervention in the market as improving either equity or efficiency. They tend to identify the efficient allocation of resources as that which would occur, given a distribution of income and assuming no public goods problems and no externalities, as a result of free consumer and producer choice. Government intervention is needed (but may not work) to solve the problems of public goods and externalities.[9]

Economists tend to identify equity with less inequality in the size distribution of income (Okun, 1975). I would like to discourage this simplistic tendency. As my review of the goals of the SCI system and of the conflicting mentalities of SCI advocates indicates, the standards of fairness and efficiency that appear to guide redistribution via private and public programs are not easy to summarize. In particular, it would be wrong to conclude that these numerous purposes all boil down to one, namely, the reduction of inequality in the size distribution of income. It would also be wrong to conclude that each and every reduction of inequality would meet the requirements of all of the mentalities.

What can be called the American standard method of representing the size distribution of income, as developed by the Bureau of the Census, is a highly simplified statement of a complex reality (Lampman,

---

[9]Achieving economies of scale and reducing information and transaction costs are also relevant reasons for government intervention in some cases.

1973). It, along with the Gini ratio, which is used as a summary measure of inequality of that distribution, is hardly an ideal measure of inequality for all purposes. It is limited by its necessarily fixed definitions of income, income-receiving unit, and income period.

While political philosophy exhibits a drift toward defining the limiting of income inequality as a goal, it is interesting that political activists have not focused on a particular concept or measure of overall income inequality. No political party has adopted a slogan of "A .300 Gini ratio or fight!" Perhaps one of the reasons for caution in adopting change in the American standard distribution as a goal is that it measures inequality of result, while political interest attaches to the processes that limit inequality of opportunity among children. It is interesting that we do not have a good index of the latter type of inequality. Perhaps the best such indicator is a measure of black-white, male-female, national origin, religious, and other intergroup income differences.

Further, measured inequality of income has had only scattered use as a guide for social intervention on behalf of the economic losers and in restraint of the winners. The classification of rich and poor for income tax or public assistance purposes hardly duplicates the American standard distribution. In actually legislating and administering programs with redistributive effects, little overt attention is given to the facts revealed therein. Moreover, large changes in such programs as income taxation and public assistance may do relatively little to alter the distribution.

That is to say, each program for redistribution, be it public education, unemployment insurance, or public housing, has its own philosophy that may have little in common with the philosophy that informs the design of the American standardized distribution of income. The latter is, then, a performance indicator to which no social policy is directly keyed. The hiatus is significant. It means that the income distribution is not used in deciding who should help whom. It may also mean something else: namely, that Americans do not really seek any particular degree of inequality in the size distribution of income, but rather seek a system of sharing that recognizes human needs, restrains certain arbitrary or capricious inequalities, and serves a variety of defined social purposes as stated in the four mentalities previously identified.

What should the reader conclude about how to rank the seven goals I identified? In the end, this is a matter of preference or informed judgment for each individual evaluator. It may be helpful to consider the range of judgments offered by different experts in the field. To serve this end I have discussed the several mentalities that weigh the goals of SCI differently. The controversy among persons of competing mentalities is often exacerbated and sometimes brought to a dead end by mutual misunderstanding of vocabularies as well as concepts and practices which are peculiar to each. These four mentalities coexist in balance—or tension—in our system of SCI. None of them speaks to the strong points of any of the others, yet each puts some constraint on the others.

Between 1950 and 1978 the ratio of SCI to GNP increased from 17.2% to 27.6%. Public benefits, particularly those intermediated by the federal government, grew faster than private benefits. Cash benefits for retirement and health care benefits grew faster than most other benefits.

The 60% increase in the SCI ratio was driven, I assert, by four explicit goals which have historic roots in American experiences with SCI institutions. These goals, along with three other goals that are often brought forward in justifying a high SCI ratio, are useful in undertaking an evaluation of the social benefit side of a benefit-cost study of the 1950–1978 changes. The social benefits of the change, to the extent that there are any, will be found in added attainment of these seven goals, which are listed in Table 4.12.

I make the judgment that the nation did realize positive added attainment of five of the seven goals as a result of the rise in the SCI ratio. I also make the judgment that the goals which get positive scores are ones to which I assign the greatest weight. Hence, I conclude that substantial gains in social benefits flowed from the 1950–1978 changes. However, the reader is invited to do his or her scoring and weighting, to reach a different conclusion, and to then proceed to the second half of the evaluation—which has to do with the social costs of the same changes. The bottom line for the evaluator is, have the added benefits been worth the added costs?

A Guide to Reading

A number of difficult issues have been raised in this chapter on social benefits. Here I suggest some readings related to those issues.

Changes in Family Size and Composition

Hutchens. 1979. Welfare, remarriage, and marital search.
Michael, Fuchs, and Scott. 1978. Changes in household living arrangements, 1950–1976.

Selecting the Income Period for Study of Redistribution

Aaron. 1982. *Economic effects of social security.* Chapter 6.
Cowell. 1979. The definition of lifetime income.
Danziger, van der Gaag, Smolensky, and Taussig. 1983. The life-cycle hypothesis and the consumption behavior of the elderly.
Layard. 1977. On measuring the redistribution of lifetime income.
Lillydahl and Singell. 1982. The scope of the grants economy and income distribution: An examination of intergenerational transfers of income.
Moss. 1978. Income distribution issues viewed in a lifetime income perspective.
Nicholson. 1970. Redistribution of income: Notes on some problems and puzzles.

Identification of Social Goals

Arrow. 1963. Uncertainty and the welfare economics of medical care.
Gordon. 1982. *Welfare, justice, and freedom.*
Journal of Social Policy. 1982. Freedom and the welfare state.
Margolis. 1982. *Selfishness, altruism and rationality.*
Pinker. 1979. *The idea of welfare.*
Rauscher. 1978. The necessity for, and the limits of, the social welfare state.
Tobin. 1970. On limiting the domain of inequality.
Weisbrod. 1968. Income redistribution effects and benefit-cost analysis.

Productivity Gains from Better Health Care

Fuchs. 1966. The contribution of health services to the American economy.
Fuchs. 1974. *Who shall live?*
Fuchs. 1983. *How we live.*
Hadley. 1982. *More medical care, better health?*
Mushkin. 1962. Health as an investment.
Wilson and Wilson. 1982. *The political economy of the welfare state.* Chapter 6.

CHAPTER   5

Social Costs of the 1950–1978 Changes in the Secondary Consumer Income System and a Comparison with Social Benefits

In the previous chapter I discussed the numerous social benefits that may be attributed to the recent growth in the scale and scope of the American system of SCI. Most of them are intangible and all of them are hard to quantify. I now turn to a discussion of the added social costs incurred by increase in the scope and scale of the system during the period 1950–1978.

It is important to note at the outset that taxes and contributions paid to finance cash SCI benefits are not good indicators of the burden or social cost of the SCI system. The flow of cash from one part of the household sector to another does not have a direct effect on the total or average level of private consumption. The outcome is quite different from that of a program which draws money out of the household sector and, by exhaustive expenditures on, for example, national defense, reduces the ability of households to consume. Social cost is best thought of as a reallocation of resources that results in less output of consumer goods. In accord with that thought, this chapter considers social cost as arising from (1) resources used up to expand collection, compliance, and administrative activities of both cash and in-kind SCI programs; (2) the shifting of potential labor time induced by the expansion of the SCI system from the labor market to such nonmarketed uses as schooling, home production, and leisure; (3) loss of productivity per hour at work; and (4) reallocation of resources to the provision of additional health care, education, and other SCI goods and services.

In this chapter I follow the pattern of Chapter 4 in measuring each of the costs, assigning weights to the several costs, and summing all costs. In addition, I attempt to balance the benefits of SCI against its costs over the period 1950–1978.

Collection, Compliance, and Administrative Costs

The overhead costs of delivering SCI benefits include the use of land, labor, and capital to raise the funds for and make and implement decisions about who should and who should not receive benefits. These costs also include the time and effort of those private citizens who comply with rules and regulations concerning taxes and contributions on the one hand and the receipt of benefits on the other. The overhead costs form a wedge between what is paid into the SCI system and what the beneficiaries receive.

The data presented in Tables 2.1 and 2.2 do not show a uniform treatment of these overhead costs. Collection costs are generally not included in these data; the principal exceptions are the social insurance programs. Administrative costs of public programs are generally included but those of private programs generally are not, although "the costs of providing this protection" are included for private health insurance. Compliance costs are generally not included.

Musgrave and Musgrave (1980, p. 302) report that the cost of federal tax administration is about half a cent per dollar of federal revenue. They estimate compliance cost, based on a calculation of taxpayer time spent per return filed, at about 1.0% for individual and corporate income tax returns. This total of 1.5% of revenue raised for collection and compliance costs is probably near the minimum range for SCI programs. State and local governments, which lack the federal economies of scale, tend to have higher ratios. Private insurance companies and philanthropic organizations have special costs of selling policies and soliciting funds. Pension funds collect some of their income in the form of return on investments, which must be managed. Even direct interfamily giving may have a counterpart to collection and compliance costs. Consider the case of several siblings trying to reach and carry out an agreement on how to share the burden of supporting an aged parent. The fact that a considerable amount of money passes from one intermediary to another suggests a special kind of collection and compliance cost. Thus, a state government or a philanthropic agency may have to spend time and effort to win an SCI grant from the federal government. Recognizing that there is great variability, I hazard the guess that collection and compliance costs on the revenue side may amount to as much as 5% of the total funds collected for all SCI purposes. (I am leaving out of account the cost of noncompliance, that is, the distortion of effort toward nontaxed activity in the so-called underground economy [Lindbeck, 1981].)

Expending SCI funds may involve both administrative and compliance costs distinct from those having to do with collecting the funds (Goetschius & Wicks, 1971). However, these are often hard to separate from the costs of delivering and consuming the benefits. Administrative costs pertinent here are those that involve finding and selecting clients who are eligible for the benefit. Schobel (1981) reports that administrative and collection costs of OASDI in 1978 amounted to 1.6% of benefit payments. Compliance costs involve such things as the time of clients, who must gather information about the benefits and supply the information necessary to establish eligibility. A special case arises when the SCI benefit is compulsory, as is true for school attendance. Education and health care, to be effective, require not only compliance but active cooperation of clients (Fuchs, 1968).

In general, what writers have in mind in discussing administrative costs is the activity that falls somewhere between the policymaking level and the direct provision of the benefit to the client. Thus, in the case of a school, the school board makes policy, the classroom teacher delivers the benefit (indeed, the service by the teacher *is* the benefit), and the administrators are those who stand between the board and the teacher.[1] For another example, consider the case of a health insurance company that carries out the terms of a collectively bargained plan. The insurance company collects contributions via the employers and makes determinations as to which persons are eligible for which benefits and how much money should be paid to which providers of health care. Note that these administrative duties may save time of both doctors and patients. Again, it is hard to draw a sensible line between administrative expense and the provision of an SCI benefit. Also, it is difficult to determine what level of such expense is optimal.

---

[1] It is interesting that comment on these concepts is often ill-informed. Some writers call the administrators and the teachers beneficiaries of SCI expenditures, overlooking the possibility that some people who are presently teachers might be employed in other industries if education funding were diminished. It is, of course, true that some teachers may be getting paid more than their opportunity costs and in that sense may be receiving rents. For this and other reasons they may have a self-interest in promoting larger school budgets.

What is wanted is a definition of the discrepancy between the value of the contributions made by donors and the benefits received by the clients of SCI programs. (It should be noted that if less were devoted to collection and compliance there would be more tax evasion, and, on the expenditure side, less administrative effort would lead to more errors and to more fraud and abuse by clients and providers.) An outside guess for the administrative cost average for all such programs, public and private, is 5% of all SCI benefits. That may be added to the 5% estimated to cover collection and compliance costs on the revenue side, for a grand total of 10%. That 10% of SCI revenues was equal to $60 billion in 1978, which amounted to about 3% of GNP. If the scope and scale of the SCI system in 1978 had been the same as in 1950, then collection, compliance, and administrative costs might have been only 2% of GNP. The difference between 3% and 2%, namely 1% of GNP, is a social cost of the 1950–1978 expansion of the SCI system.

Loss of Time at Market Work

This section examines one hypothesis concerning the welfare state, namely, that increases in the relative importance of SCI spending cause reductions in the quantity of market labor supplied.[2] More specifically, the question is: Would the current labor supply be larger than it actually is if the great increase in SCI spending in the years 1950–1978 had not occurred?

SCI money and nonmoney benefits come to households in the form of a nonlabor income. That is, the recipient does not get them as a market return for labor in the current period. Households do pay for them, however, via taxes and contributions. Hence, it is at least arguable that the existence of such benefits may reduce work effort at two points, one where the beneficiary receives the nonlabor income, and the other where the worker suffers a wage loss because of the taxes or contributions. Following this line of thought, many people see a conflict between the welfare state goals of security, adequacy of income, and minimum levels of selected services for all, on the one hand, and the high employment required for a satisfactory level of production on the other hand.[3]

---

[2]This section is a revision and adaptation of Lampman (1983).
[3]For an excellent, but less quantitative, inquiry into a number of these issues, see Lindbeck (1981).

TABLE 5.1

Civilian Labor Force Participation Rates, Employment and Unemployment Rates, Selected Years, 1950–1978

Year	Civilian labor force participation rate			Civilian employment rate[a] (%)	Unemployment rate (%)
	Total (%)	Males (%)	Females (%)		
1950	59.2	86.4	33.9	55.2	5.3
1960	59.4	83.3	37.7	54.9	5.5
1970	60.4	79.7	43.3	56.1	4.9
1978	63.2	77.9	50.0	58.6	6.0

Source: *Economic Report of the President* (1981), Table B-27, p. 264 (columns 1–3, 5), and Table B-29, p. 267 (column 4).
[a]The percentage of the working-age population that is employed in civilian jobs.

The Recent Changes in Labor Supply

Rates of participation in the labor market rose somewhat in the period under study. The employment rate went up from 55% in 1950 to 59% in 1978. Similarly, the civilian labor force participation rate (LFPR) rose from 59 to 63% (see Table 5.1). This overall change resulted from a decline of the labor force participation of men from 86 to 78% and a sharp rise in participation by women from 34 to 50%.

The LFPR of men fell in every age group except the groups under age 25. However, the greatest declines were registered by men aged 55 and older. Offsetting the declining participation of men was the rising LFPR of women in every age group except the 65-and-over group (see Table 5.2). A most striking increase in participation was registered by married women with husbands present, whose LFPR went up by 21 points, from 24 to 45% (not shown in any table).

The measured rise in the overall participation rates is doubtless an overstatement of the rise in full-time equivalent participation, since it does not account for changes in the number of people seeking only part-time work. The annual average data do correct for part-year participation by counting a person who is in the labor force for only part of the year as a fraction of a participant. However, no similar correction is made for participants who seek year-round work but at less than full-time. We do know that the percentage of all workers in the business sector who worked part-time (under 35 hours per week) rose from 11.1 in 1948 to 19.0 in 1976 (Denison, 1979, p. 41). It is interesting to note that

TABLE 5.2
Civilian Labor Force Participation Rates, Annual Average, by Sex and Age, Selected Years, 1954–1978

Sex and year	Total, 16 years & over (%)	16 and 17 years (%)	18 and 19 years (%)	20 to 24 years (%)	25 to 34 years (%)	35 to 44 years (%)	45 to 54 years (%)	55 to 64 years (%)	65 years and over (%)
Both sexes									
1954	58.8	37.9	60.0	61.6	64.3	68.8	68.4	58.7	23.9
1960	59.4	37.6	50.5	65.2	65.4	69.4	72.1	60.9	20.8
1970	60.4	41.0	59.9	69.2	70.0	73.1	73.5	61.8	17.0
1978	63.2	48.8	67.4	76.9	78.2	78.0	73.6	56.6	13.4
Male									
1954	85.5	47.1	71.5	87.0	97.3	98.1	96.5	88.7	40.5
1960	83.3	46.0	69.3	88.1	97.5	97.7	95.7	86.8	33.1
1970	79.7	47.0	66.7	83.3	96.4	96.9	94.2	83.0	26.8
1978	77.9	51.9	73.0	86.0	95.4	95.7	91.3	73.5	20.5
Female									
1954	34.6	28.7	50.4	45.1	34.4	41.2	41.1	30.1	9.3
1960	37.7	29.1	50.9	46.1	36.0	43.4	49.8	37.2	10.8
1970	43.3	34.9	53.6	57.7	45.0	51.1	54.4	43.0	9.7
1978	50.0	45.5	62.1	68.3	62.1	61.6	57.1	41.4	8.4

Source: *Employment and Training Report of the President* (1981), Table A-5, pp. 126–127.

TABLE 5.3

Average Weekly Hours of Work, by Selected Categories of Workers, Selected Years, 1950–1978

| | | Wage and salary workers in nonfarm business | | | |
| | | Males | | Females | |
Year	Production workers on private payrolls (1)	Full-time (2)	Part-time (3)	Full-time (4)	Part-time (5)
1950	39.8	43.1	19.7	39.9	22.0
1960	38.6	42.3	18.1	38.7	18.3
1970	37.1	41.5	18.0	37.3	17.9
1978	35.8	a	a	a	a

Sources: Column 1 is from *Employment and Training Report of the President* (1981), Table C-4, p. 214. Columns 2–5 are from Denison (1979), Table 3-7, p. 37.

a Denison did not give numbers for 1978.

LFPR rates for young persons fell with increasing school attendance until the early 1950s, then rose again as more and more students took part-time jobs.

The greater significance of part-time work is one important reason for the decline in average hours worked from 39.8 hours per week in 1950 to 35.8 hours in 1978 (see Table 5.3). The table also shows that hours worked by both male and female part-time workers fell at greater rates than did those of full-time workers.

It is hard to know how to adjust the labor force participation rates for the fall in hours worked, because the latter was no doubt induced by changes in demand as well as supply. I can suggest two possible ways to make the adjustment. One is to compare the percentage changes in labor force participation of +6.8 (from 59.2% in 1950 to 63.2% in 1978) with the percentage change in hours worked of −10.1% (from 39.8 hours per week in 1950 to 35.8 hours in 1978). This would suggest a decline in labor supply of 3.3% (i.e., +6.8 − 10.1 = −3.3). A second way to make the adjustment is to concentrate on the rise in part-time workers. Let us assume that every part-time worker is looking for half-time work and hence is only half of a participant in the labor force. This would mean that we should adjust the LFPR for 1950 down from 59.2 to 53.7% by subtracting one-half of the 11.1% of all workers who were part-time, and the LFPR for 1978 down from 63.2 to 53.7 (by subtracting one-half of the 19.0% of all workers who were part-time). This suggests no change in "full-time participation" from 53.7% in 1950 to 53.7% in 1978.

I conclude that there probably has been a slight relative decline in the supply of market labor, with the reduction of hours more than offsetting the rise in the LFPR "unadjusted for hours." As noted above, the changes in participation have varied considerably among age and sex groups.

The divergent trends of men and women with regard to work were apparent in the years antecedent to the "explosion" of SCI benefits. Men have tended to start full-time work later and retire earlier and women have tended to participate in market work more and more since at least the turn of the century.[4] The "liberation" of women from home work is attributable in some measure to changes in fertility, to changes in laws and customs imposing responsibilities for relatives outside the nuclear family, and to the invention of appliances that ease the burden of household chores. It may also be due in some part to shifts in the structure of work opportunities away from agriculture and toward the service occupations. The trends toward less work by men may be explained in part by changes in laws related to work; such as child labor laws and those that determine the age a child may leave school; and to falling relative prices of goods, such as travel and television, which are complementary to leisure. But perhaps the primary reason to suspect that the trend toward less work began—and might have accelerated—in the absence of a rise in SCI benefits is that wage rates, family incomes, and accumulated savings were rising. It is plausible that as people get richer, they tend to take more leisure. More about this particular proposition later.

All of these explanations for observed changes in labor supply overlap and are entangled with the hypothesis that labor supply has responded negatively to the expansion of SCI benefits. Without that expansion, would the labor supply of men have declined less, and/or would that of women have increased more? It is, of course, quite impossible empirically to represent the counterfactual general equilibrium appropriate to answering that question. One is driven to (1) deductive

---

[4]Glen G. Cain is developing a lifetime measure of labor supply for cohorts born after 1890, using Census information on LFPRs and hours worked. By assuming 16 hours per day of discretionary time during the ages 14 to 70, he calculates the ratio of hours worked to hours available. According to his unpublished tabulations, around 1900 the average woman could expect to spend about 8% of her adult life discretionary time in market work. By 1970 this had increased to 13%. The average man in 1900 could expect to spend about 43% of his adult life in market work, and by 1970 only 25% (1984).

For a graphic account of change in work patterns in this century see Levitan and Johnson (1982), Chapter 3.

Labor Supply Effects of Taxes and Benefits

The conventional price-theoretic approach to the question of how taxes and benefits financed by taxes affect the supply of labor often begins with the assumption that "the" labor supply curve slopes upward and to the right. Suppose that a tax is imposed on wages and that the wage rate net of tax therefore falls. One would expect that workers would work less. This is consistent with imagining that workers have decided that since leisure "costs" less than it did before the tax, they will substitute leisure for income (the "substitution effect"), even though they understand that if they want to maintain their pretax purchasing power they must work more hours. The latter understanding is referred to as an income effect, which, in this case, only partially offsets the substitution effect of the tax.

Other outcomes of income and substitution effects follow if the labor supply curve is assumed to be inelastic with respect to the wage rate or is seen as backward bending. In the first case, a tax on wages would not affect the quantity of labor offered or employed at the pretax or nominal wage. In the second case, such a tax would induce more work effort in the upper wage range than was forthcoming before the tax was imposed.

Suppose now that instead of having a positive tax on wages, we have the obverse, namely, a subsidy to wages. Here, assuming that the labor supply curve slopes upward and to the right, the result is that workers will move their supply curve up and out and offer more labor than at each presubsidy wage rate. The designs of the wage tax and the wage subsidy are shown in Figure 5.1, panel A. Wage-rate subsidies (or earnings subsidies) are relatively rare in the American system of benefits but are represented by the earned income tax credit of 1976.

A more common design for a benefit is the offer of a lump-sum grant unrelated to wages. An example of this is the provision of free schooling to pupils without regard to the income of their parents. Such a benefit does not affect the wage rate, but rather, appears in the household budget as nonlabor income (see Figure 5.1, panel B). To the extent the parents were paying for schooling before the lump-sum grant was initiated, one might suppose that they would believe that their living standard (net of taxes) had gone up and that they could afford to work less. Since the wage rate is unaffected, the decision can be represented as a shift of the supply curve to the left. The outcome of a reduced labor

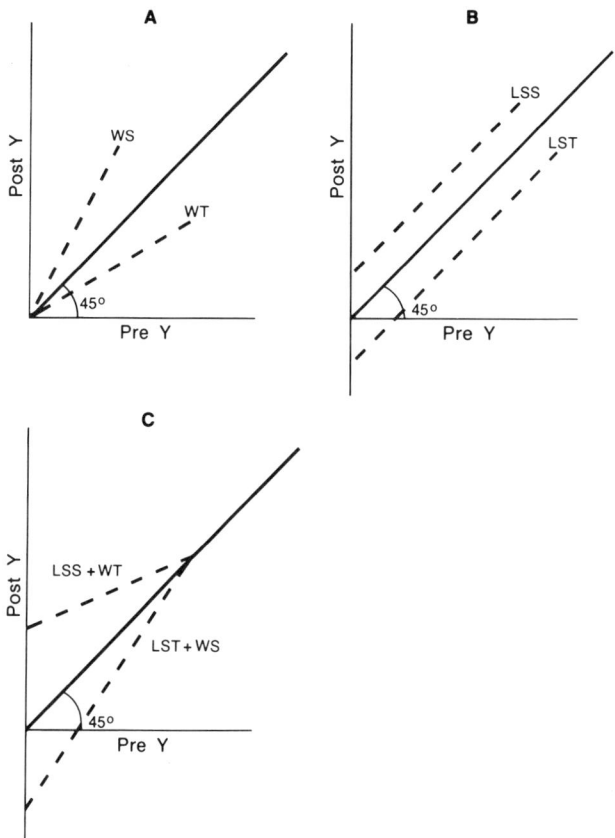

FIGURE 5.1 Designs for taxes and benefits, showing relationship to earnings. Y = income; Pre = before tax or transfer; Post = after tax or transfer; WS = wage subsidy; WT = wage tax; LSS = lump-sum subsidy; LST = lump-sum tax. (Figure by University of Wisconsin Cartographic Laboratory.)

supply would be the same whatever the slope of the labor supply curve. The obverse type of tax to a lump-sum benefit is, of course, a lump-sum tax. Such a tax reduces nonlabor income and thereby induces or coerces more work effort.

Another design for benefits is to relate them inversely to wages. Two variations can be distinguished. One, which we may call the work-conditioned design, is to pay a benefit only in cases where a person is deemed totally unable to work and, moreover, does no market work. One might think that, by definition, this benefit design cannot have a work disincentive effect. However, it may encourage some to feign inability either to work or to find work. Moreover, it may have the indirect effect of freeing a relative of the burden of providing support for the direct beneficiary, hence, adding to the relative's nonlabor income, and thereby shifting his or her supply of labor curve to the left.

Only a small portion of all benefit programs fit this description of a work-conditioned grant under which all benefits are denied if one has any earnings. Perhaps the best examples of such a design are disability insurance and unemployment insurance in states that do not allow for partial benefits, and general assistance in some jurisdictions. AFDC for unemployed fathers has some of this design with its denial of all benefits if the father works more than 100 hours in a month.

The second variation of benefits related inversely to wages is one that may be called the income-conditioned or earnings-conditioned benefit. In this more common variation of the two, the benefit is scaled to diminish to zero as earnings or total incomes rise (see Figure 5.1, panel C). This scaling may involve a benefit-reduction rate of (as in the case of the "notch" in Medicaid benefits) more than 100%, or as is the case in the Food Stamp program, far less than 100%. The earnings-conditioned benefit may be seen as having two parts. One is a lump-sum grant, which adds to nonlabor income and is assumed to have an income effect of shifting the supply of labor to the left. The other part is the benefit-reduction rate, which is like a tax in that it reduces the wage rate. This reduction in wage rate has both an income and a substitution effect and will, if the supply curve of labor slopes upward and to the right, move the beneficiaries to a lower point on their new labor supply curves. Presumably, a 100% benefit-reduction rate would lower the net wage to zero, and the beneficiaries would not willingly offer labor in that range. Thus, both the lump-sum grant or guarantee and the benefit-reduction rate contribute to a reduction in work effort. This design is the obverse of a lump-sum tax in tandem with a wage subsidy (see Figure 5.1, panel C). The two parts of the latter design together would theoretically provide the maximum incentive to work. An alternative to the lump-sum tax is a tax on earning capacity as opposed to actual earnings (Akerlof, 1978; Baumol & Fischer, 1979). To further promote work, one could add to this design a tax on goods that are complementary to leisure and a subsidy on goods, such as child day care, commuter service, and training, that are complementary to work.

The contemporary American SCI system may be characterized as having three main features: first, it is largely financed by what can be treated as taxes on earnings. Second, its benefit side is dominated by lump-sum and earnings-conditioned grants. About one-third of all benefits, most notably certain education and health care benefits, are distributed on a per capita basis and are invariant to earnings. These fit the description given above of lump-sum grants. Almost two-thirds of all benefits—some of them in cash and some in kind—are earnings-conditioned benefits. These include OAI, public assistance, food stamps, public housing, Medicaid, some higher-education benefits, and child day care. Wage subsidies and work-conditioned benefits make up only small parts of the overall total of SCI benefits. The third feature is that the greater part of the earnings-conditioned benefits go by design to categories of people who are "not expected to work," namely aged and disabled persons and female heads of families.

Both the taxes that go to finance the benefits and the benefit-reduction rates in the earnings-conditioned benefits have the effect of reducing wage rates. The lump-sum grants and the guarantee element of the income-conditioned grants add to the nonlabor income of beneficiaries. According to the theory reviewed above, a reduction in the wage rate will have the effect of reducing the quantity of labor supplied, assuming that the labor supply curve slopes upward and to the right. At the same time, an increase in nonlabor income will induce less work whether or not the labor supply curve slopes upward and to the right. One might guess that noncash benefits such as education and health care have less effect per dollar in this regard than do cash benefits, but all of the effects work in the same direction. It is this reinforcing of work disincentive that leads to the conclusion that there is an inevitable trade-off between income redistribution and labor supply and, in the extreme case where all earnings are taxed away and all goods are distributed free of charge to consumers, the final trade-off is between security for and free choice by workers. As one text puts it:

> This, indeed, is the dilemma of utopian communism, where a person should contribute to the community's output according to his ability, and compensation (the distribution of goods among individuals) should be according to need. In the absence of self-interest oriented economic motivation, another mechanism of work allocation and stimulus to effort would be needed. (Musgrave & Musgrave, 1980, p. 666)

However, theory cannot tell us how strong the effect of an increase in nonlabor income may be, nor can it tell us, since it does not establish what the slope of the labor supply curve is, what either the direction or the magnitude of the effect of a wage-rate reduction may be. Hence, it is of critical importance to find empirical evidence of labor responses to wage-rate changes and to additions to nonlabor income.

Studies of Labor Supply Response to Nonlabor Income and to Wage-Rate Reduction

Household surveys of income by source, together with information on wage rates; hours worked; health status; age, sex, and family status; school attendance; and so on, provide an entrée for econometric study of work response to nonlabor income. Such cross-section data enable one to compare the work behavior of those who have a high level of nonlabor income with those of like characteristics who do not. Numerous studies using such data have been done (see Cain & Watts, 1973). They vary as to methodology. Some exclude spouses' earnings; others leave out work-conditioned benefits; most count social benefits net of the effect of benefit-reduction rates as nonlabor income. (The latter procedure, as opposed to counting the gross benefit, may result in an overstatement of the effect per dollar of nonlabor income.) Some exclude persons who are unable to work. All such studies find it hard to fill all the cells, so to speak. For example, most data bases provide few cases of people with low wage rates who have much private nonlabor income.

All such studies tend to find that work effort declines with increases in nonlabor income. One of these studies, done by Masters and Garfinkel (1977), finds a smaller response than do most earlier ones.[5] According to this study, each annual increase of $1000 in nonlabor income is associated with a reduction of 1% in the labor supply of prime-age, healthy men. This response is greater among aged persons, for whom it is 10%. It is about 4% for prime-age women and for young, single persons. None of these studies tell much about how higher-wage earners respond to nonlabor income nor about how people in general respond to in-kind benefits. However, they do confirm the hypothesis drawn from theory that people do work less in response to provision of nonlabor income.

Theory, as reviewed above, tells us that SCI may discourage work in another way, namely, by reducing the net wage rate by a combination of benefit-reduction rates and tax rates. What do empirical studies tell about work response to reduction in wage rates? The leading studies on this question have been done by P. H. Douglas (1934) and his followers, who have estimated labor supply functions using time series of hours

---

[5]A number of other scholars believe that Masters and Garfinkel have understated the response. They bring up the problem of selection bias in the data, the problem of fixed costs of going to work, and the problem of nonlinearity of budget lines due to progressivity in tax rates and irregularities of benefit-reduction rates. See Brown (1950, pp. 46–57); Keeley (1981); Heckman and MaCurdy (1982).

worked per year in several industries and cross-section data on hours worked and LFPRs (Bowen & Finegan, 1969). Their major finding is that men's labor supply curve is highly inelastic and slightly backward-sloping with respect to wage rates. They find that married women have a supply curve that slopes upward and to the right (Mincer, 1963; Cain, 1966). This would suggest that men respond one way to a wage-rate reduction and married women respond in another way. The difference is thought to be due to the fact that while men substitute leisure for work, married women substitute market work for home work.

Three widely cited studies of the effects of changes in marginal tax rates on high-income earners reported no significant change in work effort. Sanders (1951) studied the effect of taxes on 160 executives in the United States. Break (1957) asked 306 solicitors and accountants in England about their change in work after a particular tax change, and Barlow, Brazer, and Morgan (1966) asked similar questions of 957 high-income individuals. These studies are consistent with the Douglas finding that the supply of labor for men is inelastic. A recent paper presents econometric findings that the author claims will unsettle the generally held view that a progressive income tax has only trivial effects on work effort (Hausman, 1981). He finds, as have others, that tax-caused changes in net wage rates lead to only a 1% reduction in hours worked by prime-age husbands. However, he finds a 7% reduction in response to a special effect which he and some earlier writers associate with progressive tax rates, namely a change in "virtual" nonlabor income as one moves from one income tax bracket to another. He hypothesizes that the worker behaves as if the move to a higher tax bracket were accompanied by a gift of nonlabor income, the size of which is indicated by extending the slopes of the two net wage lines to intercept the income axis at the level of zero hours of work.

Studies based on household surveys have not established that variations in benefit-reduction rates make much difference in work supplied by men. The Masters and Garfinkel study did estimate, however, that a 10 percentage point increase in the benefit-reduction rate would lead female heads of families to reduce work effort by 2%, and wives to reduce work effort by 4% (Masters & Garfinkel, 1977, Chapters 7 and 8). The method used in that study compares the work behavior of similar individuals who have the same level of nonlabor income but different wage rates. The different wage rates are a stand-in for varying benefit-reduction rates. Not surprisingly, surveys provide few examples of people working at a zero-wage rate. Hence, it is not possible to estimate the effect of benefit-reduction rates approaching 100%.

This review of empirical studies of the effects of changes in wage rates (the study by Hausman excepted) leads to the conclusion that men do not work much less, if they reduce their labor supply at all, in response to a "moderate" reduction in wage rates, but that married women and women who head families do work less in response to such a change. Empirical studies also suggest that work effort declines with increases in nonlabor income, with the greatest responses by the aged and the young and by women. Additional evidence on the difference in responses to disincentives by husbands and wives was provided by experiments with negative income taxation. The New Jersey experiment found that in the experimental families considered as a group, male family heads reduced hours worked by 6% and wives by 30% (Watts & Rees, 1977, pp. 23–32). In the Seattle-Denver experiment, among the families that were offered a guarantee at the poverty line and a 50% benefit-reduction rate, husbands reduced hours of work by 6% and wives by 22% (Keeley, Robins, Spiegelman, & West, 1978).

Application of Empirical Findings

The particular findings of the previous section should be set alongside the fact that the present-day American SCI system directs the greater part of its cash and in-kind benefits to the minority of the population who are aged (age 62 or older), disabled, or in female-headed families with children. Table 5.4 shows that 25% of the population aged 16 years and older are in these categories. The same table also illustrates the point made earlier that most of the benefits are earnings-conditioned and hence increase the beneficiaries' nonlabor income and at the same time reduce their net wage rates. Additionally, Table 5.4 presents "back of the envelope" assignments by the author of the several types of benefits to several categories of people referred to above. Column 2 indicates that about 56% of all benefits go to the quarter of the population in the three categories.

The other 75% of the population gets about 44% of total benefits, but most of that is in the form of health and education benefits that are not earnings-conditioned. This means that the greatest disincentive effects are aimed at categories of people who are least expected to work. Conversely, those who are most clearly expected to work are relatively shielded from disincentives of nonlabor income and benefit-reduction rates. However, this group is subjected to the disincentive caused by taxes on earnings occasioned by the SCI benefits.

The question I set out in this section is: Would the labor supply of men have declined less and/or would that of women have increased more than each did if the great increase in SCI benefits in the years 1950–

TABLE 5.4

Distribution of SCI Benefits, by Type, among Categories of Population, 1978

Characteristics of recipients	Percentage of population 16 years and over (1)	Percentage of SCI benefits			
		Total (2)	Earnings-conditioned[a] (3)	Not earnings-conditioned	
				Health[b] (4)	Education (5)
Aged 62 and older[c]	17	38	50	34	0
Disabled, under age 62[d]	5	10	10	14	5
Female family heads with children[e]	3	8	10	5	3
All others[f]	75	44	30	47	92
Totals (persons in millions; benefits in billions of dollars)	164 million persons	598	384	100	113

Sources: Column 1 percentages are derived from U.S. Department of Commerce, *Current Population Reports,* P-23, No. 107; P-20, No. 352 (1980), except for disabled, which is from U.S. Department of Health and Human Services (1980). Columns 2–5 are derived from Appendix Tables A.1–A.4.

[a]Includes Medicaid and all of "welfare and other services" as well as all cash benefits.

[b]Medicaid benefits are included in "earnings-conditioned" benefits.

[c]Benefits assigned to this group include those paid out by OAI, SI (aged only), SSI (aged only), cash interfamily (aged only), retirement benefits for public and private employees and veterans, half of Medicaid, most of Medicare, part of other health services, and part of food, housing, and other welfare services.

[d]Benefits assigned to this group include those paid out by DI, SSI (disabled only), workers' compensation, veterans' compensation, part of Medicare and other health programs, a per capita share of education, and part of food, housing, and other welfare services.

[e]Benefits assigned to this group include those paid out by SI (children present only), AFDC, part of Medicaid and other health programs, a per capita share of education, and part of food, housing, and other welfare services.

[f]Benefits assigned to this group are the residuals after assignments to the first three groups.

1978 had not occurred? I can offer a first tentative answer to that question. The growth of benefits has increased nonlabor income and has reduced net wage rates by means of higher benefit-reduction rates and tax and contribution rates. It is this *increase* in disincentives that is most relevant to our inquiry.

TABLE 5.5

Size of 1978 Full-Time Labor Force if SCI Benefits and Taxes to Pay for Them Were on the Scale of 1950, by Characteristics of Participants

Characteristics of recipients	Numbers in population, 16 years of age and older (millions) (1)	Actual numbers in civilian labor force, 1978 (millions) (2)	1950–1978 Increase in disincentive to work (3)	Responsiveness to disincentive (4)	Hypothetical increase in labor force full-time equivalents if benefits were on scale of 1950 (millions) (5)
Total	164	100			5.8
Aged 62 and over	28	6	High	High	1.9
Disabled, under age 62	8	2	High	High	0.6
Female family heads with children	5	3	High	High	0.5
Age 16–24, not disabled, not female head with children	30	21	Low	Moderate	1.0
Women age 24–61, not disabled, not female head with children	48	27	Low	High	1.4
Men age 24–61, not disabled	45	41	Low	Low	0.4

Sources: Column 1, with the exception of the disabled, is from U.S. Department of Commerce, *Current Population Reports*, P23, No. 107; P-20, No. 352 (1980). The number of disabled is derived from charts in U.S. Department of Health and Human Services (1980). Column 2 is from *Employment and Training Report of the President* (1981), Table A-4, p. 123, Table A-6, p. 129. Columns 3, 4, and 5 are explained in the text.

Nonlabor income in the form of SCI benefits amounted to $598 billion in 1978. That is $226 billion greater than it would have been if such benefits were equal to 17.2% of GNP as they were in 1950 (derived from Tables 4.1 and 4.2). The $226 billion of extra benefits can be distributed by type as follows: cash, $98 billion; health, $86 billion; education, $37 billion; and welfare and other services, $2 billion (derived from Tables 4.1 and 4.2). In the interval per capita benefits rose from $878 to $2730 in constant 1978 consumer prices. Break-even points do not appear to have changed much relative to median incomes. The share of benefits that are earnings-conditioned changed little, but benefit-reduction rates are somewhat higher. Moreover, since 1950, tax and contribution rates have had to rise to accommodate the expansion of benefits from an amount equal to 17.2% of GNP to 27.6%. The latter point alone means that net wage rates could have been about 10% higher in 1978 than they in fact were (Lampman, 1966a and 1975a; Watts & Skidmore, 1977).

In Table 5.5, column 3, I rank several categories of population with respect to the increase in disincentive to work posed for them by the 1950–1978 increase in benefits and associated taxes. This ranking, which accords a "high" increase in disincentive to aged, disabled, and female heads of households, is based upon our knowledge that the increases in cash benefits and other earnings-conditioned benefits, which carry severe benefit-reduction rates, have been disproportionately targeted on those three groups. The share of total benefits going to these three groups rose from 31% in 1950 to 56% in 1978 (Tables 4.5 and 5.4). On the other hand, the extra benefits going to the other three groups, namely, the young, and "other" men and women, are mainly non-earnings-conditioned benefits. However, these groups do face an extra disincentive due to the higher tax and contribution rates. The increases in nonlabor income (the $216 billion identified in Table 5.6) for the first three categories were about $5073 per person; and for persons in the other three categories they averaged only $65 (derived from Tables 5.5 and 5.6). The increase in benefit-reduction rates faced by the first three categories averaged about 20 percentage points, while the increase in benefit-reduction rates and tax rates combined faced by the other three groups went up by a little more than 10 percentage points.

To answer our research questions about changes in labor supply we need to know not only how work disincentives have been increased since 1950, but also how various groups of people may have responded to those increased disincentives. As mentioned above, Masters and Garfinkel (1977) found that percentage changes in hours worked per $1000 increases in nonlabor income were −10% for people aged 62 and over;

−4% for women and for young single persons; and −1% for prime-age healthy men. They also found that a 10 percentage point increase in the benefit-reduction rate induces female heads of families to reduce work effort by 2% and wives to reduce such effort by 4%. Other studies suggest that men are relatively unresponsive to changes in net wage rates (and hence to tax-rate changes) but that married women are quite responsive to net wage-rate changes. With that information, it is possible to at least rank the groups in Table 5.5 according to responsiveness. Column 4 shows that the aged, disabled, female household heads, and also "other women" have a "high" responsiveness to work disincentives. Young people have only a "moderate" responsiveness.

By applying the Masters and Garfinkel coefficients to the increases in work disincentives imposed since 1950, we get a rough idea of how much decrease in labor supply may be involved (see column 5 of Table 5.5). For people aged 62 and over, guarantees—indicated by total benefits for the aged divided by the total number of aged persons—went up by about $3000. The labor supply response to that, assuming a 10% reduction for every $1000 of nonlabor income, was −30%. Tax rates and benefit-reduction rates combined went up by 10 percentage points. The predicted labor supply response to that was −1%. Hence, the predicted labor supply response for this group is 31% of 6 million (or 1.9 million persons), greater than it actually was in 1978. The same reasoning applied to the disabled yields an increase of .6 million persons.

For female household heads, guarantees went up by about $3000 and combined tax and benefit-reduction rates went up by 20%. Their predicted labor supply response is −4% per $1000 of nonlabor income and −2% for each 10% increase in tax or benefit-reduction rates. From this, it is concluded that the labor supply for this group would have been .5 million (or 16%) greater than it actually was in 1978.

Some young people aged 16–24 may receive survivor benefits or other stipends if they are in school. This may influence some to work less, and so may the tuition subsidy to higher education. The number of students in higher educational institutions rose from under 3 million in 1950 to over 11 million in 1978 (Table 4.7). Some of that increase in enrollment would have occurred without the extra subsidy as parental income, including the earnings of mothers, went up. Enrollments might have risen even without such a rise in income simply because people became more interested in higher education. But it is probably fair to say that the rise in public spending on education contributed to a reduction in labor time from young people. Young people appear to be moderately responsive to work disincentives, so it is estimated that a 5% increase in their labor supply—or 1 million persons—would accompany the assumed change in benefits and taxes.

The last two categories in Table 5.5, women who are neither household heads with children or disabled, and prime-age, nondisabled men, are not likely to be eligible for many benefits other than UI, food stamps, and education benefits for their children. They are, of course, liable for payment of the 10-point increase in taxes associated with higher benefits. It is assumed that these women, most of whom are married, have a higher responsiveness to disincentive than do the men. Although they tend to receive a small quantity of benefits, these women are exposed to the disincentive of higher taxes. Hence, it is estimated that their labor supply would have been 5% greater than it actually was.[6] This translates into a change of 1.4 million persons in the national labor supply. The prime-age men, according to empirical studies, have a very low labor supply responsiveness to nonlabor income and to taxes on wages. Moreover, they tend to receive a relatively small quantity of transfers. Hence, their labor supply changes by only a nominal 1 percentage point—or .4 million persons.

My "guesstimate" is that the total "loss" of labor time due to the change in the scale of SCI benefits and of the taxes and contributions to pay for them from 17.2 to 27.6% of GNP is on the order of 5.8% of the 1978 total of labor time. One-half of that loss is allocable to adult women other than heads of families with children and to the aged. Most of the rest of the loss is identified with the disabled, female heads of families with children, and young people.

Studies of Response to Specific Program Benefits

In the preceding discussion, the effort was to separately identify work response to nonlabor income on the one hand and to reduction in the net wage rate on the other hand. This effort was made in order to gain a perspective on the work response to the broad range of benefits and contributions. Another approach to this topic is to study specific programs and, for each, to identify and measure the response to the several features of the program. These features include the conditions of eligibility and the formula for determining benefits payable to eligibles.

---

[6]One recent study finds that the great bulk of "underutilized earnings capacity" is still that of females. Excluding the aged, students, and military personnel, 21% of the total of such "slack" is attributed to male heads and 11% to female heads and 68% to wives. See Garfinkel and Haveman (1977, p. 25); see also Ross and Sawhill (1975).

The findings of such studies should provide a check on the plausibility of my guesstimate of 5.8%.

Program records from public assistance and social insurance files can be used to study the work effects of these types of nonlabor income. Comparing program records from two or more jurisdictions having varying levels of benefits or for people eligible versus those not eligible for a benefit may provide a measure of marginal change in work effort. So might the before-and-after work effort associated with a change in benefits in one program in a single jurisdiction. In both instances, one has to take account of variations across space or time in all relevant program characteristics and in all relevant environmental conditions and personal attributes. Cross-sectional and longitudinal studies using program records have been done with reference to specific public assistance and social insurance program variations. They tell us, with varying degrees of credibility, that more people will apply for and receive assistance benefits if benefit levels are more generous, people will retire earlier if eligibility is extended to younger workers, and people will work less if UI benefits are raised and extended for longer periods (Brehm & Saving, 1969).

Danziger et al. (1981) reviewed the growing literature on quantitative effects on labor supply due to specific programs. They listed 11 recent empirical studies of OAI. They noted that most of the studies suggest that labor supply is reduced and retirement age is advanced by the program. However, they say the size of the disincentive is still in doubt. They hazard the guess that OAI induces a reduction in the national total of work hours of about 1.2%. (For further discussion of these same studies of OAI, see Aaron, 1982, Chapter 5. He emphasizes the importance of assumptions about the timing of worker response to benefits.)

Danziger et al. listed three studies of disability insurance (DI) and suggested a total labor supply effect of about 1.2%. A year after the publication of the 1981 article, the authors informed me that new research (Haveman & Wolfe, 1982) leads them to believe that this number of 1.2% should be revised to a substantially lower number. On the basis of discussions with them, I will use 0.4% as the measure of labor supply loss due to DI. They review nine studies of UI that find no effect on quit rates but a substantial effect on duration of unemployment spells. They conclude that UI may cause a loss of labor supply of about 0.3%. They also cite five empirical studies of AFDC, which lead them to believe that this program is responsible for a labor supply loss of 0.6%.

For OAI, DI, UI, and AFDC, these researchers suggest a combined loss of 2.5%. They found no empirical studies of other programs but do suggest that the likely effects of workers' compensation programs, Railroad Retirement, veterans' disability compensation and pensions, Medicare and Medicaid, SSI, food stamps, and housing assistance would raise the total loss of work hours to 4.0%. They are careful to say that the program-by-program method of study is apt to overstate the effect of a single program, since recipients under one program may be responding to benefits from a second program. For example, the research studies on which they rely may attribute a work response to AFDC that may in fact be a response to AFDC, food stamps, and Medicaid.

The counterfactual used in calculating that loss is the economy of the late 1970s with a complete absence of the listed benefits but with taxes unchanged. How can one relate the response of −4.0% guesstimated by Danziger et al. to the increase in work disincentive set forth in column 3 of Table 5.5 where I suggested a counterfactual of the 1950 ratio of SCI expenditures and of the level of taxes and contributions which went with them? The retreat to the 1950 SCI ratio would mean that such expenditures in 1978 would have been only $372 billion, or $226 billion less than they actually were. Danziger et al. do not consider

TABLE 5.6

Comparison of Benefit Reductions and Increased Hours Worked in Two Studies

Characteristics of recipients	Benefit reductions (billions of dollars)		Increased hours worked by transfer recipients and taxpayers as a percentage of total work hours of all workers	
	D-H-P[a] (1)	Lampman (2)	D-H-P[a] (3)	Lampman (4)
Total	201	216	4.0	5.8
Aged 62 and over	117	140	1.4	1.9
Disabled, under age 62	28	38	0.7	0.6
Female family heads with children	32	30	0.7	0.5
All others	24	8	1.2	2.8

Sources: Column 1 is based on 1978 totals for programs listed by D-H-P with benefits assigned to population categories on the basis of knowledge of target groups of each program. Column 2 is derived from Table 5.4, column 2, and Table 4.5, column 1. Column 3 is from D-H-P, with the percentage for each category based on assignments of programs for column 1. (See text for discussion of change with respect to disability insurance.) Column 4 is from Table 5.5, column 5.

[a]D-H-P = Danziger, Haveman, and Plotnick.

all the SCI expenditures. The complete elimination of all the benefits they consider would mean a reduction for 1978 of $201 billion. However, they showed a $50 billion greater reduction than I do in cash benefits, but a $67 billion smaller reduction than I do in in-kind benefits. This would suggest that the response they estimate would be smaller than that expected from our larger total of benefit changes.

The total of $201 billion assumed to be eliminated in the Danziger et al. exercise can be distributed among several population categories as shown in column 1 of Table 5.6. By using the labor supply loss they assigned to each program, I derive the labor supply change for population categories shown in column 3. By comparing columns 3 and 4, one can see that the principal difference is in the "other" category. This is primarily due to taxes and contributions. The bottom line of 4% conforms roughly with my guesstimate of 5.8%, since Danziger et al. took account of a smaller quantity of SCI benefits and took no account of tax or contribution changes.

Why My Estimate of Reduction in Labor Supply May Be Too High

In offering these several speculations about the ways in which public SCI welfare spending may alter conventional labor market measures, I am painfully aware of the partial nature of the analysis that underlies them. There have been important changes on the demand side of the labor market which were not examined. Moreover, there are numerous interactions and intertemporal adjustments among family members and between public and private transfers which have not been accounted for.

Consider first the interactions among family members. It is interesting to note that if SCI benefits were smaller, today's married women would have less nonlabor income in the form of benefits (thus urging them to work more), but they would have more nonlabor income in the form of husbands' earnings net of taxes and contributions (thus urging them to work less). The loss of labor time due to young people staying in school longer may be partly offset by an induced increase of labor by their parents, who respond to the need to cover the living costs of the students. (Also, see Chapter 4 on the social benefits of higher productivity due to education.) It is also possible that social security may have led to reduced private interfamily transfers from children to their aged parents and thereby encouraged less work by those children. (See the discussion of the slide of benefits in Chapter 4.)

Second, consider intertemporal adjustments. The loss of labor time associated with retirement may be at least partially offset by extra labor time expended by workers and perhaps by their spouses in preretirement years in order to accumulate a larger capital sum in anticipation of extra needs during a longer retirement. Some workers may work harder in order to gain entitlement for a higher OAI or UI benefit. Thus, with respect to OAI, workers may accept benefits as soon as they are eligible (at age 62) or they may delay acceptance to a later date. They may be influenced in that decision by the provision for benefit recomputation, which allows workers to substitute current earnings for those in the lowest year in their earnings history (Blinder, Gordon, & Wise, 1980). Workers under age 62 may respond to the fact that a benefit-reduction rate of 50% will affect them after they accept benefits and hence substitute work before retirement age for work after retirement (Burkhauser & Turner, 1978).

Thus, several points suggest that 5.8% loss of labor time should be considered an upper-bound estimate of labor supply response to recent increases of SCI benefits and the taxes and contributions to pay for them.

The next step in identifying social cost is to translate the loss in labor time into loss of GNP. Since most of the time lost is that of the aged, disabled, and women, it seems likely that the production loss is smaller than would be the case if a broader cross-section of the adult population were involved. Since wages equal three-fourths of GNP, a production loss of 4% of GNP would be the highest plausible number, but it is the one I select. The distinction between potential and actual GNP is relevant. It is easier to believe that if the labor force had risen by 5.8 million persons, then *potential* GNP would have gone up by 4%, than it is to believe that *actual* GNP would have gone up by that amount. To believe the latter, one must believe that the unemployment rate, already high, would not have risen.[7] I suggest that the reader consider 4% as the loss of potential GNP.

---

[7]The weakness of demand for labor is emphasized in the following comment by Levitan and Taggart (1976):
> There is surely a tradeoff between higher welfare standards and the number of persons who work. But considering the low productivity of the workers, their difficulty in finding employment and the number of workers they would displace if they found employment, the drag on the economy from their being on welfare is small. It is proper to resent handouts to those who can find work, but it is wrong to view most recipients of social welfare as loafers. As long as the policy of fighting inflation with unemployment continues, the majority of beneficiaries do not have any choice between work and welfare. This loss in output due to withdrawal from the work force because of the availability of welfare payments is dwarfed by involuntary unemployment. (pp. 285–286)

Loss of Productivity per Hour Worked

SCI benefits and taxes and contributions appear to have the direct effect of reducing the amount of time devoted to work. It is not so clear what net effect they may have on the productivity per hour worked.

Abramovitz (1981) reviews the claim that the growth of welfare statism may be a cause of the massive decline after 1973 in the rate of increase in productivity per hour. He finds that most contemporary analyses leave a substantial part of the retardation unconnected with any identified and measured contributory source. He goes on to say that "in this state of factual uncertainty, it is not hard to propose estimates of the source of retardation which assign substantial responsibility to factors connected with the government's welfare and regulatory activities" (p. 7). He lists as suspects the effects of taxes and benefits and inflation on work, saving, investment, and research and development. He cites William Fellner's guess that the cause of at least 1 percentage point annual slackening of the trend in output per worker's hour can be found among the "suspects." It is perhaps unnecessary to point out that a 1 percentage point reduction in the rate of productivity increase, if sustained for any period of time, means a tremendous reduction in realized GNP. Abramovitz cautions that "such numbers and the argument that leads to them should be understood to be no more than what they are—a *prima facie* indication that something very substantial may be involved in the choice we make between productivity growth and alternate welfare goals" (p. 8).

A central part of the argument that the SCI system may contribute to a fall in the production per hour worked is that it may lead to less capital formation and hence to less capital per worker. There is a certain plausibility to the idea that the growth of SCI might hold down personal saving, which is about one-fourth of total national saving. Personal saving, defined as disposable personal income less personal consumption, was 5.3% of disposable personal income in 1950 and 4.9% in 1978. This ratio is relatively low in international terms—in West Germany it is 14%—and it is possible to imagine that it might have run up to 10% or more if it had not been for the growth of SCI. Had it been 10%, it might have led to a rise in the share that gross investment is of GNP—which has long been stable at 15–20% or even higher. This would, of course, have contributed to a considerably faster rise in the nation's stock of capital and, presumably, to a higher level of productivity per worker.

Taxes on personal income are probably higher than they would have been if SCI had stayed at 17.2% of GNP. Economic theory tells us that such taxes—considered aside from benefits—tend to discourage saving first by reducing disposable income and hence the capacity to save, and second by reducing the net rate of return to the lender. The lower return makes future consumption less attractive than it was relative to present consumption. However, there may be an offset to those two effects in that savers may have targets for accumulation or targets for a given annual property income and will therefore save more rather than less when tax rates go up.

These conflicting predictions lead one to reflect on motives people have for saving. One is precautionary; the second is to build an income for retirement, and a third is to make a bequest to one's children. It is worth noting that SCI benefits are responsive to several of these motives. Future benefits may be as good as money in the bank and therefore may be said to have an asset or wealth value. Although they do not help one directly in making a bequest to adult children, they do make it less necessary to save for a "rainy day," since they offset income loss due to unemployment and disability and they cover some costs of medical care. They reduce the family need to save to provide education for children. At the same time, they reduce the need to dissave for these purposes, so the net effect on total personal saving in a given year may be zero. Further, they reduce the need to save for retirement, which is a principal purpose for life-cycle saving. Such saving is assumed to be positive prior to retirement and negative after, and to result in zero principal at the time of the worker's death.

OAI funded on a pay-as-you-go basis under social security has been singled out for special study as a possible depressor of personal saving for retirement (M. Feldstein, 1974). The theoretical base is that the promise of retirement benefits substitutes for year-by-year saving by a worker. This effect was probably strongest during the start-up period of social security, since Congress decided to pay benefits far in excess of contributions to the entire first generation of retirees. As Munnell (1980) puts it: "This noncontributory component increased the lifetime wealth of individuals in the first generation, inducing them to consume more and save less (prior to retirement)." On the other hand, "since most young people working today will pay in payroll taxes at least as much as they will receive in benefits, this generation would not be expected to reduce its saving because of social security." More precisely:

> a social security system where workers contribute payroll taxes that are exactly equal in present value terms to the benefit received in retirement . . . would have no effect on lifetime resources of covered workers and therefore would have no effect on their consumption and saving. For although workers would reduce their private saving by the amount of social security contributions, the subsequent benefit payments would reduce the dissaving required to support retirement consumption. (p. 1628)

If there is a "lifetime wealth effect" of social security, which induces workers to save less, it may be offset by an "induced retirement effect," which leads workers to save more in order to finance the longer period in planned retirement. There is another reason to doubt that the "lifetime wealth" effect of social security will fully translate into a lower personal savings ratio for the nation. New social security benefits for person A may result in less interfamily transfers from person B to person A. This substitution may not result in any more consumption by A, but it may lead, in a "slide" fashion, to more saving by B (see Chapter 4). Alternatively, higher social security benefits may not lead individuals to increase their consumption but to make gifts or bequests to adult children who are struggling to pay the higher payroll tax (Barro, 1974). Such gifts may go to increased investment in human capital, which was discussed in Chapter 4.

Theory cannot tell us which of these offsetting effects on saving dominates. Empirical study of this question leaves the controversy unresolved. Time-series analyses of savings rates, cross-section studies of assets accumulated by workers at certain ages, and cross-national comparisons of savings rates and retirement benefits have failed to yield agreement. There may be an effect of social security on personal saving for retirement but econometricians have thus far failed to agree on what it is (see Danziger et al., 1981; Aaron, 1982; Cagan, 1982; Leimer & Lesnoy, 1982; Munnell, 1982, p. 88).

Private pensions, unlike pay-as-you-go social security, have been building financial reserves steadily throughout the period under study. In 1975, pension plans in private industry collected $29.9 billion in contributions and paid out $14.8 billion in benefits. Assets of these plans amounted to $212.6 billion in that year (Munnell, 1982, p. 11). It is important to know whether the enormous growth in reserves constitutes a net increase in asset accumulation or merely a shift in the form of assets. Munnell reviews all studies that have attempted to answer that question and concludes that:

> the most useful hypothesis for policy purposes now appears to be that, at any given time, consumers reduce saving in other forms to compensate for the promise of pension benefits. To guess about the magnitude of this offsetting effect would be hazardous in light of the scant empirical evidence. Nevertheless, a reasonable conjecture might be that workers reduce saving by 65 cents for each dollar of saving through pension plans, resulting in a net increase in aggregate saving of 35 cents. (Munnell, 1982, p. 77)

This suggests that about one-third of the $212.6 billion of assets of pension funds represents a net addition to the nation's capital stock.

To summarize this section, it appears that some features of SCI contribute to a gain of productivity per hour worked and some to a loss. Although there is a widespread suspicion that the growth of SCI beyond some unspecified point may have contributed to the dramatic decline grams are usually set up with a sum-certain appropriation, which is insufficient to assure provision for all in the income class. The available provisions are then rationed on some nonprice, nonincome basis. Since these funds are so small relative to total private expenditures for these purchases, it is concluded that they too do little to change the share of GNP allocated to the goods in question.

The Medicaid program also offers a subsidy confined to low-income families. Unlike food stamps, however, Medicaid benefits are not tapered, but are flat to a stated income level, at which point they are abruptly reduced to zero. This "notch" is somewhat abated by a "spend-down" provision, whereby countable income is reduced by medical expenses. Although it is true that families eligible for Medicaid would undoubtedly have spent part of their income on health care, it is likely that making health care available at zero price does increase the allocation to health care. It is worth mention here that the largest part of Medicaid funding goes to nursing-home care, which is a substitute for home care by relatives. Hence, some part of Medicaid is not a genuine reallocation of resources to health care, but is merely a shift of responsibility for its provision.

A fourth way to encourage allocation to a selected good is to offer an in-kind grant that is not related to income. This is exemplified by private health insurance and also by Medicare, which is restricted only by age and disability status. Under these programs, benefits are sometimes limited as to services that are covered and by small deductibles and maximum dollar totals. However, within limits, the beneficiary is faced by a zero price for health care. This undoubtedly encourages the beneficiaries to use more health care than they would use in the absence of such a benefit. Exactly how much more depends, of course, on the elasticity of demand for health care. Experts in the economics of health care point out that consumer demands in this field are brokered by physicians and other professionals who have a self-interest in the decision. They also call attention to the fact that any increase in demand occasioned by third-party payment will, assuming less-than-perfect elasticity of the supply of health care, drive up the price at the same time that it expands the allocation of resources to such care.

Public provision of elementary and secondary education encourages allocation to a selected good by providing it at zero price, but unlike the health insurance case, does so in a fixed quantity per person. In this case, demand is fortified by legislating compulsory attendance in schools that meet certain minimum standards. However, no public subsidy is payable to a child who attends a private school. This sets up a difficult choice for some parents who would like to take advantage of the

TABLE 5.7

Effects of Noncash SCI Benefits on Allocation of Resources to Selected Goods

Item	Nature of benefit	Effect
1. Per unit subsidy	Reduces price of open-ended quantities of selected good. (Not used in U.S. SCI system, but approached by item 4a.)	Induces substitution of subsidized items for others
2. Income tax subsidies	Reduces price of health care and owner-occupied housing; limited to upper half of income scale	Induces substitution of these items for others
3. Income-conditioned benefits		
a. Food stamps	Provides fixed quantities of food to low-income families; sum-sufficient appropriation	Induces more consumption of food by only lowest 2% of families
b. Public housing, day care, etc.	Provides fixed quantities of services to limited number of low-income families; sum-certain appropriation	Induces more consumption of services by small fraction of population
c. Medicaid	Provides open-ended quantities of health care to low-income families; sum-sufficient appropriations	Induces more consumption of health care by lowest 10% of families
d. Pell grants	Provides stipends for low-income students in higher education; sum-certain appropriations	Induces more consumption of higher education by lower half of families
4. Non-income-conditioned benefits		
a. Social and private health insurance	Provides virtually open-ended quantities of health care to families at all income levels; sum-sufficient appropriation; approaches 100% per unit subsidy	Induces more consumption of health care by majority of population

TABLE 5.8

Social Costs Attributable to 1950–1978 Changes in SCI

Added costs	Percentage of 1978 GNP
1. Collection, compliance, and administrative costs	1
2. Loss of GNP due to reduction of hours at work	4
3. Adjust 2 for positive value of extra leisure	−2
4. Loss of GNP due to reduction of productivity per hour at work from less capital per worker	0
5. Reallocation of resources to education, health care, and other selected goods	4
6. Adjust 5 for positive consumption value of extra education, health care, and other selected goods	−2
7. Total costs net of 3 and 6	5

native uses of resources forgone because of the existence of the SCI programs. These costs are of several kinds. One is the resources used up in enforcing and complying with the provisions necessary to the funding and targeting of the benefits. These costs include not only the time of paid administrators of several intermediaries in the SCI system, but also the time of contributors and beneficiaries. This sort of "transaction cost" is found even in direct interfamily giving. A rough guess is that this amounts to about 10% of the extra funds that pass through the system, or about 1% of GNP in 1978.

I have tried to quantify the social cost arising from loss of work effort that may have been caused by increasing SCI programs. It is my best guess that the increase in the SCI ratio since 1950 has caused the total of current hours at work to be about 6% smaller than it otherwise would be. The effect of this change has been to reduce GNP by about 4%. A third type of cost is the possible loss of measured GNP caused by lower productivity per hour of work. The latter is due to disincentives that may have led to less capital per worker and to a reduced intensity of work effort. I enter a zero for the quantitative scale of this effect.

The rise in the SCI ratio signals another kind of loss, this one arising out of the "distortion" of consumer choice by subsidies to education, health care, and other selected goods. The 1950–1978 increase in SCI may have reallocated about 4% of GNP away from other investments and consumer goods to these two services over and above what a free market would have allocated. Adding together the market value of the goods thus forgone, the value of measured GNP lost due to disincentives, and the value of resources devoted to collection, compliance, and administration, yields the total gross cost. The sum of these social costs before adjustment for offsetting welfare gains amounts to 9% of GNP.

Just as there are problems in weighting social benefits, there are also problems in appraising the significance of the several social costs I have been discussing. The way to get at the appraisal is to ask: Why isn't the loss of GNP due to reduction in hours at work fully offset by the value (benefit) of hours gained for nonmarket activity? And: Why isn't the value of the resources reallocated to education, health care, and other selected goods fully offset by the value (benefit) received by the consumers of such goods? The quick answer to these questions is that the consumers of the extra leisure and the extra "selected goods" did not make a free and individual choice for the quantities of those items which they are actually consuming. They were in effect "bribed" to consume the extra amounts. But that does not necessarily mean that there should be no offset at all; the issue is whether the offset should be a high fraction or a low fraction of the 4% of GNP shown for reduction in hours of work and the 4% of GNP shown for education and health care in Table 5.8.

Is less time spent at work in the market a goal or a cost of SCI? On the one hand, it would seem that more leisure or time for nonmarket work is an implicit goal of cash benefit programs aimed at retired workers, women left with children to care for, and disabled persons. On the other hand, there is considerable controversy about the appropriateness of "early" retirement, the withdrawal of some welfare mothers from the paid labor force, and the nature of disability that should qualify one for benefits. Some of the controversy turns on the question of who is at fault for the wage loss to be offset. Similarly, there are questions about the degree to which it is appropriate to expand the resources devoted to health care and education. Perhaps more leisure and more "selected goods" should be tagged as goals for which marginal utility diminishes sharply; or perhaps these items are associated with goal achievement up to some point and with cost beyond that point.

The argument is that a free choice by individual consumers would have called forth a bundle of goods that yielded more satisfactions to consumers than did the collective choice for health care and education. To comprehend this argument we need to set forth the rationale for the free-market solution to the allocation problem. The individuals as producers and consumers are assumed to maximize their personal welfare or satisfactions given their factor endowments; hence the community total of personal satisfaction is, in logic, greatest when such choices are made without distortion by regulation or tax or subsidy. The market organizes production so that each factor is allocated among alternative products to yield equal marginal returns in all employments. All products are produced in quantities that give the greatest satisfaction to all consumers given their income. This prediction can be extended to cover voluntary gifts whereby the donors equate the marginal benefit they get from making an extra gift with the satisfaction they get from the last unit of income they allocate to their own direct consumption.

Market economic theory is an exercise in deductive logic which shows that unrestricted choice, in the absence of public goods, economies of scale, and externalities, will yield an outcome that maximizes the total of individual satisfactions, given the distribution of income. This outcome is the one from which no redistribution or reallocation can be made to make one individual better off without making some other person worse off. This stern stricture against change (Pareto) is frequently relaxed to admit a change that makes some people better off if the winners' gain of satisfaction exceeds the satisfaction lost by those who are disadvantaged by the change. The question for the evaluator working from a background of market economics is whether the SCI system yields net gains for some people that are exceeded by the net losses it imposes on other people.

What can we say about the outcome of less work and hence less production from both taxpayers and benefit recipients? We are on the right track in thinking of the burden and the gain in terms of satisfactions rather than measured output of goods. The redistribution makes the taxpayer worse off and the beneficiary better off, but the nation as a whole is worse off if the added leisure is valued by those taking it as less than equal to the loss in value of measured output from work. Needless to say, GNP as measured attributes no value to extra leisure and therefore biases our impressions of the balance of burden versus benefit of redistribution. The 4% loss of GNP doubtless means a loss of less than 4% in consumer satisfaction, so a correction is called for.

What can we say about the distortion of consumer choices associated with the substitution of education and health care for other goods and services that are apparently more valued by individual consumers? In this case no loss of measured GNP is involved. However, in this case again the taxpayer is made worse off and the beneficiary is better off, but the nation as a whole is worse off and suffers a social cost if the added education and health care as valued by those taking them is worth less than the money given up by the taxpayers. The 4% distortion doubtless means a less than 4% loss of satisfactions, so a correction is called for.

Some readers will want to relate this discussion to what is called

TABLE 5.9

Social Benefits and Social Costs in 1978 Attributable to 1950–1978 Changes in SCI

Item	Added benefit	Added cost
Nonquantifiable items		
1. Reduction of insecurity with respect to income loss	+	
2. Reduction of insecurity with respect to irregular and extraordinary expenditure	+	
3. Reduction of income poverty	+	
4. Fair sharing of SCI taxes and contributions	0	
5. Reduction of income inequality	+	
6. Improvement of the social and political environment	+ or −	
7. Total of nonquantifiable benefits (items 1–6)	+	
Quantifiable items		
8. Production increases due to improved education, health, and economic security of the work force	4% of GNP	
9. Production increases from more effective automatic stabilization	0	
10. Collection, compliance, and administrative costs		1% of GNP
11. Loss of potential GNP due to reduction of hours at work (+4%), adjusted for positive value of extra nonmarketed time (−2%)		2% of GNP
12. Loss of GNP due to reduction of productivity per hour at work from less capital per worker		0
13. Reallocation of resources to selected goods (+4%), adjusted for positive consumer valuation of selected goods (−2%)		2% of GNP
Summary items		
14. Quantifiable benefits (items 8 and 9) and quantifiable costs (items 10–13)	4% of GNP	5% of GNP
15. Total of nonquantifiable and quantifiable benefits (items 7–9) and total costs (items 10–13)	4 + ?% GNP	5% of GNP

Sources: Tables 4.12 and 5.8.

Relationship of Social Costs to Social Benefits   145

"excess burden," "deadweight loss," or "efficiency loss." This concept shows how taxes and benefits change relative prices and thereby change the pattern of consumption and of resource use. The emphasis on price change directs attention solely to substitution effects and ignores income effects. The excess burden of a tax on income is seen as the move by the taxpayer to a lower indifference curve in response to a single change, namely, a reduction in the price of leisure. Similarly, the efficiency loss of a subsidy to a particular consumer good is the move by the consumers to a combination of goods which places them on a lower indifference curve than they would have enjoyed if the subsidy had not altered relative prices. I want to take account of this insight concerning lower indifference curves in evaluating the extra leisure and extra consumption of selected goods induced by the expansion of SCI.

Following this line of thought, in Table 5.8 I subtract the value of the extra leisure from the loss of GNP, and I subtract the consumption value of the extra health care and education from the value of the composition of production forgone. The "values" referred to here are utilities or satisfactions rather than market price values. The offset rate used is 50%, but the evaluator is, of course, free to select a higher or lower offset rate. With the subtractions indicated, the net social costs are shown to equal 5% of GNP.

Table 5.9 is based on Tables 4.12 and 5.8. It rearranges the benefits and costs into quantifiable and nonquantifiable items. The total of quantifiable costs less the quantifiable benefit in the form of added GNP due to improved education is shown (at line 14) as about 1% of GNP. That amount should be set against the reader's evaluation of the net total of nonquantifiable benefits (in line 7). Do the added benefits exceed the added costs? That is the judgment that we face as evaluators of the great changes that have occurred in the SCI system over the last 30 years. The quantifiable social costs of increasing the SCI ratio from 17.2 to 27.6% of GNP are 5% of GNP. The one quantifiable social benefit, namely, more GNP due to more education, almost offsets the social costs. To get a strong positive benefit-to-cost ratio, one has to believe that the six nonquantifiable social benefits are sufficiently valuable to more than offset the remaining 1 percentage point of net quantifiable social costs shown in item 14. I, for one, have no trouble in believing that the reductions in insecurity and income poverty (items 1, 2, and 3) are sufficiently valuable to do that. However, the main point of this exercise is to move you, the reader, to make your own benefit-cost calculation and to come to your own conclusions about whether the nation as a whole is better or worse off as a result of the great rise in SCI which occurred in the last three decades.

A Guide to Reading

Identifying and measuring social costs has been a favorite topic for economists in the last decade. The following titles include some of the more recent research efforts, grouped by question.

Disincentives to Work and Saving

Aaron. 1982. *Economic effects of social security.*
Brown (ed.). 1981. *Taxation and labor supply.*
Danziger, Haveman, and Plotnick. 1981. How income transfer programs affect work, savings, and the income distribution.
Heckman and MaCurdy. 1982. New methods for estimating labor supply functions.
Keeley. 1981. *Labor supply and public policy.*
Leimer and Lesnoy. 1982. *Social security and private saving: New time-series evidence.*

Welfare Loss Associated with In-Kind Benefits

Olsen. 1971. Some theorems in the theory of efficient transfers.
Paglin. 1980. *Poverty and transfers in-kind.*
Smeeding. 1982. Alternative methods for valuing in-kind transfer benefits.
Smolensky, Stiefel, Schmundt, and Plotnick. 1977. Adding in-kind transfers to the personal income and outlay account.
Thurow. 1974. Cash v. in-kind transfers.

CHAPTER 6

Future Directions for the Secondary Consumer Income System

This chapter turns away from describing and evaluating the SCI system as it exists now in the United States and looks to other nations and to the future. It deals with the following topics: (1) the variability of SCI ratios by time and place; (2) the projection of past SCI trends into the future; and (3) the key choices that will determine the future scope and pattern of SCI.

The Variability of SCI Ratios

I begin with some descriptive material intended to show, first, the variability of SCI ratios over time within the United States and, second, currently across nations. Table 6.1, column 1, shows that social welfare expenditures under public programs have grown faster than GNP since 1890 but that they grew extraordinarily fast in the Great Depression of the 1930s and again in the 1965–1975 period. Neither selected tax savings nor private SCI (which includes group insurance, philanthropy, and direct interfamily giving) show strong trends. I hazard the guess that the ratio for public and private SCI shown in Table 6.1, column 5, of 7.4% for 1890 is not much different from the ratio that prevailed in European settlements in colonial America. In 1929 the SCI ratio stood at 9.4%; in 1950 it was 17.2%, and by 1978 it was up to 27.6%.

There are probably some less-developed nations in the world today that have SCI ratios below 7.4%. There also are some nations with ratios well above the American ratio. Table 6.2 shows how countries in the Organisation for Economic Co-operation and Development (OECD)

TABLE 6.1

Components of SCI as Percentage of GNP, Selected Years, 1890–1978

Fiscal year	Social welfare expenditures under public programs (%) (1)	Selected tax savings (%) (2)	Total government SCI (%) (3)	Total private SCI (insurance, philanthropy, interfamily) (%) (4)	Government and private SCI (%) (5)
1890	2.4	0.0	2.4	5.0	7.4
1913	2.5	0.0	2.5	5.0	7.5
1929	3.9	0.5	4.4	5.0	9.4
1935	9.5	0.5	10.0	6.0	16.0
1936	13.2	0.5	13.7	6.0	19.7
1940	9.2	0.5	9.7	6.0	15.7
1945	4.4	2.0	6.4	6.0	12.4
1950	8.2	3.1	11.3	6.0	17.2
1955	8.1	3.0	11.1	6.0	17.2
1960	10.1	3.2	13.3	6.7	19.9
1965	10.9	2.5	13.4	6.8	20.2
1970	14.6	2.0	16.6	7.5	24.0
1975	18.6	1.9	20.5	8.1	28.4
1978	18.1	1.5	19.6	8.0	27.6

Sources: Column 1: Years through 1945 are from Merriam and Skolnik (1968), Table III, p. 192; years from 1950 are from Bixby (1983), Table 3, p. 15, adjusted as explained in text. Column 2: years through 1945 are author's estimates; years from 1950 are from Appendix Table A.7. Column 3 = column 1 + column 2. Column 4: years through 1945 are author's estimates based in part on Lampman and Smeeding (1983); years from 1950 are from Table 4.1. Column 5 = column 4 + column 3 from 1890 to 1945. After 1945 column 5 is taken from Table 4.2.

vary in the ratio of public expenditures on education, health, and income maintenance to gross domestic product (GDP). (Note that these categories leave out some of the items I include in my SCI accounts.) The ratio in most countries is between 18 and 25%. Japan is on the bottom end with a ratio of 10.4%. Western European countries have clearly led the world in the development of democratic welfare state institutions. In this respect there is great interest in comparing the United States to one of those leaders, namely, the Federal Republic of Germany.

The German government in recent years has published what they call the *Social Budget*. This *Sozialbudget* is part of the *Social Report* (*Sozialbericht*) published biennially to document social policy legislation and trends. It is based on a conceptual view that is similar to the one I have set forth in this book. Thus, it includes private group insurance and tax savings as I do. However, it excludes some items I include and vice versa. To achieve comparability I adjust the German "social budget" by

TABLE 6.2

Public Expenditures in Selected OECD Countries on Health, Education, and Income Maintenance, 1975 (percentage of gross domestic product)

Country	Health care (%)	Education (%)	Income maintenance (%)	Total (%)
Australia	4.8	4.7	6.3	15.8
Canada	4.8[a]	7.1	7.4[b]	19.3
France	5.3[b]	3.1[a]	13.8	23.5
Germany	6.0	5.0	15.6	26.6
Japan	3.8	3.9	2.7[a]	10.4
Sweden	6.0	5.3	10.0	21.3
United Kingdom	4.7	5.2	12.6	23.1
United States	3.4	5.6	8.8	17.8

Sources: GDP data are from OECD (1980).

For Australia, the health expenditures are calculated from OECD (1977), p. 95, using averages of fiscal-year expenditures and GDP. The education number is from OECD (1980), p. 42. Income maintenance is calculated from data in Scotton and Ferber (1978), p. 23, and (1980), p. 8.

For Canada the health number is from OECD (1977), p. 101. The education number is calculated from Minister of Supplies and Services (1981), p. 236. The income maintenance expenditure is from OECD (1976b), p. 1.

For France the health number is from OECD (1977), p. 10. Education expenditures are from OECD (1976a), p. 93. The income maintenance number is from Commission of the European Communities (1979), pp. 97–98.

For Germany, the health number is from OECD (1977), p. 109. Education expenditure is calculated from Bundesminister für Bildung und Wissenschaft (1981), p. 190. The income maintenance number is from Commission of the European Communities (1979), pp. 97–98.

For Japan the health expenditures are calculated from OECD (1977), p. 11. The education number is from OECD (1980), p. 32. The income maintenance number is from OECD (1976b), p. 11.

For Sweden, the health and education expenditures are from OECD (1980), p. 202. The income maintenance number is 1972 public income maintenance expenditure from OECD (1976b), p. 119, times ratio of 1975 to 1972 government fiscal consumption expenditure as calculated from OECD (1980), p. 202. This whole term is divided by 1975 GDP from OECD (1980), p. 201.

For the United Kingdom, the health number is from OECD (1977), p. 131. Education expenditures are from OECD (1980), p. 226. The number for income maintenance is from Commission of the European Communities (1979), pp. 97–98.

For the United States, all data are from Table 4.1 and Appendix Table A.1. Income maintenance includes items 3–8, 13–17, 19–21, 23–25 of Table A.1. The GDP number is from OECD (1980), p. 19.

Note: Data for Germany do not match Table 6.3 because of the different year and the definition of "public expenditures" used in national accounts.

[a]Number for 1973.
[b]Number for 1974.

TABLE 6.3

Selected SCI Benefits in the United States Together with Comparable Items in the Federal Republic of Germany, 1978 (percentage of GNP)

Type of benefit	United States (%)	Germany (%)
Cash	10.8	17.2
Retirement	6.6	11.4
Government	5.2	11.0
Private group insurance	1.4	.4[a]
Disability	1.5	1.3[b]
Loss of family breadwinner	0.9	.8[c]
Unemployment	1.1	.7[d]
Other[e]	0.6	3.0
Child allowances	—	1.3[f]
Aid to mothers	—	.2
Assistance to victims of political events	—	.7
Miscellaneous	0.6	.8
Health care	5.5	9.2[b]
Government	3.5	9.2
Private group insurance	2.0	n.a.
Education	4.9	5.0[g]
Government	4.9	5.0
Food, housing, and other welfare services	1.9	2.4
Food	0.4	—
Housing	1.0	.7
Employment training and mobility	—[h]	.7
Other welfare services	0.5	1.0
Total I	23.1	33.8
Balancing items		
Philanthropy	+0.6	n.a.
Interfamily	+4.0	n.a.

(1) adding education and (2) dropping "promotion of saving" and tax-saving due to income splitting by spouses. I exclude philanthropic and direct interfamily giving from the American column, since I have no good estimates of such transfers for West Germany. To the extent that these excluded items are relatively greater in the United States, my final ratios overstate the differences between the two countries. After making these several adjustments, I have a ratio of modified SCI to GNP of 23.1% for the United States and 33.8% for West Germany. By rearranging the German items under classifications familiar to us, I can show in more detail how their system compared to that of the United States (see Table 6.3).

TABLE 6.3 (Continued)

Type of benefit	United States (%)	Germany (%)
Education		−5.0
Promotion of savings		+1.4[i]
Tax splitting		+1.1[j]
Total II		
SCI	27.6	
Social Budget		31.3

Sources: Data for United States are compiled from Tables 3.1, 3.3–3.4, 3.9. German data are from *Social Budget* (Deutscher Bundestag, 1980), p. 79, Table 7; and Grund- und Strukturdaten (Bundesminister für Bildung und Wissenschaft, 1981), p. 181.

Notes: Total I shows GNP shares of public expenditures for comparable purposes in both the United States and Germany. Programs without equivalents in one country were counted for the other country only. Total II brings the American SCI back to the definition used in this book (see Table 4.1) and brings the German Total I as shown here back to the *Social Budget* total (Deutscher Bundestag, p. 79, Table 7).

n.a. = data not available. Dash = no program. Sums may not add to totals due to rounding.

[a]Private group insurance for Germany is 3.5% of the retirement total of 11.4% of GNP, i.e., .4% of GNP (Deutscher Bundestag, p. 87, paragraph 67). These are benefits from voluntary or negotiated employer contributions only.

[b]Health expenditures for Germany are 8.4% for curative and preventive health care and .8% for industrial accidents and occupational diseases (Deutscher Bundestag, p. 79, Table 7). The German National Health Insurance spends 62% of this sum (= 5.7% of GNP). Other public bodies spend the remainder. Private group health insurance data were not available but, if available, should be *added* to the 9.2% of GNP shown here. Also, disability income benefits are taken out of the health expenditure category (Deutscher Bundestag, p. 79, Table 7). The noncash component of disability expenditures is minor (Deutscher Bundestag, p. 85, Table 11).

[c]These are benefits for surviving spouses only in the *Social Budget* (Deutscher Bundestag, p. 87, footnote 1). Payments to orphans are negligible, amounting to less than 0.02% of GNP in 1979 (Deutscher Bundestag, p. 82, Table 9).

[d]Unemployment compensation only.

[e]Other cash benefits in Germany cover welfare programs without equivalent in the United States. Other cash benefits in he United States are essentially tax exemptions for children under age 18 (Appendix Table A.1.).

[f]Child allowances for 1978 were calculated as .6 times the 2.1% of GNP allocated to children (Deutscher Bundestag, p. 79, Table 7). This 2.1% of GNP includes orphans' allowances and tax deductions for families with children. The ratio .6 is approximately the share of child allowance in the 1979 and 1980 budget totals for children (Deutscher Bundestag, p. 82, Table 9).

[g]The German education percentage includes 4.3% for elementary, primary, secondary, and higher education and .7% for vocational and further education (Bundesminister für Bildung und Wissenschaft, p. 181).

[h]Employment training for the United States is included in other welfare services (line below).

[i]Deutscher Bundestag, p. 79, Table 7.

[j]Deutscher Bundestag, p. 82, Table 9 and paragraph 42; p. 129, Table 47.

The West German *Social Budget* gives more emphasis than does the comparable part of the U.S. system to income maintenance (17.2% of GNP vs. 10.8%) and health care (9.2% vs. 5.5%). Some of these differences are no doubt explained by the different demographic compositions of the two nations. The share of the population over age 65 is 15% in Germany and 11% in the United States. Also, Germany is like most countries other than the United States in having a child allowance.

The two systems are similar with respect to the sources of funds. About 60% of the German social welfare transfers (including education) are paid for out of "social security funds" (i.e., payroll taxes). The remainder are paid for out of general tax revenues. In the United States about half of the revenues, excluding philanthropic and direct family giving, are from payroll taxes and wage diversions.

Reasons for the Variability of SCI Ratios

Every society devises ways to share the income maintenance needs of the aged, disabled, and members of broken families, and at the same time, to spread the burden of teaching the young and healing the sick. The universality of SCI is variously explained as extension of familial love to a larger kinship circle and as recognition of societal need for the integrative power of transfers as opposed to the sometimes alienating force of pure exchange (Boulding, 1973).

It might seem reasonable to believe that a nation's SCI ratio would fall as income per capita rises, since nuclear families should be in a better position to save and handle their own minimum needs for income maintenance, education, and health care. To the contrary, however, the trend appears to run the other way. That is, the SCI ratio rises with income (Boltho, 1982). However, it does not fall with income in depressions, but rises. This is in part because GNP falls, rather than because SCI spending increases. Some students of this question deduce from this relationship that the demand for SCI is elastic to income. In other words, they conclude that people (donors as well as donees) are not satisfied with a fixed minimum of such transfers at rising income levels, but react toward them as they do toward luxuries. Curiously, however, charitable contributions and purchases of some SCI goods do not show the luxury type of response to income on the cross-section. Other writers ascribe this correlation over long periods of time not to income as such but rather to underlying structural changes associated with urbanization, industrialization, and the breakdown of the extended family. More specialization, greater mobility of both capital and labor, and rapidity of technological change have made people more interdependent (Wilensky, 1975).

The Variability of SCI Ratios

The SCI ratio appears to be sensitive to the share of the population under 20 and over 65 years of age. The aged are, of course, the major clients for income maintenance transfers and the young claim most of the education benefits. The post-World War II years have seen first a remarkable reversal and then a resumption of a long-term fall in the "dependency ratio." See Table 6.4 and Figure 6.1, which show that the ratio of the population outside the "working ages" of 20 through 64 to those in the working ages rose from a low of 0.675 in 1940 to a high of 0.950 in 1965 and then fell to 0.753 in 1980. It is likely that the current trend will continue to a low of 0.683 in 2010 and that it will then reverse. These changes in the age composition of the population are, of course, primarily due to variations in fertility rates. Of lesser importance are immigration and changing life expectancy.

Another theory is that the SCI ratio has risen because providers of health care and education have had, owing to the advance of science and technology, progressively better and more productive services to sell. This suggests a price effect, as opposed to the income effect referred to above. A related fact is that new methods of financing and delivering SCI have been introduced, together with new concepts in justification for them. For example, social insurance is an invention that underlies the growth of public income maintenance. The innovation of group insurance, with its lower transaction costs, certainly contributed to growth of private SCI. Experts thus help in setting new social goals and standards and sometimes promote them by persuasive predictions concerning the outcomes of new programs (Aaron, 1978). It is relevant to note here that programs sometimes have outcomes different from those intended by their designers. A good example of this is the nursing home, which was promoted as a way to remove chronically ill patients from the expensive acute-care hospitals. In actuality, nursing homes have, to a significant degree, served as a substitute for less expensive home-based care.

Another rather technical argument is that once a social welfare program is started, it tends to have a rather predictable period of expansion. The best example of this is OAI, which starts with limited eligibility or insured status and only gradually moves toward wide eligibility. The U.S. program, which was legislated in 1935, paid benefits to only 16% of the aged in 1950. The comparable percentage in 1978 was 92%, by which time the system was "mature." (That is, most people reaching age 65 have been in covered employment all their working lives.) Hence, some researchers introduce "age of programs" as an explanatory variable independent of per capita income.

Some scholars see the rising SCI ratio as a function of such political developments as the extension of suffrage. The new voters, who come

TABLE 6.4

Percentage Distribution of the U.S. Population by Age Groups
for Selected Years, 1850–2060
(actual to 1980; projections to 2060)

	Share of population			Dependency ratio		Covered workers per OASDI beneficiary[c]
	Under 20 (%)	20–64 (%)	65 and over (%)	Aged[a]	Total[b]	
1850	52.5	44.9	2.6	0.058	1.227	—
1870	49.7	47.3	3.0	0.063	1.114	—
1890	46.1	50.0	3.9	0.078	1.000	—
1910	42.0	53.7	4.3	0.080	0.862	—
1930	38.8	55.8	5.4	0.097	0.792	—
1940	34.5	59.7	6.8	0.114	0.675	—
1950	34.3	57.5	8.2	0.143	0.739	16.5
1955	35.9	55.6	8.5	0.153	0.799	8.6
1960	38.7	52.2	9.1	0.174	0.915	5.1
1965	39.4	51.3	9.3	0.182	0.950	4.0
1970	37.8	52.4	9.8	0.184	0.900	3.6
1975	34.9	54.6	10.5	0.189	0.828	3.2
1980	31.8	57.0	11.1	0.195	0.753	3.3
1985	29.7	58.5	11.8	0.202	0.709	3.3
1990	28.9	58.5	12.6	0.215	0.709	3.3
1995	28.5	58.4	13.1	0.225	0.713	3.2
2000	28.1	58.7	13.2	0.226	0.705	3.2
2005	27.2	59.4	13.3	0.225	0.683	3.1
2010	26.5	59.4	14.0	0.236	0.683	2.9
2015	26.2	58.3	15.4	0.265	0.714	2.6
2020	26.7	56.3	17.0	0.303	0.765	2.3
2025	26.1	54.9	19.0	0.346	0.821	2.1
2030	25.8	53.8	20.4	0.378	0.859	2.0
2035	25.7	53.6	20.7	0.386	0.864	2.0
2040	25.6	53.9	20.5	0.380	0.856	2.0
2045	25.7	54.1	20.1	0.372	0.847	2.0
2050	25.8	54.0	20.2	0.374	0.853	2.0
2055	25.8	53.8	20.4	0.378	0.858	2.0
2060	25.8	53.8	20.4	0.379	0.858	2.0

Source: Board of Trustees, Federal OASDI Trust Funds and Disability Insurance Trust Funds (1982), Table A1 and 28. Projections after 1980 are based on Alternative II assumptions, based on lifetime births per woman of 2.1, which is the median among several used by the Bureau of the Census.

Note: Dash = period when OASDI did not exist or had virtually no beneficiaries.

[a]Population aged 65 and over as a ratio to population 20–64.

[b]Population aged 65 and over plus population under age 20 as a ratio to population aged 20–64.

[c]Through 1980, actual data. After 1980, the number of covered workers is projected under assumptions of labor force participation and employment. The number of beneficiaries is projected with the help of strong assumptions about retirement rates, mortality, and disability rates. The interested reader should refer to Table 28 in the source.

FIGURE 6.1 Dependency ratio (population aged 65 and over plus population under 20, as ratio to population aged 20–64), United States, 1850–2050 (From Table 6.4. Figure by University of Wisconsin Cartographic Laboratory.)

from lower-income classes, see transfers as ways to get access to financial security and to key services which had been reserved to the rich. A related theory is that social welfare spending is positively related to the activity and influence of social democratic or labor parties. Another theory is that such spending is supported by middle- and upper-income classes out of fear of disorderly and militant behavior by the poor (Cloward & Piven, 1971). These theories must confront the awkward facts that conservatives as well as liberals, and totalitarians as well as democrats, have sponsored social welfare programs, and that few nations have ever abandoned such programs once they have implemented them. Wilensky (1981) notes the considerable overlap of values among movements and parties.

> For instance, the values invoked to defend the welfare state comprise a veritable smorgasbord. They have included equality (social democrats, Marxian socialists, modern liberals), efficiency, economic prosperity, and equality of opportunity ('efficiency socialists' such as the Fabians), harmony and social justice (Socialists and Catholic humanists alike), political order, hierarchy, and the prevention of revolution (Bismarck and the Catholic Church as well as contemporary establishment Communists) (p. 352)

Another line of political analysis focuses on the process of public choice and tends to see development of social welfare transfers as the outcome of an alliance of the middle class (particularly teachers and other SCI providers) with the poor in a scheme to exploit the rich (Stigler, 1970). In some cases, this alliance may even include some of the rich who have previously committed themselves to private transfer and see an advantage for themselves in universalizing the pattern they have adopted. For example, employers who have adopted—perhaps at the urging of a union—a voluntary health insurance plan may favor a governmental plan that would force all their competitors to meet the same costs they do. The leaders in this case would be secondary beneficiaries of the government plan (Davis & North, 1971).

One school of thought teaches that public choice with majority voting is biased toward higher public spending than individuals really want. This bias arises out of the camouflaging of the costs of social welfare benefits and the practice of log-rolling by legislators in response to pressure groups (Browning, 1975; Mueller, 1979). It follows that the treasury needs to be protected by constitutional limits on taxes and the requirement of more than a majority vote to initiate new spending. This school's concept of "government failure" may be seen as a reaction to the notion that private purchase and voluntary transfer of income maintenance, education, and health care suffer from "market failure" due to the public good and externality considerations referred to in Chapter 4.

Projecting Past SCI Trends into the Future

The Likelihood of a Higher SCI Ratio

The years since 1950—particularly from 1965 to 1975—were years of rapid growth for American SCI. Between 1950 and 1978 the ratio of SCI to GNP rose 60%. Over the same period increases in ratios to GNP for components of SCI were as follows: health care, up 250%; education, up 49%; cash benefits, up 48%; and food, housing, and other welfare services, up 4% (Table 4.2).

Projecting another 60% increase in the overall SCI ratio yields a ratio of 44.3% in the year 2010. However, the 60% increase seems unlikely because the health care ratio is unlikely to more than triple again as it did in the last 30 years. On the other hand, for our ratio to equal the present West German ratio, it would have to rise to about 35%. It is not hard to imagine an SCI ratio for the year 2010 in the range of 33–37% (see Figure 6.2).

One basis for such speculation is that new SCI programs with new goals are always in the wings and, once started, they tend to grow. Strong candidates for such a role include the following: (1) job training, (2) housing rental allowances, (3) pre-kindergarten schooling and child day care, and (4) stipends for college students. It is also possible that there could be a new surge of interest in a goal, for instance, to reduce inequality of result (as opposed to inequality of opportunity). It is also

Projecting Past SCI Trends into the Future

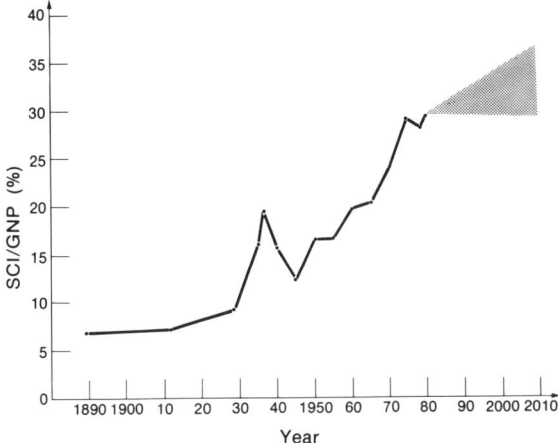

FIGURE 6.2 SCI ratios, actual, 1890–1978, projected to 2010. (Actual ratios from Table 6.1, column 5; projections as discussed in text. Figure by University of Wisconsin Cartographic Laboratory.)

likely that there will be continued growth in some well-established programs. For some examples, the income maintenance programs to offset income loss due to disability have grown at a rapid rate, and veterans' program expenditures are bound to grow as World War II veterans get older. A number of lively proposals for reform might be adopted, and most of them would add to SCI. Among these are some form of national health insurance, the mandating of private pensions for all employees, changing spouse retirement benefits under social security via the introduction of homemaker credits or a demogrant, the substitution of a universal child allowance for AFDC and the income tax exemption for children, and the indexing of numerous benefits which, unlike social security, are not now protected against inflation.

Looking at the longer term, the leading point in support of a prediction of a higher SCI ratio is the change in the age composition of the population that will occur in the second and third decades of the next century. The share of the population that is 65 or older will then leap upward from 13% in 2000 to 21% in 2035 in response to the baby boom of the early post-World War II years followed by a decline to zero-population-growth birth rates (see Table 6.4). The change in the ratio of retired to working adults will dictate a 50% increase in payroll tax rates unless changes are made in ways of financing social security or in terms of eligibility or in levels of benefits. This point is discussed more fully in a later section. Since benefits for the aged are a lion's share of SCI benefits, it follows that the SCI ratio will tend to rise. But, I repeat, that demographic change is several decades away.

The Likelihood of a Decline in the SCI Ratio

What basis might there be for predicting that there will be a decline in the SCI ratio? One good point on this side of the argument is that the ratio peaked in 1975 or 1976 and has declined since then. This change was led by an actual fall in the share of GNP devoted to public education. Not all programs were growing even in the early 1970s. AFDC rolls reached a peak in 1972–1973. Programs that pay benefits to children have had falling demand with declining birth rates. It will be some time before there will be rising numbers of jobs for college teachers.

Another point to support a prediction of a decline in the SCI ratio is that the nation is now, and has been for some time, in a period of reaction to the rapid growth of public—and some private—SCI programs. Propositions 13 (in California) and $2\frac{1}{2}$ (in Massachusetts) were aimed in part at local funds for schools. President Carter made efforts to cut back on social security and to contain hospital costs. The Reagan administration is committed to restraining the rate of growth of federal social welfare spending. It is, of course, too early to tell how long the current reaction will continue. Some of the change of direction on the public side might be offset by more rapid growth in private programs. Thus, cutting back on social security might lead to a strengthening of private pensions, and reducing Medicaid money for nursing homes may prompt a return to more direct interfamily transfers. Note that such substitutions of private for public transfers would not diminish the scale of the SCI system as I have defined it.

There are two philosophical points to be made that may lend credence to a prediction of a stable or falling SCI ratio in this decade. One is that a sympathetic reading of Chapter 4 of this book—on how the present system relates to the immediate goals of offsetting income loss, of helping to cover extraordinary or irregular purchases, of reducing income poverty, and of fairly sharing the burdens of SCI—might lead one to believe that major parts of those goals have been accomplished. Most people have some protection against the principal risks of income loss; equality of opportunity for education and health care has been advanced; income poverty, if income is defined broadly, has been substantially eliminated, particularly for the aged; and the burden of paying for benefits is fairly distributed, if the benefits-received principle is a standard for fairness. The conclusion that these goals have been achieved might lead many citizens to support policies to slow down the growth of SCI.

A second philosophical point has to do with trade-offs. Some people who might favor more aggressive pursuit of SCI goals are cautioned not to do so because of their perceptions of the associated social costs discussed in Chapter 5.

The Key Choices Determining the Future Scope and Pattern of SCI

It is useful to look back to gain understanding of how and why the American SCI system has grown over recent decades and of the range of possibilities for the future. However, such inquiry should not lead one to minimize the role of conscious choice with respect to both ends and means. The American people and their selected policymakers in both public and private organizations can certainly opt to raise or lower the SCI ratio, to change the relative importance of public and private funding in the system, and to alter the composition of benefits by type. Similarly, they can alter the pattern of ways to pay for SCI.

The SCI ratio may be taken as a rough indicator of a society's priority for economic security versus the priority accorded income growth, control of inflation, national defense, or environmental or cultural improvements. If people come to hold less interest in security against irregularity of income and uncertainty of consumer outlays and more interest in one or more other social goals, then the SCI ratio may well languish. For example, a rigorous pursuit of economic growth may dictate more encouragement of saving and investment, less incentive for workers to withdraw from the paid labor force, and more stimulus for research and development of new technology. It is true, of course, that education and some other SCI programs for children may be justified as "supply side" programs that promote economic growth, but this may not be enough to halt a slide in the SCI ratio. Concentration on the goal of improving economic growth is likely to cause some "crowding out" of public and private SCI programs. Such a concentration requires that every program meet the question: What does it do for economic growth?

The unexpectedly good performance of the American economy in the first 25 years after World War II led many Americans to take economic growth for granted and, hence, to think more expansively about redistribution of the fruits of progress. Particularly, the prospect of successive federal government budget surpluses in the mid-1960s encouraged rivalrous bids for ways to dispose of the fiscal dividends. The outcome was a surge of federal initiatives in Medicare and Medicaid, aid to education, and income maintenance. Had economic growth, as distinct from satisfactory employment levels, been more in doubt, it is likely that physical capital formation would have been ranked ahead of some of those SCI initiatives. In this connection, it is important to note that social welfare expenditure often plays a residual role to that of successful economic performance. For example, the elimination of income poverty, as called for in 1964, relied upon a given rate of growth in primary incomes. When that rate of growth was not realized, as was apparent through most of the 1970s, the responsibility for achievement of the antipoverty goal fell more heavily on SCI.

At a lower level of generality, a choice may be made to alter the balance among SCI intermediaries. The dominance of tax-funded benefits—including benefits that take the form of income tax savings—could be reduced. At the same time, the federal government role could be diminished in favor of a stronger funding role for state and local governments. (This would, of course, be a reversal of the trend since the 1930s toward federal establishment of national minimums in social programs.) Employer contributions to private pension and health insurance funds could be encouraged via more substantial tax incentives or, alternatively, they could be mandated by law. Philanthropic contributions, which now amount to only 2.3% of all SCI funds and which have been falling in relative importance since 1950, might be looked to as a way to pick up some of the burden dropped by government agencies. Direct interfamily giving, which has also dropped in relative importance, could be encouraged by tax subsidy or it could be mandated.

One question that arises from reflections on the balance of SCI intermediaries is, Who should be responsible for the planning of such system-wide change? The assumption of most planners is that the lead must be taken by the federal government and, more particularly, by the president and his Office of Management and Budget (Glennerster, 1975). The latter is in a position to look across the several executive departments and independent agencies that have responsibility for SCI programs and to identify links and interactions, overlaps, duplications, and omissions that arise in the complex of programs. At present, there is only limited integration or coordination of efforts to achieve SCI goals by the departments of Health and Human Services, Education, Agriculture, Labor, the Treasury, and by the Veterans Administration, to name only a few of the actors. One encouraging step toward integration was the establishment of the office of Assistant Secretary for Research and Planning in a number of departments.

There is a similar fragmentation of effort on the legislative side. Although a considerable part of the SCI budget goes through the House Ways and Means Committee and the Senate Finance Committee, legislative oversight for a number of such programs is exercised by two appropriations committees and numerous committees on such topics as agriculture, defense, housing, and veterans' affairs, again to name only a few. The new (since 1977) Budget Committees of the two houses are in a good position, with expert help from the Congressional Budget Office, to make judgments on priorities among SCI programs. The Joint Economic Committee has sponsored some system-wide inquiries on SCI topics. The adoption of the unified budget, which includes the OASDHI revenues and outlays, was a step in the direction of providing a system-wide view of SCI. The social welfare expenditures statistical series published by the Social Security Administration and, I hope, this book are also of help in this regard.

Another choice has to do with the target groups for benefits. At present, benefits are heavily targeted to the aged, children, and the poor. This pattern could be altered toward either more or less concentration on those groups. For example, the several elements of SCI could be redesigned to make the system much more pro-poor. (Australia is perhaps the leading example of a nation with a highly pro-poor SCI system. Many of its public benefits are means-tested, and payroll taxation is not used.) We could address each element with the question, What does it do for the poor (or the truly needy)? The programs that score high in answer to that question could be sustained and those that score low could be cut back. This choice confronts us with the issue of selective versus universal programs, which is a perennial issue for social planners (Garfinkel, 1982). Are selective programs such as public assistance to be preferred over more nearly universal (or less selective) programs such as social insurance? Should broad-based subsidies to all users of a particular good (for example, subsidized college tuitions) be converted to an income-conditioned subsidy? Is an affirmative action or compensatory approach to the problems encountered by racial or other minorities to be favored over more broadly targeted programs?

Current issues about targeting of benefits include the following: How far should we go in extending eligibility for DI benefits? What level of expenditure should schools be required to make for children with "learning disabilities"? Should income-conditioned benefits be redesigned to take more or less account of beneficiaries' assets and income from assets? (Institute for Research on Poverty, 1977). Should a special insurance benefit be available for unemployed youth? What about a new income maintenance program for so-called displaced homemakers, those who are ineligible for child-related benefits but too young for OAI benefits? Should OAI and other benefits be readjusted to be less generous to the stereotypical nonworking wife relative to other women? (Burkhauser & Holden, 1982).

People tend to be guided in making their choices with respect to targeting of benefits by what I referred to earlier as mentalities or philosophies. Those with a public assistance mentality emphasize aid to the categorical, not-expected-to-work poor, while those with a social insurance mentality give priority to those who experience income loss due to an insurable risk. Those who stress the efficiency of social investment would target benefits wherever the social rate of return is highest. Those who are swayed by the philosophy that emphasizes horizontal and vertical equity would set aside all traditional categories and selected risks and target benefits by means of a simple ranking of income with an adjustment for family size.

The long-standing controversy among the proponents of the first three philosophies was much enlivened by the arrival in the 1960s of the horizontal-vertical equity school, which sought to recast much of the SCI system into a unitary cash benefit to be federally administered in conjunction with and as an extension of the individual income tax. This negative income tax movement may be said to have run out of steam by the mid-1970s, but by that time it had achieved a number of legislative landmarks, including the Food Stamp program, SSI, and the earned income credit (Lampman, 1977a). More recently, the promoters of the NIT have been challenged from another side by those who favor a shift away from income taxation to consumption taxation, perhaps by use of a value-added tax as a major source of revenue for SCI benefits.

Future choices of the relative priority to be accorded SCI goals vis à vis economic growth and other goals, choices concerning the balance among intermediaries, the emphasis on alternative target groups for benefits, and the influence to be accorded the competing methods of financing and delivering benefits are likely to be taken in a less than systematic manner. However, the philosophy that people come to hold concerning these underlying matters will no doubt influence the positions they take on more specific questions.

One can order a discussion of these more specific questions by reference to what I earlier called the immediate goals of the SCI system, namely, offsetting income loss; helping people to buy education, health care, or other selected goods reducing income poverty; and fairly sharing the burdens of SCI.

Offsetting Income Loss

Over half of SCI benefits for income maintenance are addressed to retirement. Roughly equal amounts are paid out in OAI benefits and in pensions for private and public employees. Less than 2% of all retirement benefits are in the form of public assistance (SSI) and only about

10% are direct interfamily benefits. Recent controversies have turned on the role to be played by OAI, as opposed to private pensions on one hand and SSI on the other (Boskin, 1977b; R. Campbell, 1977; Munnell, 1977; Stein, 1979). The 1972 decision to index OAI benefits was, of course, an important step in strengthening that program, as was the 1977 decision to extend the base of the payroll tax and hence the wages used in computing retirement benefits. The latter decision has been criticized by some for trespassing upon the territory of private pensions. OAI has also been criticized for being too redistributive downward and hence of violating the principles of insurance equity under which each earnings class would pay a premium proportional to its share of total benefits (Burkhauser & Warlick, 1981). The remedy for this breach of insurance equity is, according to these critics, to use SSI, which is funded by general revenues (or a negative income tax or a flat payment per aged person) to supplement "insurance fair" OAI payments. What the balance will be among the three methods of funding retirement benefits will no doubt be an open question for some time.

As I noted earlier, a major political problem for OAI will arise in conjunction with the demographic crunch of 2010. Table 6.4 shows this change in age composition. It may help in discussing this situation to identify retirement classes in 30-year intervals, starting with the group that retired in 1980 (Lampman, 1977). The second generation, which will retire in 2010, represents the post-World War II baby boom. The third generation, retiring in 2040, is made up of children born in 1975, and the fourth, retiring in 2070, will be born in 2005. All four of these generations are involved in the transition to a radically different relationship between the number of retirees and the number of taxpaying workers.

We can assume that the tax rate will need to rise rapidly around 2010 when the postwar babies, in their great numbers, start to retire. This increase in tax rate will fall first on the retirement class of 2040, that is, the relatively small group born in 1975. Each worker in the class of 2010, which is now in the working ages, has to pay current retirement costs of one-third of an aged person; but the worker in the class of 2040 will need to pay for one-half of an aged person (see Table 6.4). The 50% jump in this ratio will require a 50% jump in the tax rate. If replacement rates are held constant, the retirement class of 2040 will get a relatively bad deal. (Table 6.5 raises some questions about whether replacement rates will, in fact, be held constant. Column 1 shows the 50% jump in payroll tax rates, but column 2 shows a less than 50% rise in OASDI cost as a percentage of GNP. Some of this discrepancy is explained by a projected fall in the percentage that taxable wages are of total compensation.) The 2040 class will pay more per capita than their parents did and

TABLE 6.5

OASDI Cost Rates as a Percentage of Taxable Payroll and GNP, 1950–2060 (actual to 1980, projections to 2060)

	OASDI cost rate	
	As a percentage of taxable payroll (1)	As a percentage of GNP (2)
1950	1.17	n.a.
1955	3.34	n.a.
1960	5.89	1.94
1965	7.93	2.78
1970	8.12	3.30
1975	10.65	4.46
1980	10.72	4.67
1982	11.78	5.16
1985	11.70	5.05
1990	11.64	4.94
1995	11.42	4.76
2000	11.03	4.48
2005	10.95	4.36
2010	11.53	4.51
2015	12.82	4.92
2020	14.44	5.44
2025	15.97	5.90
2030	16.83	6.10
2035	17.02	6.05
2040	16.80	5.86
2045	16.66	5.70
2050	16.72	5.62
2055	16.81	5.54
2060	16.81	5.44

Source: Board of Trustees, Federal OASDI Trust Funds and Disability Insurance Trust Funds (1982), Tables 29 and 30. Intermediate Alternative II-A projections are presented here.

Note: Cost rate is defined as annual cost of OASDI as a percentage of taxable payroll in the first column and GNP in the second column. Taxable payroll is that portion of wages and salaries taxable under the payroll tax. Contributions to private pensions and health insurance are excluded from the payroll tax base.

n.a. = data not available.

and get the same share of earnings replaced. In other words, they will get a lower rate of return on their contributions than will the class of 2010. It is unlikely that the retirement class of 2070 will get that kind of a bad deal, that is, a lower rate of return than their parents. That would happen only if population growth were to fall substantially below zero in 2005.

OAI is a treaty among generations and that treaty is likely to be quite strained as a result of this demographic twist. It is worth pointing out that the rate of return of a pay-as-you-go, fixed-replacement-rate system is bound to fall as it matures even without any other change. The system has already registered such a fall, but it has been gradual. The current decline in the rate of population growth will cause a further reduction in the system's rate of return. A zero population growth rate may mean that the only factor remaining to cause the rate of return to be positive is a positive rate of growth of the average real wage and some people have doubts about the future of that variable.

Is it fair to plan to impose a payroll tax rate as high as 17% on the retirement class of 2040, knowing that their rate of return is going to be low? Is it fair for their parents (the retirement class of 2010) to have a relatively easy time in paying the current retirement cost of the class of 1980 without helping to lighten the burden for their children in the class of 2040? This class of 2010, after all, has a lower child-dependency burden than did the class of 1980 as well as a lower old-age dependency burden than the class of 2040.

In the pursuit of fairness, should the class of 1980 volunteer now to accept lower replacement rates than they are scheduled to enjoy? That class, it may be said, is the one that is at fault. They caused the prospective jump in the tax rate to be so extraordinarily great by departing dramatically from the historic downward trend in the fertility rate. Should this class (my own) of senile delinquents pay now for their youthful follies of creating such a large retirement class in 2010? Or should we honor their use of the classic defense of "no malicious intent"?

Would it be more fair for the retirement class of 2010, who have virtuously returned the nation to its historic fertility trend, to now accept lower replacement rates or an increase in the typical retirement age from 65 to 68, effective in 2010, and thereby hold down the taxes their children will have to pay at that time? Since the median benefit is now projected to be about $10,000 a year (in 1977 prices) in 2010, it would not seem like a great hardship to accept a somewhat lower replacement rate. Alternatively (and this is reminiscent of the trust fund controversy "settled" in the 1950s), should they volunteer to pay higher payroll taxes now in order to accumulate a trust fund that could be used to reduce the payroll taxes to be paid after 2010 by the class of 2040? Should that fund be drawn down by 2040, or maintained as an earning asset for the class of 2070?

Who should answer these mind-boggling questions? Should they be voted on by the class of 2010 alone, or should the class of 1980 also have a say in a decision that will affect their grandchildren? Some of these questions were at least tentatively answered by the 1983 amendments to the Social Security Act.

Quite aside from the issue of intergenerational fairness is the question of how to hold all earners in the system when the average rate of return falls to low levels. The redistributive tilt in the benefit formula and the relatively low replacement rate for people earning the maximum taxable wage produce a low return for high-income earners now. But this could turn into a negative rate of return for them if the average rate falls sharply. Will they want, then, to withdraw from the system and direct their contributions to private pensions? Alternatively, will they use political pressure to modify the distributional tilt in the formula to eliminate dependents' benefits and to push more of the retirement burden onto general-revenue-funded SSI? Will more and more low-income workers try to escape from the effect of higher payroll taxes via earned income credits of the type introduced into the income tax in 1975? Is it possible that, because of such political pressure, OAI will disintegrate into SSI and private pensions?

These questions would all be easier to answer if the rate of return could be protected by maintaining a higher growth in the real wage base, which, of course, equals the number of covered earners times the average real wage. One way to raise the rate of increase in real wages is to stimulate a higher rate of increase in plant and equipment per worker. One method to finance that extra investment would be to raise payroll taxes to accumulate a permanent social security trust fund in advance of the year 2010. Some critics see use of this method as a logical corollary of the plausible but unproved notion that our present rate of saving would be higher if workers did not have the promise, discussed in Chapter 5, of future retirement benefits to be paid for on a pay-as-you-go basis.

Reducing Insecurity with Respect to Irregular and Extraordinary Purchases

The persistent rise in the share of GNP going to health care has caused and, at the same time, has been caused by the spectacular growth of SCI health care benefits. A decision to arrest this rapid growth in spending will confront the very difficult choice of either cutting back on consumer rights of access to high-quality care or departing from the traditional practice of allowing decentralized decisions on who gets what health care. It would appear that widespread health insurance with comprehensive benefits is incompatible with fee-for-service methods. However, quality of care may suffer if a ceiling is put on health care expenditures in a manner similar to that followed in the field of education, or in the British National Health Service (LeGrand, 1982).

Rather than force a confrontation between the principles of third-party payment and fee-for-service, some would seek control over cost by regulatory and technological change. Such changes include regulatory control—or alternatively, deregulation and appeal to competition for control—over the number of physicians and of hospital beds, penalties for "unnecessary" surgery and hospitalization, increasing supplies of paramedical personnel, the development of social service models as opposed to hospital models for nursing homes, and deinstitutionalizing the care of mental patients. This approach takes the analyst inside the industry in the search for technical efficiency (i.e., the most cost-effective method for producing a given health outcome).

Unlike health care, education is currently on a downward spending trend. The percentage of GNP going to education has been falling since 1975. There are, nonetheless, important choices to be exercised with respect to the financing of education. Some of these have to do with new target groups, such as children under 5 years of age, physically handicapped children and those with learning disabilities, and older adults who seek retraining or refresher courses. Other issues arise with respect to the goal of statewide equality of opportunity for elementary and secondary education. Currently the trend is toward heavier state financing and control of local outlays per student. Another set of issues arises from an interest in greater diversity of education providers. Some see the answer to this in a tax credit in the individual income tax for tuition paid. Others see it in a voucher to be issued by a state government for use in any public or private school. Again, as in health care, full evaluation of alternative education policies will take the analyst into cost-effectiveness comparisons.

It is of interest to note that arrangements could be made via a voucher system to give parents a choice of schools that spend above the subsidized level and require them to pay the difference. Whether this would result in a significantly greater total resource allocation to education is debatable. The competition among schools that would be encouraged by this scheme might also improve the technical efficiency of schooling expenditure.

By 1972, with the passage of the Pell program, it was apparent that there was a strong movement to increase the percentage of total student cost covered by private funds. The strategy of some who promoted this program was to raise state tuition fees toward the full cost of education, thereby improving the competitive chances of private colleges, and to make means-tested grants to students in both public and private colleges to cover a part of tuition and living costs. Whether this effort to privatize a more substantial part of the cost of higher education will be successful is problematical. It may turn out that the Pell grants will be converted into a scheme to cover the living costs of virtually all students, along the lines of programs in the United Kingdom, Germany, and a number of other nations (Woodhall, 1978). This would relieve parents of interfamily giving by a public transfer but do little to reduce the scope of the overall SCI system. In the meantime, there is little evidence to indicate that the grants program has expanded enrollment of students from disadvantaged family backgrounds (Hansen & Lampman, 1982; Manski & Wise, 1983). If most of the Pell money goes to students who would have attended college anyway, then the subsidy is, from one point of view, redundant and amounts to a pure rent to recipients.

Like education, the food, housing, and other welfare services are not maintaining their share of GNP. Housing is the heaviest user of SCI funds in this miscellaneous category, and the leading program is tax saving for owner-occupants. One important choice here may concern the expansion of income-conditioned housing allowances or rental vouchers (Bradbury & Downs, 1981; Lowry, 1982). Other important choices may involve the cashing out of food stamps; the expansion of energy assistance programs; new programs to help people pay for legal assistance; the purchase of social services from private, nonprofit agencies; the expansion of job-training programs and child day care services.

Reducing Income Poverty

About one-third of all cash and noncash SCI benefits in 1978 went to the 20% of the population who were pretransfer poor. However, a disproportionate share of those benefits went to the aged. A struggle continues to find ways to provide more cash benefits to families with children. AFDC, which in 1978 paid 2% of the total of SCI benefits, was the storm center of welfare reform efforts of the Nixon-Carter period. A child allowance, which is found in many other nations, and a negative income tax were considered as possible replacements for AFDC and the income tax exemption for children. An alternative way to deliver cash benefits to some children is to mandate a formula for payments by absent parents to the custodial parents of their children, with collections to be managed by the Internal Revenue Service (Garfinkel & Uhr, 1984). Continuing change in the public attitude toward work by women with children promises that the "reform" of AFDC will continue to be a live issue in years to come.

Children in families headed by noncategorical or "working poor" persons are helped by relatively few cash, health care, or housing benefits. Should the federal government mandate national minimums for AFDC-UP (unemployed parent), Medicaid, and rental allowances? Alternatively, should the emphasis be on job training, job creation, and other programs designed to increase this group's share of wage income? (Lampman, 1977a).

Fair Sharing of SCI Burdens

In recent decades, the payroll tax and private wage diversion schemes have risen in relative importance as ways to pay for SCI benefits. The local property tax has fallen in relative importance as states have assumed responsibilities formerly shared by local governments. Philanthropy and direct interfamily giving have declined relatively. The role of the federal government in funding SCI has risen dramatically, mainly because of the growth of payroll taxation.

There is much current discussion about using consumption-based taxes, such as the value-added tax, as substitutes for income and payroll taxes to fund SCI programs. There is also a vigorous controversy about reducing the role of the federal government in the SCI system, which would tend to reduce the importance of income taxation and of tax savings. At the same time there are strong pressures to broaden the use of tax savings for numerous purposes. Some that I mentioned earlier are tuition tax credits for private schools, for child day care, and, of course, the negative income tax or the credit income tax. It is worth emphasizing that many of the SCI benefits could be converted to benefits delivered via the tax savings route.

Where We Stand

Some Americans still living have seen the ratio of public and private SCI to GNP rise fourfold. They have seen two great bursts in that ratio—once in the Great Depression of the 1930s and again in the prosperous period of the late 1960s and early 1970s. They have also witnessed the enthusiasm for welfare state schemes in many other nations in the post-World War II years.

In some decades the growth of SCI has been led by education, in some, by cash benefits for the aged, and in others by health care. Similarly, there has been variation in which institution has been the most dynamic—in some instances it has been the local school district, in others, social insurance or private group insurance.

Altogether, the growth of the American system of SCI can be called a social revolution. What are the reasons for this remarkable development? The leading explanations offered by scholars who specialize in this topic include the following: (1) structural changes associated with urbanization, industrialization, and the breakdown of the extended family; (2) changes in the age composition of the population, with emphasis on the share of the population aged 65 years and older; (3) rising demand for, and improved quality of, health care and education; (4) inventions of new institutions such as social insurance; (5) political factors such as the extension of suffrage, the qualities of leaders and parties, and cross-class alliances; and (6) what can be called government failure to resist political pressures of minority groups with selfish interests.

Has this social revolution run its course, or has it only paused to gather energy for another great leap forward? A case can be made for the likelihood of little or no growth in the SCI ratio between now and the year 2010. That case rests on a prediction of a stable fertility rate, the maturity at present of public and private retirement plans, and the probability that health care will not claim an ever larger share of GNP. It also rests on the assumption that public opinion will be less receptive than it has often been in the past to proposals for quite new kinds of SCI benefits, a number of which are on the horizon. However, shortly after 2010, a sharp rise in the proportion of aged in the total population is likely to cause a several-point rise in the SCI ratio. Since the aged receive one-third of all SCI benefits—equal to about 9% of GNP—a 50% rise in their benefits would be a rise in the SCI ratio of 4.5 percentage points (i.e., from 27.6 to 32.1%).

What will actually happen to that ratio and, perhaps equally important, what will happen to the composition of SCI benefits and the methods used to pay for them, will depend on decisions made by people in their roles as citizens and as participants in private organizations. Most fundamental among these decisions will be the priority assigned to goals served by SCI, namely, security against income loss and against irregular and extraordinary consumer outlays and reduction of income poverty, as compared to the priority selected for economic growth and other goals. Other important choices have to do with the balance among intermediaries and among the several immediate or internal goals of SCI. Finally, there are many choices that need to be taken in determining the significant details of specific programs or groups of programs aimed at each of the SCI goals.

Answers to these questions—both the broad and the narrow—often depend on the knowledge that people have concerning the alternatives and their likely outcomes. If this book helps you, the reader, to make better-informed and more careful policy choices with respect to SCI, it will have served its purpose.

A Guide to Reading

The following list of selected readings is divided into (1) historical and comparative studies that help to explain why SCI ratios vary; (2) political or public choice writings that shed light on why the American SCI system is what it is; (3) proposals for integrating or rationalizing certain sets of existing programs; and (4) other proposals for change.

Historical and Comparative Studies

Anderson and Hill. 1980. *The birth of a transfer society.*
Beckerman. 1979. *Poverty and the impact of income maintenance programmes.*
Davis and North. 1971. *Institutional change and American economic growth.*
Easterlin. 1980. *Birth and fortune: The impact of numbers on personal welfare.* (About the baby-boom generation.)
Flora and Heidenheimer (eds.). 1981. *The development of welfare states in Europe and America.*
Heclo. 1974. *Modern social politics in Britain and Sweden: From relief to income maintenance.*
Higgins. 1981. *States of welfare: A comparative analysis of social policy.*
Kaim-Caudle. 1973. *Comparative social policy and social security: A ten-country study.*
LeGrand. 1982. *The strategy of equality.*
Matthews and Stafford (eds.). 1982. *The grants economy and collective consumption.*
Pritchard and Saunders. 1978. Poverty and income maintenance in Australia—a review article.
Rimlinger. 1971. *Welfare policy and industrialization in Europe, America, and Russia.*
Scotton and Ferber (eds.). 1980. *Public expenditures and social policy in Australia.*
Wilson and Wilson. 1982. *The political economy of the welfare state.*

Political Studies

Aaron. 1978. *Politics and the professors: The Great Society in perspective.*
Browning. 1975. Why the social insurance budget is too large in a democracy.
Browning. 1981. A theory of paternalistic in-kind transfers.
Burke and Burke. 1974. *Nixon's good deed.* (About Supplemental Security Income.)

Campbell, C. D. 1969. Social insurance in the U.S.: A program in search of an explanation.
Cloward and Piven. 1971. *Regulating the poor.*
Derthick. 1979. *Policymaking for Social Security.*
Dobelstein. 1980. *Politics, economics and public welfare.*
Edelman. 1977. *Political language: Words that succeed and policies that fail.*
Feder. 1977. *Medicare: The politics of federal hospital insurance.*
Friedman and Hausman. 1977. Welfare in retreat: A dilemma for the federal system.
Fuchs. 1976. From Bismarck to Woodcock: The "irrational" pursuit of National Health Insurance.
Glennerster. 1975. *Social service budgets and social policy: British and American experience.*
Grønberg. 1977. *Mass society and the extension of welfare.*
Hirschman. 1982. *Shifting involvements: Private interest and public action.*
Inglehart. 1977. *The silent revolution: Changing values and political styles among western publics.*
Jennings. 1979. Competition, constituencies, and welfare policies in American states.
Klein. 1980. The welfare state: A self-inflicted crisis?
Logue. 1979. The welfare state: Victim of its success.
Lovell. 1978. Spending for education: The exercise of public choice.
Meltzer and Richard. 1981. *A rational theory of the size of government.*
Organisation for Economic Co-operation and Development. 1981. *The welfare state in crisis.*
Stigler. 1970. Director's law of public income redistribution.

Proposals for Integrating Programs

Barth, Carcagno, and Palmer. 1974. *Toward an effective income support system.*
Garfinkel (ed.). 1982. *Income-tested transfer programs: The case for and against.*
Lurie (ed.). 1975. *Integrating income maintenance programs.*
Organisation for Economic Co-operation and Development. 1974. *Negative income tax: An approach to the coordination of taxation and social welfare policies.*
U.S. Congress. 1973. *Studies in public welfare.*
Worthington and Lynn. 1977. Incremental welfare reform: A strategy whose time has passed.

Other Proposals for Change

Abel-Smith and Maynard. 1978. *The organization, financing, and cost of health care in the European Community.*
Akerlof. 1978. The economics of "tagging" as applied to the optimal income tax, welfare programs, and manpower planning.
American Enterprise Institute for Public Policy Research. 1974. *National health insurance proposals.*
Anderson, M. 1978. *Welfare: The political economy of welfare reform in the U.S.*
Bloomquist. 1979. *The health care business: International evidence on public versus private health care systems.*
Boskin (ed.). 1977b. *The crisis in social security: Problems and prospects.*
Bradbury and Downs (eds.). 1981. *Do housing allowances work?*
Davis. 1975. *National health insurance: Benefits, costs, and consequences.*
Fox. 1977. Options for national health insurance.
Garfinkel and Uhr. 1984. Child support and the public interest.
Harris and Seldon. 1979. Over-ruled on welfare: The increasing desire for choice in education and medicine.

A Guide to Reading

Horlick. 1979. Mandating private pensions: Experience in four European countries.

Institute for Research on Poverty. 1977. *The treatment of assets and income from assets in income-conditional government benefit programs.*

Keniston and the Carnegie Council on Children. 1977. *All our children.*

Kleiler. 1978. *Can we afford early retirement?*

Marmor and Christianson. 1982. *Health care policy: A political economy approach.*

Myers. 1979. Expansion or contraction of Social Security: Serious side effects.

Neugarten (ed.). 1982. *Age or need? Public policies for older people.*

Ozawa. 1982. *Income maintenance and work incentives: Toward a synthesis.* (Proposes substitution of child allowances and other demogrants for means-tested benefits.)

Pechman (ed.). 1980. *What should be taxed—income or expenditure?*

Struyk and Bendick (eds.). 1981. *Housing vouchers for the poor: Lessons from a national experiment.*

U.S. Department of the Treasury. 1977b. *Blueprints for basic tax reform.*

Appendix

TABLE A.1
SCI Cash Benefits, Grouped by Risk, 1950–1980 (billions of dollars)

Type of benefit	1950	1955	1960	1965	1970	1975	1978	1980
1. Total (lines 2 + 12 + 18 + 22 + 26)	26.8	38.4	56.4	73.9	116.2	219.1	301.7	389.9
2. Retirement (lines 3–11)	6.7	12.7	22.6	32.8	55.5	110.2	157.7	213.2
3. Old Age Insurance	0.5	3.4	8.0	11.6	19.3	40.4	58.7	75.7
4. Survivors' Insurance (aged)	0.1	0.4	1.1	1.9	3.8	9.2	13.3	17.2
5. Supplemental Security Income (aged) or Old Age Assistance	1.4	1.6	1.8	1.8	1.9	2.7	2.6	2.8
6. Public employee retirement	0.8	1.4	2.6	4.5	8.6	20.1	29.9	39.5
7. Railroad Retirement	0.3	.6	.9	1.1	1.6	3.1	4.0	4.8
8. Veterans' pensions	0.4	0.5	0.6	0.7	0.9	1.3	1.7	1.9
9. Additional income tax exemptions for aged and blind, and credit for the elderly	0.7	0.7	1.0	1.0	1.3	1.7	2.2	2.5
10. Private pensions[a]	1.0	1.9	3.5	6.0	11.7	21.6	31.4	51.3
11. Interfamily (aged)	1.5	2.2	3.1	4.2	6.4	10.1	13.9	17.5
12. Disability (lines 13–17)	2.3	3.5	5.1	7.4	11.7	23.2	32.4	41.4
13. Disability Insurance	0	0	0.7	1.7	3.5	8.5	12.8	15.6
14. Supplemental Security Income (aid to blind and disabled)	0.1	0.2	0.3	0.5	1.0	3.4	4.6	5.4

(continued)

TABLE A.1 (*Continued*)

Type of benefit	1950	1955	1960	1965	1970	1975	1978	1980
15. State and railroad temporary disability insurance	0.1	0.3	0.4	0.5	0.7	1.0	1.1	1.4
16. Workers' compensation	0.4	0.6	0.9	1.3	2.0	4.0	5.9	9.6
17. Veterans' compensation	1.7	2.4	2.8	3.4	4.5	6.3	8.0	9.4
18. Loss of family breadwinner (lines 19–21)	1.3	1.8	2.8	4.1	8.6	16.2	20.5	23.5
19. Survivors' Insurance (children present)	0.2	0.6	1.2	1.8	3.1	5.6	7.4	8.8
20. Aid to Families with Dependent Children	0.6	0.7	1.1	1.9	5.0	10.0	12.5	14.0
21. Veterans' life insurance	0.5	0.5	0.5	0.4	0.5	0.6	0.6	0.7
22. Unemployment (lines 23–25)	2.6	2.5	3.5	3.8	6.0	18.4	24.1	29.6
23. Unemployment Insurance and Employment Service[b]	2.3	2.2	3.1	3.1	3.9	13.9	12.7	18.3
24. General and emergency assistance	0.3	0.2	0.3	0.3	0.6	1.3	1.5	1.7
25. Other public aid[c]	0	0.1	0.1	0.4	1.5	3.2	9.9	9.6

26. Other (lines 27–29)	13.9	17.9	22.4	25.8	34.4	51.1	67.0	82.2
27. Exemptions for children under 18	6.5	7.7	9.7	8.4	8.4	10.6	11.9	12.8
28. Earned income tax credit	—	—	—	—	—	—	0.1	0.5
29. Interfamily (nonaged)	7.4	10.2	13.4	17.4	26.0	40.5	55.0	68.9

Sources: Lines 3, 4, 13, and 19 are derived from the *Social Security Bulletin, Annual Statistical Supplement* (1982), pp. 105–107. The *Statistical Supplement* presents data for calendar years so these were adjusted to a fiscal-year basis and checked against the fiscal-year totals for OASDHI shown in Bixby (1981), p. 4, and for 1980 in Bixby (1983), p. 10.

Lines 5 and 14 are derived from the *Statistical Supplement* (1982), pp. 4, 225, 247–249. SSI replaced Old Age Assistance and Aid to the Blind and Disabled in 1974. Lines 6, 7, 15, 16, 21, 23, and 25 are from Bixby (1981), p. 4, and for 1980 from Bixby (1983), p. 10. Lines 8 and 17 appear as a combined total in Bixby (1981), p. 4, and for 1980 from Bixby (1983), p. 10, but were divided with 17% going to pensions and the remainder to compensation. Lines 9, 27, and 28 are from Table A.7.

Line 10 is from McMillan and Bixby (1980), p. 15. Lines 11 and 29 are from Table A.6 (lines 6 and 3). Lines 20 and 24 are derived from the *Statistical Supplement* (1982), p. 247 (Table 188), and p. 249 (Table 190). The calendar year data were adjusted to a fiscal-year basis and checked against the fiscal year totals for Public Assistance in Bixby (1981), p. 4, and Bixby (1983), p. 10, for 1980.

Note: Dash = program did not exist.

[a]Includes benefits for disability, loss of breadwinner, and unemployment.

[b]Includes Railroad Unemployment Insurance.

[c]Work relief, other emergency aid, surplus food for the needy, repatriate and refugee assistance, temporary and emergency assistance, and work experience training programs under the Economic Opportunity Act and Comprehensive Employment and Training Act.

TABLE A.2

SCI Benefits for Health Care, by Funding Source, 1950–1980 (billions of dollars)

Type of benefit	1950	1955	1960	1965	1970	1975	1978	1980
1. Total (lines 2 + 15 + 16)	4.5	7.3	11.8	28.1	40.9	80.5	120.4	148.1
2. Government (lines 3–14)	3.3	4.7	6.8	9.5	25.4	51.6	75.9	98.2
3. Medicare	—	—	—	—	7.2	14.8	25.2	35.0
4. Medicaid	0.1	0.2	0.5	1.4	5.2	13.5	20.4	27.4
5. Hospital and medical care	1.2	2.0	2.9	3.5	5.3	9.4	10.7	12.2
6. Veterans' health and medical care	0.6	0.7	0.9	1.1	1.7	3.3	4.9	5.8
7. Workers' compensation (health care only)	0.2	0.3	0.4	0.6	1.0	2.5	3.8	3.7
8. Vocational rehabilitation (health care only)	0	0	0	0	0.1	0.2	0.3	0.3
9. State temporary disability insurance (health care only)	0	0	0	0.1	0.1	0.1	0.1	0.1
10. Maternal and child health	0	0.1	0.1	0.2	0.4	0.6	0.7	0.8
11. School health	0	0.1	0.1	0.1	0.3	0.3	0.4	0.6

	1950	1955	1960	1965	1970	1975	1978	1980
12. Other public health facilities	0.4	0.4	0.4	0.7	1.4	2.9	5.0	6.9
13. Construction of medical facilities	0.5	0.4	0.6	0.7	1.0	2.0	2.5	2.8
14. Income tax deductions of medical expenses (tax savings)	0.3	0.5	0.9	1.1	1.7	2.0	1.9	2.6
15. Group insurance	0.9	2.2	4.5	17.8	14.5	27.3	42.3	47.0
16. Philanthropy	0.3	0.4	0.5	0.8	1.0	1.6	2.2	2.9

Sources: Lines 3–13 are from Bixby (1981), p. 4, and Bixby (1983), p. 10 for 1980. Line 14 is from Table A.7, line 6. Line 15 equals line A minus line B, below. This includes Blue Cross, Blue Shield, independent group plans, and group insurance by insurance companies. Lines A and B are from *Social Security Bulletin* (June 1977), p. 15 for 1950–1975, and *Health Care Financing Review* (Sept. 1981), p. 75 for calendar year 1978. The figures below are in billions of dollars.

	1950	1955	1960	1965	1970	1975	1978	1980
A. Total private health insurance	1.0	2.5	5.0	18.7	15.7	28.9	45.0	
B. Individual policies (health)	0.1	0.3	0.5	0.9	1.2	1.6	2.7	

Line 16 is from Table A.5, line 5.
Note: Dash = program did not exist.

TABLE A.3
SCI Benefits for Education, by Funding Source, 1950–1980 (billions of dollars)

Type of education	1950	1955	1960	1965	1970	1975	1978	1980
1. Total (lines 2 + 8)	10.1	13.0	19.7	30.5	55.2	90.9	113.2	134.4
2. Government	9.4	11.8	18.0	28.1	51.6	85.4	106.1	125.2
3. Elementary and secondary	5.6	9.7	15.1	22.4	38.6	59.8	73.2	86.8
4. Higher	0.9	1.2	2.2	4.8	9.9	16.4	21.9	26.1
5. Vocational and adult	0.2	0.2	0.3	0.9	2.1	4.4	6.1	7.4
6. Veterans' education benefits	2.7	0.7	0.4	0	1.0	4.4	3.4	2.4
7. Basic Education Opportunity Grants	—	—	—	—	—	0.6	1.5	2.5
8. Philanthropy (lines 9 + 10)	0.7	1.2	1.7	2.4	3.6	5.5	7.1	9.2
9. Elementary and secondary	0.4	0.6	0.8	1.0	1.2	1.8	2.6	3.2
10. Higher	0.3	0.6	0.9	1.4	2.4	3.7	4.5	6.0

Sources: Lines 3–6 are from Bixby (1981), p. 4. Line 7 is from U.S. Department of Education (1981), p. 10, the number for 1975 is the average of the 1974–1975 and 1975–1976 award periods. Lines 9 and 10 are from Table A.5.

Note: Dash = program did not exist.

TABLE A.4

SCI Benefits for Food, Housing, and Other Welfare Services, by Funding Source, 1950–1980 (billions of dollars)

Type of benefit	1950	1955	1960	1965	1970	1975	1978	1980
1. Total (lines 2 + 16 + 17)	8.0	9.9	12.7	16.9	26.1	49.9	62.6	83.2
2. Government (line 3–15)	2.8	3.7	6.0	8.5	15.2	33.0	41.1	56.4
3. Food stamps	—	—	—	0	0.6	4.7	5.1	9.1
4. Child nutrition	0.2	0.2	0.4	0.6	0.9	2.5	3.6	5.3
5. Public housing	0	0.1	0.1	0.2	0.5	1.5	3.6	5.3
6. Other housing	0	0	0	0.1	0.2	1.7	1.6	1.9
7. Income tax savings on owner-occupied housing	1.4	2.9	4.6	5.9	8.6	13.6	16.3	22.2
8. Veterans' welfare services	0.9	0.2	0.2	0.2	0.4	0.9	0.8	0.9
9. Public assistance social services	—	—	—	—	0.7	2.6	2.8	2.3
10. Vocational rehabilitation (excluding medical)	0	0	0.1	0.2	0.5	0.8	1.0	1.0
11. Institutional care	0.2	0.2	0.4	0.8	0.2	0.3	0.4	0.5
12. Child welfare	0.1	0.1	0.2	0.4	0.6	0.6	0.8	0.8
13. Income tax savings on child care and dependent care expense	—	—	—	—	0.2	1.3	0.6	0.9
14. Special OEO and ACTION programs	—	—	—	0.1	0.8	0.6	0.9	2.3
15. Social welfare not elsewhere classified	0	0	0	0	1.0	1.9	3.6	3.9
16. Philanthropy	0.7	0.9	1.1	1.4	2.0	3.0	4.3	5.2
17. Interfamily for food and housing	4.5	5.3	5.6	7.0	8.9	13.9	17.2	21.6

Sources: Lines 3–6, 8–12, 14, and 15 are from Bixby (1981), p. 4. Lines 7 and 13 are from Table A.7, line 8–9. Line 16 is from Table A.5, line 6. Line 17 is from Table A.6, line 7.

Note: Dash = program did not exist.

TABLE A.5
SCI Benefits, Philanthropy, 1950–1980 (billions of dollars)

Type of benefit	1950	1955	1960	1965	1970	1975	1978	1980
1. Total (lines 2 + 5 + 6)	1.7	2.5	3.3	4.6	6.6	10.1	13.6	17.3
2. Education (lines 3 + 4)	0.7	1.2	1.7	2.4	3.6	5.5	7.1	9.2
3. Elementary and secondary	0.4	0.6	0.8	1.0	1.2	1.8	2.6	3.2
4. Higher (all postsecondary)	0.3	0.6	0.9	1.4	2.4	3.7	4.5	6.0
5. Health	0.3	0.4	0.5	0.8	1.0	1.6	2.2	2.9
6. Food, housing, and other welfare services	0.7	0.9	1.1	1.4	2.0	3.0	4.3	5.2

Sources: Line 3, which is the same as line A below, was derived from fragmentary sources reflected in lines B, C, and D below, in billions of dollars.

	1949–1950	1954–1955	1959–1960	1964–1965	1965–1966
A. To education, primary and secondary	0.4	0.6	0.8	1.0	1.1
B. Independent primary and secondary			0.03	0.07	0.11
C. Roman Catholic parochial school operation and construction			0.99	1.15	
D. Nonpublic primary and secondary					
E. Total private primary and secondary (lines B + C)			1.02	1.23	

	1969–1970	1971–1972	1973–1974	1974–1975	1977–1978
A. To education, primary and secondary	1.2	1.3		1.8	2.6
B. Independent primary and secondary	0.11	0.13			
C. Roman Catholic parochial school operation and construction	1.42	1.49			
D. Nonpublic primary and secondary			1.12		
E. Total private primary and secondary (lines B + C)	1.54	1.63			

Lines B and C are from Nelson (1977), p. 130. Line D is from Erickson (1977), p. 595 and footnotes on pp. 610–611. For those years in which E has a number, 0.8 times line E was used for line A. This correction is to exclude the value of donated labor time, which is consistently excluded in this book. Erickson estimates that at least 25% of philanthropic contributions are in the form of donated time, principally by teachers in Roman Catholic parochial schools. For the years for which line E shows a number, line A assumes that a constant percentage of GNP went to primary and secondary education. The 1980 number was calculated by using the 1978 percentage of GNP.

Line 4, which is the same as line A below, is line B multiplied by 1.1 to bring the numbers closer to the estimates in line F. Lines C, D, and E are from *Digest of Educational Statistics* (1982), p. 139, Table 127 and (1969), p. 88, Table 120. Line F is from Nelson (1977), p. 130. Line G is from Jenny and Allan (1977), p. 586. The latter numbers represent only a selected sample of educational institutions. They were drawn from reports by the Council for Financial Aid to Education, which is the same source used by Nelson (line F) to estimate total contributions to all institutions. All numbers are in billions of dollars.

	1949–1950	1954–1955	1959–1960	1963–1964	1964–1965	1965–1966	1969–1970
A. To higher education	0.3	0.6	0.9	1.3	1.4	1.5	2.4
B. Total lines C + D + E	0.26		0.79	1.18		1.34	2.14
Private gifts and grants							
C. Current fund income	0.12		0.38	0.55		0.64	1.00
D. Plant fund receipts	0.07		0.20	0.32		0.37	0.73
E. Other fund receipts	0.07		0.21	0.31		0.33	0.41
F. Higher education			1.23		1.94		2.49
G. Higher education					1.1		1.4

(*continued*)

TABLE A.5 (Continued)

	1971–1972	1973–1974	1974–1975	1975–1976	1977–1978	1979–1980
A. To higher education		3.3	3.7	4.1	4.5	6.0
B. Total lines C + D + E		3.01		3.72	4.04	5.36
Private gifts and grants						
C. Current fund income		1.43		1.92	2.32	2.81
D. Plant fund receipts		1.10		1.28	1.15	1.51
E. Other fund receipts		0.49		0.53	0.58	1.05
F. Higher education	2.85					
G. Higher education						

Line 5 is from *Health Care Financing Review* (Sept. 1981), p. 36. The numbers used are those labeled "All Third-parties—Private—Other than Insurance." On pp. 42 and 44 of the same review, these numbers appear as "Philanthropy and Industrial In-Plant." Over half of these numbers represent the amount spent on hospital care and other professional services. Nelson (1977, p. 130) found that "health and hospital services" plus "medical facilities construction" was $.747 billion, $1.236 billion and $1.8 billion for the years 1960, 1965, and 1970, respectively. These are higher than the numbers used here.

Line 6 is from McMillan and Bixby (1980), p. 16. The 1980 number was calculated by using the 1978 percentage of GNP times the 1980 GNP.

TABLE A.6

SCI Benefits, Interfamily, 1950–1980 (billions of dollars)

Type of benefit	1950	1955	1960	1965	1970	1975	1978	1980
1. Total (lines 2 + 7)	13.4	17.7	22.1	28.6	41.3	64.5	86.1	108.0
2. Cash (lines 3 + 6)	8.9	12.4	16.5	21.6	32.4	50.6	68.9	86.4
3. Nonaged (18–64) (lines 4 + 5)	7.4	10.2	13.4	17.4	26.0	40.5	55.0	68.9
4. Children enrolled in postsecondary schools and not at home	0.6	0.7	1.1	1.8	3.3	5.6	7.5	8.8
5. Others	6.8	9.5	12.3	15.6	22.7	34.9	47.5	60.1
6. Aged (65 and older)	1.5	2.2	3.1	4.2	6.4	10.1	13.9	17.5
7. Food and housing (lines 8 + 11)	4.5	5.3	5.6	7.0	8.9	13.9	17.2	21.6
8. Nonaged (18–64) (lines 9 + 10)	3.8	4.5	4.8	6.0	7.9	12.6	15.7	19.8
9. Children enrolled in postsecondary schools and living at home	0.2	0.3	0.4	0.7	1.4	2.3	2.8	3.5
10. Others	3.6	4.2	4.4	5.3	6.5	10.3	12.9	16.3
11. Aged (65 and older)	0.7	0.8	0.8	1.0	1.0	1.3	1.5	1.8

Sources: Line 2 is from Lampman and Smeeding (1983), p. 53, Table 2, line 2, which is identified as interhousehold gifts of cash. Line 3 is line 2 minus line 6.

Line 4 is the number of students age 18 or over who are not living at home multiplied by the average parental contribution to such students. Two-thirds of all the students shown in line A are assumed to be not living with parents or other relatives. This is the ratio reported in U.S. Department of Commerce, *Current Population Reports*, Series P-20, No. 245 (1973), cf. Morgan et al. (1962), p. 408. The average parental contribution is assumed to equal 72% of the cost of room and board at public institutions shown in line B.

(continued)

TABLE A.6 (Continued)

	1950	1955	1960	1965
A. Total attendance at postsecondary schools (millions)	2.7	2.7	3.6	5.3
B. Costs of room and board at public institutions (dollars)	433	533	620	707

	1970	1975	1978	1980
A. Total attendance at postsecondary schools (millions)	8.0	10.2	11.3	11.6
B. Costs of room and board at public institutions (dollars)	864	1381	1381	1582

Line A is from *Digest of Educational Statistics* (1982), p. 94, and (1965), p. 74. Line B is from *Digest of Educational Statistics* (1982), p. 41.
Line 5 is line 3 minus line 4.
Line 6 is calculated as a percentage of line 2. The percentage used is the ratio of independent units headed by a person aged 18 or older to all independent units headed by a person aged 65 or older. Note that all dependent units are excluded from this calculation. Relevant numbers are shown in lines A, B, and C below, in millions of units.

	1950	1955	1960	1965	1970	1975	1980
A. Independent units headed by a person 18 or older	(55.0)	(55.0)	59.4	64.4	71.1	(81.1)	92.0
B. Independent units headed by a person 65 or older	(9.5)	(9.5)	11.2	12.4	13.9	(16.2)	18.7
C. Percentage 65 or older of all independent units (line B ÷ line A)	17.0	17.3	18.9	19.3	19.6	20.0	20.3

Lines A and B were calculated by subtracting the number of spouses of householders from the total population in the age group. Sources used are U.S. Department of Commerce, *Current Population Reports*, Series P-20, and Series P-25. From Series P-20, I used No. 56 (1954), pp. 9–10; No. 105 (1960), p. 11; No. 144 (1965), p. 15; No. 212 (1970), p. 13; No. 271 (1974), p. 18; No. 365 (1980), p. 13. From Series P-25, I used No. 265 (1950), p. 21; 1955 same as 1950; No. 483 (1960–1965), pp. 2–3; No. 917 (1970–1980), pp. 9–10, 12–13, 17–18, 24–25. Numbers in parentheses in line A and B are extrapolated from nearby years.

Line 7 is from Lampman and Smeeding (1983), p. 53, Table 2, line 6, which is identified as "intrahousehold gifts in-kind" (food and housing).

Line 8 is line 7 minus line 11.

Line 9 is calculated as a percentage of line 8. The percentage used is the ratio of dependents enrolled in postsecondary school and living at home to all dependents aged 18–64. One-third of all such students are assumed to live at home. The percentage used for each year is as follows: 5.8% for 1950 and 1955; 8.0% for 1960; 11.2% for 1965; 17.4% for 1970; 18.0% for 1975, 1978, and 1980.

Line 10 is line 8 minus line 9.

Line 11 is calculated as a percentage of line 7. The percentage used is the ratio of dependents aged 65 and older to all dependents aged 18 and older. Relevant numbers are shown in lines A, B, and C below.

	1950	1954	1955	1960–1961	1965	1970	1974	1975	1978	1980
A. Adult dependents who are 18 and older (millions)	(14.4)	18.0	(14.4)	17.6	18.7	19.9	20.9			23.8
B. Adult dependents who are 65 and older (millions)	2.6	2.6		2.5	2.6	2.4	2.0			2.0
C. Percentage of adult dependents who are 65 and older (line B ÷ line A)	(14.4)	14.4	(14.4)	14.2	13.9	12.1	9.6	(9.4)	(8.8)	8.4

Lines A and B are derived from U.S. Department of Commerce, *Current Population Reports*, Series P-20 and Series P-25 (same references as for line 6 of this table). Numbers in parentheses are extrapolated from nearby years.

Discussion: Table A.6 is the least satisfactory of the several Appendix tables. This is because of the paucity of data on interfamily cash and in-kind transfers. Most of the data are calculated in terms of households rather than families. Moreover, since the definition of family I use in this book is different from that used by the Bureau of the Census, I cannot make direct connections with most census data. The best estimates in Table A.6 are lines 2 and 7. Line 2, which is based on Bureau of Labor Statistics surveys, assumes that all gifts of cash are interhousehold gifts and ignores the fact that some cash gifts flow from one family to another within a household. On the other hand, line 7, which is based on a 1959 survey by Morgan, assumes that all in-kind gifts occur within a household and ignores the fact that some in-kind gifts flow from a family in one household to a family in another household. These data shortcomings compound the difficulties of dividing the benefits among several groups, which I attempt in lines 3–6 and lines 8–11. The reader is cautioned against making any critical use of those lines. It should also be mentioned that here, as elsewhere in the book, I exclude all gifts of time, which are substantial between families. See Morgan, Dye, and Hybels (1977). The President's Commission on Pension Policy conducted a household survey in 1979 which included extensive questions on interfamily transfers. I did not learn of this survey early enough to incorporate the results in this book. A forthcoming paper by Cox and Raines is the first attempt to utilize this survey with respect to interfamily transfers as a source of income. (Cox and Raines's paper will be published in the NBER Conference on Research in Income and Wealth Series.)

TABLE A.7
SCI Benefits, Selected Tax Savings, 1950–1980 (billions of dollars)

Type of savings	1950	1955	1960	1965	1970	1975	1978	1980
1. Total (lines 2 + 6 + 7)	8.9	11.8	16.2	17.4	20.2	29.2	33.0	41.0
2. Cash (lines 3 + 4 + 5)	7.2	8.4	10.7	10.4	9.7	12.3	14.2	15.3
3. Additional exemptions for aged and blind and credit for the elderly	0.7	0.7	1.0	1.0	1.3	1.7	2.2	2.5
4. Exemptions for children under 18	6.5	7.7	9.7	8.4	8.4	10.6	11.9	12.8
5. Earned income tax credit	—	—	—	—	—	—	0.1	0.5
6. Health, medical deduction	0.3	0.5	0.9	1.1	1.7	2.0	1.9	2.6
7. Housing and other (lines 8 + 9)	1.4	2.9	4.6	5.9	8.8	14.9	16.9	23.1
8. Owner-occupied housing	1.4	2.9	4.6	5.9	8.6	13.6	16.3	22.2
9. Child and dependent care expenses	—	—	—	—	0.2	1.3	0.6	0.9

Sources: Line 3, tax savings from additional exemptions for aged and blind, is calculated as follows: The tax saving per exemption, which is the dollar value of the exemption multiplied by the average tax rate, is shown in line C below. This amount multiplied by the number of additional exemptions claimed on tax returns is shown in line F.

	1950	1955	1960	1965	1970	1975	1978	1980
A. Dollars per exemption	600	600	600	600	600	750	1,000	1,000
B. Average tax rate (total tax as percentage of taxable income)	.232	.232	.230	.202	.210	.210	.183	.200
C. Tax savings per exemption (line A × line B)	139	139	138	121	126	158	183	200

	1950	1955	1960	1965	1970	1975	1978	1980
D. Additional exemptions for the aged (millions)	4.1	4.1	6.8	7.9	8.9	9.9	11.0	11.9
E. Additional exemptions for the blind (millions)	{	0.1	}	0.1	0.1	0.2	0.2	0.2
F. Total tax savings (billions of dollars) [line C × (line D + line E)]	0.6	0.6	0.9	1.0	1.1	1.6	2.1	2.4
G. Tax credit for the elderly (billions of dollars)	0.1	0.1	0.1	0.0	0.2	0.1	0.1	0.1

Lines B, D, E, and G are from U.S. Department of the Treasury, *Statistics of Income*. Sources for line B are all from *Statistics of Income*, 1950 same as 1955; (1955), p. 37; (1960), p. 65; (1965), pp. 54, 56, 57 (used income tax before credits minus total tax credits, all divided by taxable income of taxable returns); (1970), p. 171; (1975), p. 105; (1978), p. 6; (1980), p. 37. Lines D and E are from *Statistics of Income*, 1950 same as 1955; (1955), p. 12; (1960), p. 18; (1965), p. 35; (1970), p. 107; (1975), p. 59; (1978), p. 65; (1980), p. 60. Line G is from *Statistics of Income*, 1950 same as 1955; (1955), p. 23; (1960), p. 39; (1965), p. 38; (1970), p. 156; (1975), p. 88; (1978), p. 125; (1980), p. 86. Lines F and G combine to equal line 3.

Line 4, tax savings from exemptions for children, is based on lines A and B below. Line C is the same as line 4.

	1950	1955	1960	1965	1970	1975	1978	1980
A. U.S. population under age 18 (millions)	47.0	55.4	70.5	69.7	66.8	67.2	64.8	63.7
B. Tax savings per exemption (from line C above)	139	139	138	121	126	158	183	200
C. Total tax savings (billions of dollars) (line A × line B)	6.5	7.7	9.7	8.4	8.4	10.6	11.9	12.8

Line 5 is from U.S. Department of the Treasury, *Statistics of Income*. For 1978, I used *Statistics of Income* (1978), p. 78; for 1980, same source (1980), p. 87.

Line 6 is the total medical care costs deducted from adjusted gross income (line A below) minus the amount deducted for health insurance premiums (line B), with the remainder multiplied by the average tax rate for each year. Lines A and B are from U.S. Department of the Treasury, *Statistics of Income*. Line A is from *Statistics of Income* (1955), pp. 16, 84; (1960), p. 13; (1965), p. 210 (number for 1964 since medical deduction was not tabulated in 1965); (1970), p. 120; (1975), p. 53; (1978), p. 53; (1980), p. 55. Line B is .25 times number in line A for years 1950–1965. This is the same ratio as 1970. For years 1970, 1975, 1980, same references as for line A. The number for 1978 is average of 1975 and 1980 numbers.

(*continued*)

TABLE A.7 (Continued)

	1950	1955	1960	1965	1970	1975	1978	1980
A. Medical deduction from AGI (billions of dollars)	1.5	3.0	5.2	7.1	10.6	11.4	12.2	15.0
B. Amount deducted for insurance premiums (billions of dollars)	0.4	0.8	1.3	1.8	2.3	1.8	1.9	2.0

Line 8 is the average tax rate multiplied by the sum of property taxes on owner-occupied housing, and net imputed rent from such housing. Net imputed rent is defined as the gross rental value minus necessary expenses of ownership, which consist of interest on mortgage debt, property taxes, depreciation, repairs and maintenance, and casualty insurance. As Goode (1976) points out:

> Homeowners may now deduct interest and taxes, even though imputed rent is not included in AGI. The taxation of imputed net rent, therefore, would involve an addition to taxable income equal to gross rent minus expenses other than interest and taxes. This increase in the tax base would equal the sum of imputed net rent and the personal deductions now allowed for mortgage interest and property taxes on owner-occupied dwellings. Merely to increase the tax base by the amount of net rent would imply double deductions for interest and property taxes, one set in the form of the personal deductions now granted and a second set in the computation of net rent.
>
> The omission of imputed net rent from AGI and the personal deductions for mortgage interest and property taxes discriminate in favor of homeowners compared with renters and with other investors. Homeowners obtain a tax-free return on their investment and at the same time are allowed to deduct important items of housing costs that tenants also pay as part of their rent but without obtaining a tax deduction. (p. 118)

Relevant numbers for calculating line 8 are shown below. Line F is the same as line 8.

	1950	1955	1960	1965	1970	1975	1978	1980
A. Property tax on owner-occupied housing (billions of dollars)	1.7	3.0	5.2	8.2	14.3	20.7	26.0	27.4
B. Mortgage interest on owner-occupied housing (billions of dollars)	1.8	3.6	7.0	11.1	16.5	34.3	52.9	75.3
C. Net imputed rent on owner-occupied housing (billions of dollars)	2.5	6.0	7.7	9.8	10.3	9.7	9.9	8.5
D. Sum of lines A, B, and C (billions of dollars)	6.0	12.6	19.9	29.1	41.1	64.7	88.8	111.2
E. Average tax rate (total tax as percentage of taxable income)	0.232	0.232	0.230	0.202	0.210	0.210	0.183	0.200
F. Total tax savings (line D × line E) (billions of dollars)	1.4	2.9	4.6	5.9	8.6	13.6	16.3	22.2

Lines A, B, and C are listed by the Bureau of Economic Analysis under the heading of "owner-occupied nonfarm housing" as "indirect business tax," "net interest," and "rental income of persons with capital consumption adjustment" respectively. Sources for lines A, B, and C are as follows. The years 1950–1970 are from *Survey of Current Business Supplement, The National Income and Product Accounts of the United States, 1929–74 Statistical Tables* (July 1981), pp. 304–305. The year 1975 is from *Survey of Current Business* (July 1977), p. 60. The year 1978 is from *Survey of Current Business Supplement, National Income and Product Accounts 1976–79* (July 1981), p. 78, Table 8.8. The year 1980 is from *Survey of Current Business* (July 1983), p. 96, Table 8.8.

Note: Dash = program did not exist.

TABLE A.8
Sources of Funds for SCI Benefits, 1950–1978 (billions of dollars)

Source of funds	1950	1955	1960	1965	1970	1975	1978
1. Total (lines 2 + 7 + 8 + 9)	49	69	101	139	238	440	598
2. Taxes, total (lines 3 + 4 + 5 + 6)	31	43	64	86	154	296	396
3. Payroll	4	9	16	23	46	103	146
4. Property	3	5	8	11	19	30	36
5. State general revenue	7	10	14	22	40	69	92
6. Federal general revenue	17	19	26	30	49	94	122
7. Wage diversion	3	5	12	19	36	69	103
8. Philanthropy	2	3	3	5	7	10	14
9. Interfamily	13	18	22	29	41	65	86

Sources: Line 1 figures are rounded from Table 4.1, line 1. Line 3 is from Bixby (1981), p. 4. It equals the amount shown for social insurance benefits less those for public employee retirement. Line 4 assumes that property taxes pay one-half the amount spent by state and local governments for elementary and secondary education and vocational and adult education (see Bixby, 1981, p. 6). Line 5 is derived from Bixby (1981), p. 6. It equals the total for state and local expenditures less those identified as social insurance and less line 4. Line 7 is derived from Tables A.1 and A.2 and includes public and private employee pensions and private health insurance. Line 8 is from Table A.5. Line 9 is from Table A.6.

Appendix

TABLE A.9
SCI Benefits, by Type and Source of Funding, 1978

Type of benefit	Amount of benefit (billions of dollars)	Source of funding
Total	598	
Cash	302	
Social insurance	117	Payroll tax
Employee benefits (public and private)	61	Wage diversion
Other public benefits	55	State $12b, federal $43b
Interfamily	69	Gifts to families
Health care	120	
Social insurance	29	Payroll tax
Employee benefits	42	Wage diversion
Other public benefits	47	State $18b, federal $29b
Philanthropy	2	Gifts to philanthropies
Education	113	
Elementary, secondary and vocational	79	Local $36b, state $37b, federal $6b
Higher	22	State $16b, federal $6b
Veterans' educational benefits and Basic Educational Opportunity Grants	5	Federal
Philanthropy	7	Gifts to philanthropies
Food, housing and other welfare services	63	
Public benefits	42	State $9b, federal $33b
Philanthropy	4	Gifts to philanthropies
Interfamily	17	Gifts to families

Sources: Tables 4.1, 3.1, 3.3, 3.4, 3.9, and A.8, and Bixby (1981), Table 1, pp. 4–6.
Note: Sums may not add to totals due to rounding.

TABLE A.10

Funding source	Amount (billions of dollars)
Total	598
Payroll tax	146
Income maintenance (cash)	117
Health care	29
Wage diversion (public and private employers)	103
Income maintenance (cash)	61
Health care	42
Local property tax	36
Education	36
State general revenue	92
Income maintenance (cash)	12
Health care	18
Education	53
Food, housing, and other welfare	9
Federal general revenue[a]	122
Income maintenance (cash)	43
Health care	29
Education	17
Food, housing, and other welfare	33
Philanthropy	14
Health care	2
Education	7
Food, housing, and other welfare	4
Interfamily	86
Income maintenance (cash)	69
Food, housing, and other welfare	17

Source: Table A.9.
Note: Sums may not add to totals due to rounding.
[a] Includes $33 billion to pay for tax savings.

Appendix

TABLE A.11

Type of benefit	Amount of benefit (billions of dollars) (1)	Percentage to pretransfer poor (2)	Amount to pretransfer poor (billions of dollars) (3)
Total	49.4	28	13.8
Cash (total)	26.8	34	9.2
Retirement	6.7	43	2.9
Disability	2.3	50	1.2
Loss of breadwinner	1.3	70	0.9
Unemployment	2.6	53	1.4
Other	13.9	20	2.8
Health care (total)	4.5	32	1.4
Government	3.3	47	1.6
Group insurance	0.9	5	0
Philanthropy	0.3	20	0.1
Education (total)	10.1	17	1.7
Government			
Elementary, secondary, vocational, and adult	5.8	19	1.1
Higher	0.9	10	0.1
Veterans' benefits	2.7	10	0.3
Philanthropy	0.7	19	0.1
Food, housing, and other welfare services (total)	8.0	19	1.5
Food	0.2	69	0.1
Income tax saving on owner-occupied housing	1.4	5	0.1
Other government	1.2	35	0.4
Philanthropy	0.7	20	0.1
Interfamily	4.5	20	0.9

Sources: Column 1 is from Tables A.1, A.2, A.3, and A.4. Column 2 is from Table A.12, column 2, except for the total and subtotals, for which the percentages are derived as column 3 divided by column 1. Column 3 = column 1 × column 2.

Note: Column 2 is based on the percentage of each type of benefits going to the pretransfer poor that prevailed in the 1970s. No estimates of these percentages for 1950 are available. With that caveat, this table may be compared to Table 3.10. It appears that the 1978 system was more pro-poor than the 1950 system, especially with regard to cash and food, housing, and other welfare services.

TABLE A.12

SCI Benefits by Type and Specific Program, with Percentage Received by Pretransfer Poor and by the Aged, 1978

Type of benefit	Amount of benefit (billions of dollars) (1)	Percentage to pretransfer poor (2)	Amount to pretransfer poor (billions of dollars) (3)	Amount to aged (billions of dollars) (4)	Amount to aged pretransfer poor (billions of dollars) (5)
Total	597.9	33	200.5	193.6	84.1
Cash benefits (total)	301.7	41	123.6	138.1	59.4
Retirement	157.7	43	66.7	138.1	59.4
Old Age Insurance	58.7	58	34.0	52.8	30.6
Survivors' Insurance (aged only)	13.3	58	7.7	12.0	7.0
Supplemental Security Income	2.6	89	2.3	2.6	2.3
Public employee retirement	29.9	40	12.0	26.9	10.8
Railroad Retirement	4.0	20	0.8	3.6	0.7
Veterans' pensions	1.7	43	0.7	1.7	0.7
Private pensions	31.4	20	6.3	28.3	5.7
Interfamily (aged)	13.9	20	2.8	8.0	1.6
Additional income tax exemptions for aged and blind, and credit for elderly	2.2	5	0.1	2.2	0.1
Disability	32.4	50	16.3		
Disability insurance	12.8	45	5.8		
Supplemental Security Income	4.6	89	4.1		
State and railroad temporary disability insurance	1.1	27	0.3		

Workers' compensation	5.9	45	2.7
Veterans' compensation	8.0	43	3.4
Loss of family breadwinner	20.5	70	14.3
Survivors' Insurance (children present)	7.4	40	3.0
Aid to Families with Dependent Children	12.5	89	11.1
Veterans' life insurance	0.6	40	0.2
Unemployment	24.1	53	12.8
Unemployment Insurance and employment service	12.7	21	2.7
General assistance	1.5	89	1.3
Other public aid	9.9	89	8.8
Other	67.0	20	13.5
Exemptions for children under 18 (tax savings)	11.9	20	2.4
Earned income tax credit (tax savings)	0.1	67	0.1
Interfamily (nonaged)	55.0	20	11.0
Education (total)	113.2	17	19.8
Elementary and secondary	73.2	19	14.0
Higher	21.9	10	2.2
Vocational and adult	6.1	19	1.2
Veterans' education benefits	3.4	10	0.3
Basic Educational Opportunity Grants	1.5	50	0.8
Philanthropy	7.1	19	1.3
Health care (total)	120.4	32	38.2	44.6	21.5
Medicare	25.2	35	8.8	25.2	8.2
Medicaid	20.4	90	18.4	10.0	10.0

(continued)

TABLE A.12 (Continued)

Type of benefit	Amount of benefit (billions of dollars) (1)	Percentage to pretransfer poor (2)	Amount to pretransfer poor (billions of dollars) (3)	Amount to aged (billions of dollars) (4)	Amount to aged pretransfer poor (billions of dollars) (5)
Hospital and medical care	10.7	20	2.1	2.2	0.4
Veterans' health and medical programs	4.9	50	2.5	2.5	2.5
Workers' compensation	3.8	45	1.7		
Vocational rehabilitation	0.3	45	0.1		
State temporary disability insurance (health care only)	0.1	27	0		
Maternal and child health	0.7	40	0.3		
School health	0.4	40	0.2		
Other public health activities	5.0	20	1.0		
Construction of medical facilities	2.5	20	0.5		
Income tax deductions of medical expenses (tax savings)	1.9	5	0.1	0.3	0
Group insurance	42.3	5	2.1	4.0	0.2
Philanthropy	2.2	20	0.4	0.4	0.2

Food, housing, and other welfare services (total)	62.6			
Food stamps	5.1	30	18.9	10.9 3.2
Child nutrition	3.6	69	3.5	1.3 1.3
Public housing	3.6	69	2.5	
Other housing	1.6	68	2.4	0.8 0.4
Income tax savings on owner-occupied housing	16.3	50	0.8	0.1
Veterans' welfare services	0.8	5	0.8	5.0 0.2
Public assistance social services	2.8	50	0.4	0.2 0.1
Vocational rehabilitation	1.0	50	1.4	0.6 0.1
Institutional care	0.4	20	0.2	
Child welfare	0.8	20	0.1	0.1 0.1
Tax savings on child care and dependent care expenses	0.6	50	0.4	
Special OEO and ACTION programs	0.9	5	0	
Social welfare not elsewhere classified	3.6	30	0.3	
Philanthropy	4.3	50	1.8	0.3 0.3
Interfamily for food and housing	17.2	20	0.9	1.0 0.2
		20	3.4	1.5 0.5

Sources: Column 1 is from Tables 3.1, 3.3, 3.4, 3.5, and 3.9. Column 2 is from Plotnick and Skidmore (1975), pp. 56–57 for government programs. Column 3 = column 1 × column 2. Column 4 is supplied by the author on basis of knowledge about populations targeted by each program. Column 5 = column 4 × column 2.

Note: I assume that very few aged participate in the programs left blank in columns 4 and 5.

References

Aaron, H. J. 1978. *Politics and the professors: The Great Society in perspective.* Washington, D.C.: The Brookings Institution.
Aaron, H. J. 1982. *Economic effects of social security.* Washington, D.C.: The Brookings Institution.
Abel-Smith, B., and Maynard, A. 1978. *The organization, financing, and cost of health care in the European Community.* Brussels: The European Economic Community.
Abramovitz, M. 1981. Welfare quandaries and productivity concerns. *American Economic Review, 71,* 1–17.
Ackerman, B. A. 1980. *Social justice in the liberal state.* New Haven: Yale Univ. Press.
Advisory Council on Social Security. 1978. Background papers for public hearings, Oct. 2. Washington, D.C.: U.S. Department of Health, Education, and Welfare.
Aharoni, Y. 1981. *The no-risk society.* Chatham, N.J.: Chatham House.
Akerlof, G. A. 1978. The economics of "tagging" as applied to the optimal income tax, welfare programs, and manpower planning. *American Economic Review, 68,* 8–19.
American Enterprise Institute for Public Policy Research. 1974. *National health insurance proposals.* Washington, D.C.: AEI.
Anderson, M. 1978. *Welfare: The political economy of welfare reform in the United States.* Stanford: Hoover Institution Press.
Anderson, T., and Hill, P. 1980. *The birth of a transfer society.* Stanford: Hoover Institution Press.
Arrow, K. J. 1963. Uncertainty and the welfare economics of medical care. *American Economic Review, 53,* 941–973.
Arrow, K. J. 1951. *Social choice and individual values.* (2nd ed.) New York: Wiley.
Atkinson, A. B. 1982. *Social justice and public policy.* Cambridge, Mass.: MIT Press.
Atkinson, A. B. 1983. *The economics of inequality.* (2nd ed.) New York: Oxford Univ. Press.
Atkinson, A. B., and Stiglitz, J. E. 1980. *Lectures on public economics.* New York: McGraw-Hill.
Ball, R. M. 1978. *Social Security, today and tomorrow.* New York: Columbia Univ. Press.
Barlow, R., Brazer, H. E., and Morgan, J. N. 1966. *Economic behavior of the affluent.* Washington, D.C.: The Brookings Institution.
Barro, R. J. 1974. Are government bonds net wealth? *Journal of Political Economy, 82,* 1095–1117.
Barth, M. C., Carcagno, G. J., and Palmer, J. L. 1974. *Toward an effective income support system: Problems, prospects, and choices.* Madison, Wis.: Institute for Research for Research on Poverty, Univ. of Wisconsin.

Baumol, W. J., and Fischer, D. 1979. The output distribution frontier: Alternatives to income taxes and transfers for strong equality goals. *American Economic Review, 69,* 514–525.
Beckerman, W. 1979. *Poverty and the impact of income maintenance programmes.* Geneva: International Labor Office.
Beveridge, W. H. 1944. *Full employment in a free society.* New York: W. W. Norton and Co.
Bixby, A. K. 1981. Social welfare expenditures, fiscal year 1979. *Social Security Bulletin, 44* (November), 3–12.
Bixby, A. K. 1983. Social welfare expenditures, fiscal year 1980. *Social Security Bulletin, 46* (August), 9–17.
Blaug, M. 1970. *An introduction to the economics of education.* London: Penguin.
Blendon, R. J. 1977. The changing role of private philanthropy in health affairs. In *Research papers of the Commission on Private Philanthropy and Public Needs,* Vol. 2. Washington, D.C.: U.S. Department of the Treasury.
Blinder, A. S., Gordon, R. H., and Wise, D. E. 1980. Reconsidering the work disincentive effects of Social Security. *National Tax Journal, 33,* 431–442.
Bloomquist, A. 1979. *The health care business: International evidence on private versus public health care systems.* Vancouver: Fraser Institute.
Board of Trustees, Federal OASDI Trust Funds and Disability Insurance Trust Funds. 1982. *1982 Annual Report, Federal Old Age and Survivors Insurance and Disability Insurance trust funds.* Washington, D.C.: GPO.
Boltho, A. 1982. Course and causes of collective consumption trends in the West. In R. C. Matthews and G. B. Stafford (eds.), *The grants economy and collective consumption.* New York: St. Martin's.
Boskin, M. J. 1977a. Social security and retirement decisions. *Economic Inquiry, 15,* 1–25.
Boskin, M. J. (ed.). 1977b. *The crisis in social security: Problems and prospects.* San Francisco: Institute for Contemporary Studies.
Boskin, M. J. 1978. Taxation, saving, and the rate of interest. *Journal of Political Economy, 86,* S3–S27.
Boulding, K. E. 1973. *The economy of love and fear: A preface to grants economics.* Belmont, Calif.: Wadsworth.
Boulding, K. E., and Pfaff, M. (eds.). 1972. *Redistribution to the rich and the poor: The grants economics of income distribution.* Belmont, Calif.: Wadsworth.
Bowen, W. G., and Finegan, T. A. 1969. *The economics of labor force participation.* Princeton, N.J.: Princeton Univ. Press.
Bowler, K. E. 1974. *The Nixon Guaranteed Income Proposal.* Cambridge, Mass.: Ballinger.
Bradbury, K. L. 1978. Income maintenance alternatives and family composition: An analysis of price effects. *Journal of Human Resources, 13,* 305–331.
Bradbury, K. L., and Downs, A. (eds.). 1981. *Do housing allowances work?* Washington, D.C.: The Brookings Institution.
Break, G. F. 1957. Income taxes and incentives to work: An empirical study. *American Economic Review, 47,* 529–549.
Brehm, C. T., and Saving, T. R. 1969. The demand for general assistance payments. *American Economic Review, 54,* 1002–1018.
Breton, A. 1974. *The economic theory of representative government.* Chicago: Aldine.
Brittain, J. A. 1972. *The payroll tax for Social Security.* Washington, D.C.: The Brookings Institution.
Brown, C. V. 1980. *Taxation and the incentive to work.* Oxford: Oxford Univ. Press.
Brown, C. V. (ed.). 1981. *Taxation and labor supply.* London: Allen and Unwin.
Browning, E. K. 1975. Why the social insurance budget is too large in a democracy. *Economic Inquiry, 13,* 373–388.

Browning, E. K. 1981. A theory of paternalistic in-kind transfers. *Economic Inquiry, 19,* 579–597.
Browning, E. K., and Browning, J. M. 1983. *Public finance and the price system.* (2nd ed.) New York: Macmillan.
Browning, E. K., and Johnson, W. R. 1979. Taxes, transfers and income inequality. In G. M. Walton (ed.), *Regulatory change in an atmosphere of crisis: Current implications of the Roosevelt years.* New York: Academic Press.
Buchanan, J. M., Tollison, R. D., and Tullock, G. (eds.). 1981. *Toward a theory of the rent-seeking society.* College Station, Texas: Texas A & M Univ. Press.
Budd, E., Radner, D., and Whitehead, T. C. An accounting framework for transfer payments and its implications for the size distribution of income. In M. Moon (ed.), *Social accounting for transfers.* National Bureau of Economic Research. In press.
Budget of the United States Government. (Executive Office of the President; annual, fiscal years). Washington, D.C.: GPO.
Bundesminister für Bildung und Wissenschaft. 1981. *Grund- und Strukturdaten 1980/81.* Bonn: Gersbach & Sohn.
Burdett, K. 1979. Unemployment insurance payments as a search subsidy: A theoretical analysis. *Economic Inquiry, 17,* 333–343.
Burke, V. J., and Burke, V. B. 1974. *Nixon's good deed.* New York: Columbia Univ. Press.
Burkhauser, R. V., and Haveman, R. H. 1982. *Disability and work: The economics of American policy.* Baltimore: Johns Hopkins Press.
Burkhauser, R. V., and Holden, K. C. (eds.). 1982. *A challenge to Social Security: The changing roles of women and men in American society.* New York: Academic Press.
Burkhauser, R. V., and Turner, J. A. 1978. A time series analysis on Social Security and its effect on the market work of men at younger ages. *Journal of Political Economy, 86,* 701–715.
Burkhauser, R. V., and Warlick, J. 1981. Disentangling the annuity from the redistributive aspects of social security. *Review of Income and Wealth, 27,* 401–421.
Cagan, P. (ed.). 1982. *Saving for retirement.* (Report on a mini-conference on saving held for the 1981 White House Conference on Aging). Washington, D.C.: American Council on Life Insurance.
Cahnman, W. J., and Schmitt, O. 1979. The concept of social policy (Sozialpolitik). *Journal of Social Policy, 8,* 47–59.
Cain, G. G. 1966. *Married women in the labor force.* Chicago: Univ. of Chicago Press.
Cain, G. G. 1984. Lifetime measures of labor supply of men and women. Institute for Research on Poverty Discussion Paper #749-84, Madison, Wis.
Cain, G. G., and Watts, H. M. (eds.). 1973. *Income maintenance and labor supply: Econometric studies.* New York: Academic Press.
Campbell, C. D. 1969. Social insurance in the U.S.: A program in search of an explanation. *Journal of Law and Economics, 12,* 249–265.
Campbell, R. R. 1973. *Economics of health and public policy.* Washington, D.C.: American Enterprise Institute.
Campbell, R. R. 1977. *Social Security: Promise and reality.* Stanford, Calif.: Hoover Institution Press.
Carnegie Council on Policy Studies in Higher Education. 1975. *The federal role in postsecondary education: Unfinished business, 1975–80.* San Francisco: Jossey-Bass.
Cloward, R. A., and Piven, F. F. 1971. *Regulating the poor.* New York: Random House.
Collard, D. 1978. *Altruism and economy.* Oxford: Martin Robertson.
Commission of the European Communities. 1979. *The European Social Budget, 1980–1975–1970.* Brussels: EEC.
Cohn, E. 1979. *The economics of education.* Cambridge, Mass.: Ballinger.

References

Corning, P. A. 1969. *The evolution of Medicare: From idea to law.* Washington, D.C.: GPO.
Council on Foundations. 1982. *Corporate philanthropy.* Washington, D.C.: Council on Foundations.
Cowell, F. 1979. The definition of lifetime income. Institute for Research on Poverty Discussion Paper #566–79, Madison, Wis.
Cox, D., and Raines, F. n.d. Interfamily transfers and income distribution. Washington University, Department of Economics, St. Louis, Mo. (Mimeo.)
Crew, M. A., and Young, A. 1977. *Paying by degrees: A study of the financing of higher education students by grants, loans, and vouchers.* London: Institute of Economic Affairs.
Culyer, A. J. 1980. *The political economy of social policy.* Oxford: Martin Robertson.
Current Population Reports. See U.S. Department of Commerce.
Danziger, S., Haveman, R. H., and Plotnick, R. 1980. Income transfer programs in the United States: An analysis of their structure and impacts. Special study on economic change, Vol. 6: *Federal finance: The pursuit of economic goals.* Joint Economic Committee, U.S. Congress. Washington, D.C.: GPO.
Danziger, S., Haveman, R. H., and Plotnick, R. 1981. How income transfer programs affect work, savings, and the income distribution: A critical review. *Journal of Economic Literature, 19,* 975–1028.
Danziger, S., Haveman, R. H., and Smolensky, E. 1977. The Program for Better Jobs and Income—a guide and a critique. Joint Economic Committee, Congress of the U.S. Washington, D.C.: GPO.
Danziger, S., and Lampman, R. J. 1978. Getting and spending. *Annals of the American Academy of Political and Social Science, 435,* 23–39.
Danziger, S., and Plotnick, R. In press. *Has the War on Poverty been won?*
Danziger, S., van der Gaag, J., Smolensky, E., and Taussig, M. K. 1983. The life-cycle hypothesis and the consumption behavior of the elderly. *Journal of Post Keynesian Economics, 5*(2), 208–227.
Davis, K. 1975. *National health insurance: Benefits, costs, and consequences.* Washington, D.C.: The Brookings Institution.
Davis, K., and Schoen, C. 1978. *Health and the war on poverty: A ten-year appraisal.* Washington, D.C.: The Brookings Institution.
Davis, L., and North, D. 1971. *Institutional change and American economic growth.* Cambridge: Cambridge Univ. Press.
de Jouvenel, B. 1951. *Ethics of redistribution.* Cambridge, Cambridge Univ. Press.
Denison, E. F. 1974. *Accounting for U.S. economic growth, 1929–1969.* Washington, D.C.: The Brookings Institution.
Denison, E. F. 1979. *Accounting for slower economic growth: The U.S. in the 1970's.* Washington, D.C.: The Brookings Institution.
Derthick, M. 1979. *Policymaking for Social Security.* Washington, D.C.: The Brookings Institution.
Deutscher Bundestag. 1980. *Sozialbericht 1980.* (Bundestagsdrucksache 8/4327). Bonn: Heger Verlag.
Dickinson, F. G. (ed.). 1962. *Philanthropy and public policy.* New York: Columbia Univ. Press.
Dickinson, F. G. 1970. *The changing position of philanthropy in the American economy.* New York: Columbia Univ. Press.
Digest of Educational Statistics, various issues. Washington, D.C.: U.S. National Center for Educational Statistics.
Dobelstein, A. W. 1980. *Politics, economics, and public welfare.* Englewood Cliffs, N.J.: Prentice-Hall.
Douglas, P. H. 1934. *The theory of wages.* New York: Macmillan.

Easterlin, R. A. 1980. *Birth and fortune: The impact of numbers on personal welfare.* New York: Basic Books.
Economic report of the President. 1981. (Council of Economic Advisers; annual). Washington, D.C.: GPO.
Edelman, M. 1977. *Political language: Words that succeed and policies that fail.* New York: Academic Press.
Eisner, R. Transfers in a total incomes system of accounts. In M. Moon (ed.), *Social accounting for transfers.* National Bureau of Economic Research. In press.
Eisner. R., Simons, E. R., Pieper, R. J., and Bender, S. 1981. Total incomes in the United States, 1948 to 1976. Evanston, Ill.: Northwestern University. (Preliminary mimeo.)
Employment and training report of the President. 1981. Washington, D.C.: GPO.
Erickson, D. A. 1977. Philanthropy, public needs, and nonpublic schools. In *Research papers of the Commission on Private Philanthropy and Public Needs.* Vol. 2. Washington, D.C.: U.S. Department of the Treasury.
Feder, J. M. 1977. *Medicare: The politics of federal hospital insurance.* Lexington, Mass.: Heath, Lexington Books.
Feldstein, M. S. 1974. Social Security, induced retirement and aggregate capital accumulation. *Journal of Political Economy,* 82, 905–926.
Feldstein, M. S. 1976. Social Security and the distribution of wealth. *Journal of the American Statistical Association,* 71, 800–807.
Feldstein, P. J. 1979. *Health care economics.* New York: Wiley.
Flora, P., and Heidenheimer, A. J. (eds.). 1981. *The development of welfare states in Europe and America.* New Brunswick, N.J.: Transaction Books.
Fox, A. 1982. Earnings replacement rates and total income: Findings from the retirement history study. *Social Security Bulletin,* 45 (October), 3–23, 53.
Fox, P. D. 1977. Options for National Health Insurance: An overview. *Policy Analysis,* 3, 1–24.
Fraser, D. 1973. *The evolution of the British welfare state.* London: Macmillan.
Freeman, R. A. 1981. *The wayward welfare state.* Stanford, Calif.: Hoover Institution Press.
Freeman, R. B. 1976. *The overeducated American.* New York: Academic Press.
Freeman, R. B. 1982. The changing economic value of higher education in developed economies. Working Paper No. 820. National Bureau of Economic Research, Cambridge, Mass.
Friedman, B. L., and Hausman, L. J. 1977. Welfare in retreat: A dilemma for the federal system. *Public Policy,* 25, 25–48.
Friedman, M. 1962. *Capitalism and freedom.* Chicago: Univ. of Chicago Press.
Friedman, M., and Friedman, R. 1980. *Free to choose.* New York: Harcourt Brace Jovanovich.
Fuchs, V. R. 1966. The contribution of health services to the American economy. Reprinted in M. H. Cooper and A. J. Culyer (eds.), *Health economics.* New York: Penguin.
Fuchs, V. R. 1968. *The service economy.* New York: Columbia Univ. Press.
Fuchs, V. R. 1974. *Who shall live?* New York: Basic Books.
Fuchs, V. R. 1976. From Bismarck to Woodcock: The "irrational" pursuit of National Health Insurance. *Journal of Law and Economics,* 19, 347–359.
Fuchs, V. R. (ed.). 1982. *Economic aspects of health.* Chicago and London: National Bureau of Economic Research, Univ. of Chicago Press.
Fuchs, V. R. 1983. *How we live.* Cambridge, Mass.: Harvard Univ. Press.
Garfinkel, I. (ed.). 1982. *Income-tested transfer programs: The case for and against.* New York: Academic Press.
Garfinkel, I., and Haveman, R. H. 1977. *Earnings capacity, poverty, and inequality.* New York: Academic Press.

Garfinkel, I., and Uhr, E. 1984. Child support and the public interest. *Public Interest*, Spring, pp. 111–122.

Geiger, T. 1978. *Welfare and efficiency, their interactions in western Europe and implications for international economic relations*. Washington, D.C.: National Planning Association.

Gershuny, J. 1978. *After industrial society? The emerging self-service economy*. London: Macmillan.

Gibson, R. M., and Waldo, D. R. 1981. National health expenditures, 1980. *Health Care Financing Review*, September, 1–54.

Gibson, R. M., and Waldo, D. R. 1982. National health expenditures, 1981. *Health Care Financing Review*, January, 1–35.

Gilbert, N. 1983. *Capitalism and the welfare state*. New Haven, Conn.: Yale Univ. Press.

Gilder, G. F. 1981. *Wealth and poverty*. New York: Basic Books.

Glennerster, H. 1975. *Social service budgets and social policy: British and American experience*. London: Allen and Unwin.

Godfrey, L. 1975. *Theoretical and empirical aspects of the effects of taxation on the supply of labor*. Paris: Organisation for Economic Co-operation and Development.

Goetschius, G., and Wicks, J. H. 1971. A note on administrative costs of governmental transfer payments. *National Tax Journal*, 24, 511–514.

Goldsmith, R. W. 1982. *The national balance sheet of the U.S., 1953–1980*. Chicago: Univ. of Chicago Press.

Golladay, F. L., and Haveman, R. H. 1977. *The economic impacts of tax-transfer policy: Regional and distributional effects*. New York: Academic Press.

Goode, R. 1976. *The individual income tax*. (Rev. ed.) Washington, D.C.: The Brookings Institution.

Goodin, R. E. 1982. Freedom and the welfare state: Theoretical foundations. *Journal of Social Policy*, 11 (Part 2), 149–176.

Gordon, S. 1982. *Welfare, justice, and freedom*. New York: Columbia Univ. Press.

Gornick, M. 1976. Ten years of Medicare: Impact on the covered population. *Social Security Bulletin*, 39 (July), 3–21.

Gramlich, E. M. 1981. *Benefit-cost analysis of government programs*. Englewood Cliffs, N.J.: Prentice-Hall.

Grønberg, K. A. 1977. *Mass society and the extension of welfare, 1960–70*. Chicago: Univ. of Chicago Press.

Gwartney, J., and Stroup, R. 1983. Labor supply and tax rates: A correction of the record. *American Economic Review*, 73, 446–451.

Haanes-Olsen, L. 1976. Social security funding practices in selected countries. *Social Security Bulletin*, 39 (May), 24–29.

Haanes-Olsen, L. 1978. Earnings-replacement rate of old-age benefits 1965–75, selected countries. *Social Security Bulletin*, 41 (January), 3–14.

Hadley, J. 1982. *More medical care, better health?* Washington, D.C.: The Urban Institute.

Hamermesh, D. S. 1977. *Jobless pay and the economy*. Baltimore: Johns Hopkins Press.

Handler, J. F., and Sosin, M. 1983. *Last resorts: Emergency assistance and special needs programs in public welfare*. New York: Academic Press.

Hansen, W. L., and Lampman, R. J. 1974. Basic opportunity grants for higher education. Together with Epilogue: Good intentions and mixed results: An update on the BEOG program eight years later. In R. H. Haveman and J. Margolis (eds.), *Public expenditure and policy analysis*. (3rd ed.) Chicago: Rand McNally.

Harris, R. 1980. Trends in social welfare spending: Factors that will shape the future. In Joint Economic Committee, U.S. Congress, Special Study in Economic Change, Vol. 6, *Federal finance: The pursuit of American goals*. Washington, D.C.: GPO.

Harris, R., and Seldon, A. 1979. Over-ruled on welfare: The increasing desire for choice in education and medicine and its frustration by representative government: A 15-year investigation into private preferences and public policy between state and private services. London: Institute of Economic Affairs.

Hartman, R. W. 1983. *Pay and pensions for federal workers.* Washington, D.C.: The Brookings Institution.

Hauptman, A. M. 1982. *Financing student loans.* Washington, D.C.: The Washington Office of the College Board.

Hausman, J. A. 1981. Labor supply. In H. J. Aaron and J. A. Pechman (eds.), *How taxes affect economic behavior.* Washington, D.C.: The Brookings Institution.

Haveman, R. H. (ed.). 1977. *A decade of federal antipoverty programs: Achievements, failures, and lessons.* New York: Academic Press.

Haveman, R. H., and Wolfe, B. 1982. Disability transfers, and the work effort response of older males: A reconciliation. National Bureau of Economic Research, Cambridge, Mass.

Hayek, F. A. 1944. *The road to serfdom.* Chicago: Univ. of Chicago Press.

Hayek, F. A. 1960. *The constitution of liberty.* Chicago: Univ. of Chicago Press.

Health Care Financing Review. (Monthly.) Published by U.S. Department of Health and Human Services (Health Care Financing Administration, Office of Research, Demonstrations, and Statistics).

Heckman, J. J. 1974. Effects of child-care programs on women's work effort. *Journal of Political Economy,* 82, 5136–5163.

Heckman, J. J., and MaCurdy, T. E. 1982. New methods for estimating labor supply functions: A survey. National Bureau of Economic Research, Working Paper No. 858, Cambridge, Mass.

Heclo, H. 1974. *Modern social politics in Britain and Sweden: From relief to income maintenance.* New Haven, Conn.: Yale Univ. Press.

Higgins, J. 1981. *States of welfare: A comparative analysis of social policy.* New York: St. Martin's.

Hirschman, A. O. 1970. *Exit, voice and loyalty.* Cambridge, Mass.: Harvard Univ. Press.

Hirschman, A. O. 1982. *Shifting involvements: Private interest and public action.* Princeton, N.J.: Princeton Univ. Press.

Historical statistics of the United States, colonial times to 1970. 1976. Published by U.S. Department of Commerce (Bureau of the Census). Washington, D.C.: GPO.

Hoagland, G. W. 1982. The effectiveness of current transfer programs in reducing poverty. In P. M. Sommers (ed.), *Welfare reform in America: Perspectives and prospects.* Boston: Kluwer-Nijhoff.

Hochman, H. H., and Rodgers, J. D. 1969. Pareto optimal redistribution. *American Economic Review,* 59, 542–557.

Holland, D. H. 1977. The effect of taxation on incentives in higher income groups. In *Fiscal policy and labor supply.* London: Institute for Fiscal Studies.

Horlick, M. 1979. Mandating private pensions: Experience in four European countries. *Social Security Bulletin,* 42 (March), 18–29.

Huntford, R. 1971. *The new totalitarians.* London: Penguin.

Hutchens, R. M. 1979. Welfare, remarriage, and marital search. *American Economic Review,* 69, 369–379.

Inglehart, R. 1977. *The silent revolution: Changing values and political styles among Western publics.* Princeton, N.J.: Princeton Univ. Press.

Institute for Research on Poverty. 1977. *The treatment of assets and income from assets in income-conditioned government benefit programs: Technical papers.* Washington, D.C.: Federal Council on the Aging.

References

Institute for Socioeconomic Studies. 1978a. *An inventory of federal income transfer programs.* White Plains, N.Y.: Author.
Institute for Socioeconomic Studies. 1978b. *An inventory of state and local transfer programs.* White Plains, N.Y.: Author.
Ireland, Y. R., and Johnson, D. B. 1970. *The economics of charity.* Blacksburg, Va.: Center for the Study of Public Choice.
Jackson, L. R., and Johnson, W. A. 1974. *Protest by the poor: The welfare rights movement in New York City.* Lexington, Mass.: Lexington-Heath.
Jennings, E. T., Jr. 1979. Competition, constituencies, and welfare policies in American states. *American Political Science Review, 73,* 414–429.
Jenny, H. H., and Allan, M. A. 1977. Philanthropy in higher education: Its magnitude, its nature, and its influence on college and university finance. In *Research papers of the Commission on Private Philanthropy and Public Needs,* Vol. 2. Washington, D.C.: U.S. Department of the Treasury.
Johnson, W. G., Curington, W. P., and Cullinan, P. R. 1979. Income security for the disabled. *Industrial Relations, 18,* 173–183.
Joseph, K., and Sumption, J. 1979. *Equality.* London: John Murray.
Journal of Social Policy. 1982. Vol. 2.
Kaim-Caudle, P. R. 1973. *Comparative social policy and social security. A ten-country study.* London: Martin Robertson.
Kamerman, S., and Kahn, A. 1979. The day-care debate: A wider view. *Public Interest,* Winter, 76–93.
Kasper, J., Waldren, D., and Wilensky, G. 1979. *Who are the uninsured? National Health Care Expenditures Study.* National Center for Health Services Research. Washington, D.C.: GPO.
Kass, D. I., and Panther, P. A. 1981. The administrative cost of nonprofit health insurers. *Economic Inquiry, 19,* 515–521.
Keeley, M. C. 1981. *Labor supply and public policy: A critical review.* New York: Academic Press.
Keeley, M. C., Robins, P. K., Spiegelman, R. J., and West, R. W. 1978. The labor supply effects and costs of alternative negative income tax programs. *Journal of Human Resources, 13,* 3–36.
Kendrick, J. W. 1972. *Economic accounts and their uses.* New York: McGraw-Hill.
Kendrick, J. W. 1976. *The formation and stocks of total capital.* New York: Columbia Univ. Press.
Keniston, K., and the Carnegie Council on Children. 1977. *All our children.* New York: Harcourt Brace Jovanovich.
Kienzle, E. C. 1982. Post-fisc distributions of income: Measuring progressivity with application to the United States. *Public Finance Quarterly, 10,* 355–368.
Kleiler, F. M. 1978. *Can we afford early retirement?* Baltimore: Johns Hopkins Press.
Klein, R. 1980. The welfare state: A self-inflicted crisis? *Political Quarterly, 51,* 24–34.
Kotlikoff, L., and Smith, D. E. 1983. *Pensions in the American economy.* Chicago: Univ. of Chicago Press.
Krashinsky, M. 1978. The cost of day care in public programs. *National Tax Journal, 31,* 363–372.
Krashinsky, M. 1981. *User charges in the social services: An economic theory of need and inability.* Toronto: Univ. of Toronto Press.
Kyrk, H. 1953. *The family in the American economy.* Chicago: Univ. of Chicago Press.
Lampman, R. J. 1966a. How much does the American system of transfers benefit the poor? In L. H. Goodman (ed.), *Economic progress and social welfare.* New York: Columbia Univ. Press.

Lampman, R. J. 1966b. Toward an economics of health, education, and welfare. *Journal of Human Resources*, 1, 45–53.
Lampman, R. J. 1969. Transfer and redistribution as social process. In S. Jenkins (ed.), *Social Security in international perspective*. New York: Columbia Univ. Press.
Lampman, R. J. 1970. Transfer approaches to distribution policy. *American Economic Review*, 60, 270–279.
Lampman, R. J. 1971. *Ends and means of reducing income poverty*. Chicago: Markham.
Lampman, R. J. 1973. Measured income inequality: What does it mean and what can it tell us? *Annals of the American Academy of Political and Social Science*, 409, 81–91.
Lampman, R. J. 1974. What does it do for the poor? *Public Interest*, Winter, 66–82.
Lampman, R. J. 1975a. Scaling welfare benefits to income: An idea that is being overworked. *Policy Analysis*, 1, 1–10.
Lampman, R. J. 1975b. Social accounting for transfers. In J. D. Smith (ed.), *The personal distribution of income and wealth*. New York: Columbia Univ. Press.
Lampman, R. J. 1977a. Concepts of equity in the design of schemes for income redistribution. In I. L. Horowitz (ed.), *Equity, income and policy: Comparative studies in three worlds of development*. New York: Praeger.
Lampman, R. J. 1977b. The future of Social Security, 1977–2050. In *Proceedings of the 29th Annual Winter Meeting, Industrial Relations Research Association*. Madison, Wis.: IRRA.
Lampman, R. J. 1983. How has the labor supply changed in response to recent increases in social welfare expenditures and the taxes to pay for them? In J. Barbash (ed.), *The work ethic*. Madison, Wis.: Industrial Relations Research Association.
Lampman, R. J., and Smeeding, T. M. 1983. Interfamily transfers as alternatives to government transfers to persons. *Review of Income and Wealth*, 29, 45–66.
Layard, R. 1977. On measuring the redistribution of lifetime income. In M. S. Feldstein and R. Inman (eds.), *The economics of public services*. London: Macmillan.
LeGrand, J. 1982. *The strategy of equality*. London: Allen and Unwin.
Leimer, D. R. 1979. The role of the replacement rate in the design of the Social Security benefit structure. Social Security Administration, Staff paper. no. 36. Washington, D.C.: U.S. Department of Health, Education, and Welfare.
Leimer, D. R., and Lesnoy, S. D. 1982. Social Security and private saving: New time-series evidence. *Journal of Political Economy*, 90, 606–629.
Levitan, S. A. 1980. *Programs in aid of the poor for the 1980s*. (4th ed.) Baltimore: Johns Hopkins Press.
Levitan, S. A., and Alderman, K. C. 1975. *Child care and ABC's too*. Baltimore: Johns Hopkins Press.
Levitan, S. A., and Cleary, K. A. 1973. *Old wars remain unfinished: The veterans benefit system*. Baltimore: Johns Hopkins Press.
Levitan, S. A., and Johnson, C. M. 1982. *Second thoughts on work*. Kalamazoo, Mich.: W. E. Upjohn Institute for Employment Research.
Levitan, S. A., and Taggart, R. 1976. *The promise of greatness*. Cambridge, Mass.: Harvard Univ. Press.
Levitan, S. A., and Wurzburg, G. K. 1979. *Evaluating federal social programs: An uncertain art*. Kalamazoo, Mich.: W. E. Upjohn Institute for Employment Research.
Levitan, S. A., and Zickler, J. K. 1973. *Swords into plowshares: Our GI bill*. Salt Lake City, Utah: Olympus.
Lillydahl, J. H., and Singell, L. D. 1982. The scope of the grants economy and income distribution: An examination of intergenerational transfers of income. *American Journal of Economics and Sociology*, 41, 125–139.
Lindbeck, A. 1975. *Inequality and redistribution: Policy issues, principles and Swedish experience*. Paris: Organisation for Economic Co-operation and Development.

References

Lindbeck, A. 1981. *Work disincentives in the welfare state*. Stockholm: University of Stockholm, Institute for International Economic Studies. (Reprinted from Nationaloekonomische Gesellschaft Lectures 79–80, Vienna: Manz, 1981.)

Logue, J. 1979. The welfare state: Victim of its success. *Daedalus*, Fall, 69–87.

Lovell, J. C. 1978. Spending for education: The exercise of public choice. *Review of Economic Statistics*, 60, 487–495.

Lowry, I. S. 1982. Experimenting with housing allowances: Executive summary. *Rand Report No. R-2880-HUD*. Santa Monica, Calif.: The Rand Corporation.

Lurie, I. (ed.). 1975. *Integrating income maintenance programs*. New York: Academic Press.

Macaulay, J. R., and Berkowitz, L. (eds.). 1970. *Altruism and helping behavior*. New York: Academic Press.

MacCallum, G. C. 1967. Negative and positive freedom. *Philosophical Review*, 76, 312–334.

MacDonald, M. 1977. *Food, stamps, and income maintenance*. New York: Academic Press.

MacDonald, M., and Sawhill, I. V. 1978. Welfare policy and the family. *Public Policy*, 26, 89–119.

McMillan, A. W., and Bixby, A. K. 1980. Social welfare expenditures, fiscal year 1978. *Social Security Bulletin*, 43 (May), 3–17.

MaCurdy, T. E. 1981. An intertemporal analysis of taxation and work disincentives: An analysis of the Denver Income Maintenance Experiment. Working Paper No. 624. Cambridge, Mass.: National Bureau of Economic Research.

Manski, C. F., and Wise, D. A. 1983. *College choice in America*. Cambridge, Mass.: Harvard Univ. Press.

Margolis, H. 1982. *Selfishness, altruism and rationality*. New York: Cambridge Univ. Press.

Marmor, T. R., and Christianson, J. B. 1982. *Health care policy: A political economy approach*. Beverly Hills, Calif.: Sage.

Marshall, T. H. 1977. *Social policy in the twentieth century*. (4th ed.) London: Hutchinson.

Masters, S., and Garfinkel, I. 1977. *Estimating the labor supply effects of income-maintenance alternatives*. New York: Academic Press.

Matthews, R. C., and Stafford, G. B. (eds.). 1982. *The grants economy and collective consumption*. New York: St. Martin's.

Meade, J. F. 1976. *The just economy*. London: Allen and Unwin.

Meltzer, A. H., and Richard, S. F. 1981. A rational theory of the size of government. *Journal of Political Economy*, 89, 914–927.

Mencher, S. 1967. *Poor law to poverty program*. Pittsburgh: Univ. of Pittsburgh Press.

Menchik, P. L., and David, M. 1983. Income distribution, lifetime savings, and bequests. *American Economic Review*, 83, 672–690.

Merriam, I. C., and Skolnik, A. M. 1968. *Social welfare expenditures under public programs in the U.S., 1929–66*. Washington, D.C.: GPO.

Michael, R. T., Fuchs, V. R., and Scott, S. 1978. Changes in household living arrangements, 1950–1976. Working Paper No. 262. Cambridge, Mass.: National Bureau of Economic Research.

Mincer, J. 1963. Labor force participation of married women. In National Bureau of Economic Research, Conference Proceedings, *Aspects of labor economics*. Princeton, N.J.: Princeton Univ. Press.

Minister for Supplies and Services. 1981. *Canada yearbook 1980–81*. Ottawa, Canada: Statistics Canada.

Mishan, E. J. 1982a. *What political economy is all about*. New York: Cambridge Univ. Press.

Mishan, E. J. 1982b. *Cost-benefit analysis*. (3rd ed.; 1st ed., 1971.) London: Allen and Unwin.

Moon, M. L. 1977. *The measurement of economic welfare: Its application to the aged poor*. New York: Academic Press.

Moon, M. L. (ed.). In press. *Social accounting for transfers*. Chicago: National Bureau of Economic Research, Univ. of Chicago Press.

Morgan, J. N., David, M. H., Cohen, W. J., and Brazer, H. E. 1962. *Income and welfare in the United States*. New York: McGraw-Hill.

Morgan, J. N., Dye, R. F., and Hybels, J. A. 1977. Results from two national surveys of philanthropic activity. In *Research Papers of the Commission on Private Philanthropy and Public Needs*. Vol. 1. Washington, D.C.: U.S. Department of the Treasury.

Moss, M. 1978. Income distribution issues viewed in a lifetime income perspective. *Review of Income and Wealth*, 24, 119–136.

Mueller, D. 1979. *Public choice*. Cambridge: Cambridge Univ. Press.

Munnell, A. H. 1977. *The future of Social Security*. Washington, D.C.: The Brookings Institution.

Munnell, A. H. 1980. Review of *Social Security versus private saving*, G. M. von Furstenberg ed. *Journal of Economic Literature*, 18, 1627–1630.

Munnell, A. H. 1982. *The economics of private pensions*. Washington, D.C.: The Brookings Institution.

Musgrave, R. A., and Musgrave, P. B. 1980. *Public finance in theory and practice*. (3rd ed.) New York: McGraw-Hill.

Mushkin, S. 1962. Health as an investment. *Journal of Political Economy*, Supplement, 70, 129–157.

Myers, R. J. 1979. Expansion or contraction of Social Security: Serious side effects. *Annals of the American Academy of Political and Social Science*, 443, 63–71.

Neenan, W. B. 1981. *Urban public economics*. Belmont, Calif.: Wadsworth.

Nelson, R. L. 1977. Private giving in the American economy. In *Research papers of the Commission on Private Philanthropy and Public Needs*, Vol. 1. Washington, D.C.: U.S. Department of the Treasury.

Neugarten, B. L. (ed.). 1982. *Age or need? Public policies for older people*. Beverly Hills, Calif.: Sage.

Newhouse, J. P. 1978. *The economics of medical care: A policy perspective*. Reading, Mass.: Addison-Wesley.

Ng, Y.-K. 1979. *Welfare economics: Introduction and development of basic concepts*. London: Macmillan.

Nicholson, J. L. 1970. Redistribution of income: Notes on some problems and puzzles. *Review of Income and Wealth*, 16, 273–278.

Okner, B. A. 1979. Distributional aspects of tax reform during the past fifteen years. *National Tax Journal*, 32, 11–27.

Okun, A. M. 1975. *Equality and efficiency: The big tradeoff*. Washington, D.C.: The Brookings Institution.

Olsen, E. O. 1971. Some theorems in the theory of efficient transfers. *Journal of Political Economy*, 79, 166–176.

Olsen, E. O. 1982. The role of government in the housing sector. In H. Giersch (ed.), *Reassessing the role of government in the mixed economy*. Tübingen, West Germany: J. C. B. Mohr (Paul Siebeck).

Olson, M. 1971. *The logic of collective action: Public goods and the theory of groups*. Cambridge, Mass.: Harvard Univ. Press.

Organisation for Economic Co-operation and Development. 1974. *Negative income tax: An approach to the co-ordination of taxation and social welfare policies*. Paris: OECD.

Organisation for Economic Co-operation and Development. 1976a. *Public expenditures on education*. Paris: OECD.

References

Organisation for Economic Co-operation and Development. 1976b. *Public expenditures on income maintenance programmes.* Paris: OECD.
Organisation for Economic Co-operation and Development. 1977. *Public expenditures on health.* Paris: OECD.
Organisation for Economic Co-operation and Development. 1978. *Public expenditure trends.* Paris: OECD.
Organisation for Economic Co-operation and Development. 1980. *National accounts, 1961–1978.* Vol. 2. Paris: OECD.
Organisation for Economic Co-operation and Development. 1981. *The welfare state in crisis.* Paris: OECD.
Owen, J. D. 1974. *School inequality and the welfare state.* Baltimore: Johns Hopkins Press.
Ozawa, M. N. 1982. *Income maintenance and work incentives: Toward a synthesis.* New York: Praeger.
Paglin, M. 1980. *Poverty and transfers in-kind: A re-evaluation of poverty in the United States.* Stanford, Calif.: Hoover Institution Press.
Palmer, J., and Sawhill, I. V. (eds.). 1982. *The Reagan experiment: An examination of economic and social policies under the Reagan administration.* Washington, D.C.: The Urban Institute.
Pauly, M. V. 1971. *Medical care at public expense: A study in applied welfare economics.* New York: Praeger.
Peacock, A. T., and Rowley, C. K. 1975. *Welfare economics: A liberal restatement.* London: Martin Robertson.
Pechman, J. A. (ed.). 1980. *What should be taxed—income or expenditure?* Washington, D.C.: The Brookings Institution.
Pechman, J. A., and Okner, B. A. 1974. *Who bears the tax burden?* Washington, D.C.: The Brookings Institution.
Pechman, J. A., and Timpane, P. M. (eds.). 1975. *Work incentives and income guarantees: The New Jersey Negative Income Tax Experiment.* Washington, D.C.: The Brookings Institution.
Peltzman, S. 1973. The effect of government subsidies-in-kind on private expenditures: The case of higher education. *Journal of Political Economy, 81,* 1–27.
Phelps, E. S. (ed.). 1975. *Altruism, morality, and economic theory.* New York: Russell Sage Foundation.
Pinker, R. 1979. *The idea of welfare.* London: Heinemann.
Plotnick, R. D. 1977. Social welfare expenditures and the poor: The 1965–76 experience and future expectations. Institute for Research on Poverty Discussion paper #443–77, Madison, Wis.
Plotnick, R. D., and Skidmore, F. 1975. *Progress against poverty: A review of the 1964–74 decade.* New York: Academic Press.
Poynter, J. R. 1969. *Society and pauperism: English ideas on poor relief, 1795–1834.* London: Routledge and Kegan Paul.
Pritchard, H., and Saunders, P. 1978. Poverty and income maintenance policy in Australia—A review article. *Economic Record, 54,* 17–31.
Psacharopoulos, G. 1973. *Returns to education.* San Francisco and Washington, D.C.: Jossey-Bass.
Psacharopoulos, G. 1977. Unequal access to education and income distribution: An international comparison. *De Economist, 125,* 383–392.
Rauscher, A. 1978. The necessity for, and the limits of, the social welfare state. *Review of Social Economics, 36,* 333–347.
Rawls, J. 1971. *A theory of justice.* Cambridge, Mass.: Harvard Univ. Press.

Recktenwald, H. C. 1971. *Tax incidence and income redistribution: An introduction.* Detroit: Wayne State Univ. Press.

Reinhardt, U. E. 1979. Medicare: Its financing and future. *American Economic Review*, 69, 279–283.

Rejda, G. E. 1984. *Social insurance and economic security.* Englewood Cliffs, N.J.: Prentice-Hall.

Reno, V., and Rader, A. D. 1982. Benefits for individual retired workers and couples now approaching retirement age. *Social Security Bulletin*, 45 (February), 25–31.

Reynolds, M., and Smolensky, E. 1977. *Public expenditures, taxes, and the distribution of income: The U.S., 1950, 1961, 1970.* New York: Academic Press.

Rimlinger, G. V. 1971. *Welfare policy and industrialization in Europe, America, and Russia.* New York: Wiley.

Rivlin, A. M. 1971. *Systematic thinking for social action.* Washington, D.C.: The Brookings Institution.

Robson, W. A. 1976. *Welfare state and welfare society.* London: Allen and Unwin.

Root, L. S. 1982. *Fringe benefits: Social insurance in the steel industry.* Beverly Hills, Calif.: Sage.

Ross, H. L., and Sawhill, I. V. 1975. *A time of transition: The growth of families headed by women.* Washington, D.C.: The Urban Institute.

Ruggles, N., and Ruggles, R. 1970. *The design of economic accounts.* New York: Columbia Univ. Press.

Ruggles, P., and O'Higgins, M. 1981. The distribution of public expenditure among households in the United States. *Review of Income and Wealth*, 27, 137–164.

Samuelson, P. A. 1975. Optimum social security in a life-cycle growth model. *International Economic Review*, 16, 539–544.

Sanders, T. 1951. *Effects of taxation on executives.* Cambridge, Mass.: Harvard University Graduate School of Business Administration.

Sapolsky, H. M. 1977. America's socialized medicine: The allocation of resources within the veterans' health care system. *Public Policy*, 25, 329–382.

Sawyer, M. 1976. *Income distribution in OECD countries.* Economic Outlook, Occasional Studies. Paris: OECD.

Schnitzer, M. 1974. *Income distribution: A comparative study of the U.S., Sweden, West Germany, East Germany, the U.K., and Japan.* New York: Praeger.

Schobel, B. D. 1981. Administrative expenses under OASDI. *Social Security Bulletin*, 44 (March), 21–28.

Schultz, T. W. 1960. Capital formation by education. *Journal of Political Economy*, 68, 571–583.

Schultz, T. W. 1963. *The economic value of education.* New York: Columbia Univ. Press.

Schultz, T. W. (ed.). 1972. *Investment in education: The equity-efficiency quandary.* Chicago: Univ. of Chicago Press.

Schulz, J. H. 1980. *The economics of aging.* Belmont, Calif.: Wadsworth.

Schulz, J. H., Leavitt, T. D., and Kelly, L. 1979. Private pensions fall far short of preretirement income levels. *Monthly Labor Review*, 102 (February), 28–32.

Scotton, R. B., and Ferber, H. 1978 and 1980. *Public expenditures and social policy in Australia.* Melbourne: Univ. of Melbourne.

Seers, D., and Jolly, R. 1966. The treatment of education in national accounting. *Review of Income and Wealth*, 12, 195–208.

Sen, A. K. 1970. *Collective choice and social welfare.* San Francisco: Holden-Day.

Skidmore, F. (ed.). 1981. *Social security financing.* Cambridge, Mass.: MIT Press.

Sloan, F., Cromwell, J., and Mitchell, J. B. 1978. *Private physicians and public programs.* Lexington, Mass.: Lexington-Heath.

References

Smeeding, T. M. 1982. Alternative methods for valuing selected in-kind transfer benefits and measuring their effects on poverty. Technical paper no. 50, U.S. Department of Commerce, Bureau of the Census. Washington, D.C.: GPO.

Smith, R. T., and Lilienfeld, A. M. 1971. *The Social Security Disability program: An evaluation study*. Washington, D.C.: U.S. Department of Health, Education and Welfare.

Smolensky, E., Stiefel, L., Schmundt, M., and Plotnick, R. D. 1977. Adding in-kind transfers to the personal income and outlay account: Implications for the size distribution of income. In F. T. Juster (ed.), *The distribution of economic well-being*. Cambridge, Mass.: Ballinger.

Snyder, W. W. 1970. Measuring the stabilizing effects of Social Security programs in seven countries, 1955–65. *National Tax Journal*, 23, 263–273.

Social Security Bulletin, Annual Statistical Supplement. Various years. Washington, D.C.: U.S. Department of Health and Human Services (Social Security Administration).

Statistical abstract of the United States. Various years. Washington, D.C.: U.S. Department of Commerce (Bureau of the Census).

Stein, B. 1979. *Social Security and the private pension system*. New York: Industrial Relations Counselors.

Steuerle, E., and Hoffman, R. 1979. Tax expenditures for health care. *National Tax Journal*, 32, 101–115.

Stigler, G. J. 1970. Director's law of public income redistribution. *Journal of Law and Economics*, 13, 1–10.

Stiglitz, J. E. 1974. The demand for education in public and private school systems. *Journal of Public Economics*, 3, 349–385.

Stockman, D. A. 1978. Welfare is the problem. *Journal of the Institute for Socioeconomic Studies*, 3, 39–50.

Struyk, F. J., and Bendick, M., Jr. (eds.). 1981. *Housing vouchers for the poor: Lessons from a national experiment*. Washington, D.C.: The Urban Institute.

Stubblebine, W. C., and Willett, T. D. (eds.). 1983. *Reaganomics: A mid-term report*. San Francisco: Institute for Contemporary Studies Press.

Survey of Current Business. Various years, and 1976 and 1981 Supplements: *National income and product accounts*. Washington, D.C.: U.S. Department of Commerce.

Taubman, P. 1978. *Income distribution and redistribution*. Reading, Mass.: Addison-Wesley.

Taussig, M. K., and Danziger, S. 1976. Conference on the trend in income inequality in the U.S. Special Report No. 11. Madison, Wis.: Institute for Research on Poverty.

Tawney, R. H. 1952. *Equality*. (4th ed.; 1st ed., 1932.) London: Allen and Unwin.

Thurow, L. C. 1974. Cash vs. in-kind transfers. *American Economic Review*, 64, 190–195.

Titmuss, R. 1968. *Commitment to welfare*. London: Allen and Unwin.

Titmuss, R. 1974. *Social policy*. London: Allen and Unwin.

Titmuss, R. 1976. *Essays on the welfare state*. (3rd ed.) London: Allen and Unwin.

Tobin, J. 1970. On limiting the domain of inequality. *Journal of Law and Economics*, 13, 263–277.

Tullock, G. 1982. *Economics of income redistribution*. Hingham, Mass.: Kluwer Boston, Inc.

U.K. Central Statistical Office. 1981. Effects of taxes and benefits on household income, 1980. *Economic trends* (annual series). London: Her Majesty's Stationery Office.

U.S. Congress, Joint Economic Committee, Subcommittee on Fiscal Policy. 1973–74. *Studies in public welfare* (20 papers). Washington, D.C.: GPO.

U.S. Department of Commerce (Bureau of the Census). Various years. *Statistical abstract of the United States*. Washington, D.C.: GPO.

U.S. Department of Commerce (Bureau of the Census). Various years. *Current Population Reports*, P-20, Population Characteristics. Washington, D.C.: GPO.

U.S. Department of Commerce (Bureau of the Census). Various years. *Current Population Reports*, P-23, Special Studies. Washington, D.C.: GPO.

U.S. Department of Commerce (Bureau of the Census). Various years. *Current Population Reports*, P-60, Consumer Income. Washington, D.C.: GPO.

U.S. Department of Education. 1981. *Basic grants: End of year report, 1979–80.* Washington, D.C.: GPO.

U.S. Department of Health, Education, and Welfare (Public Health Service, National Center for Health Statistics). 1978. *Current estimates from the Health Interview Survey.* National Health Survey, Series 10, No. 130. Washington, D.C.: GPO.

U.S. Department of Health and Human Services (Health Care Financing Administration, Office of Research, Demonstrations, and Statistics). *Health Care Financing Review* (Monthly). Washington, D.C.: GPO.

U.S. Department of Health and Human Services (Social Security Administration). *Social Security Bulletin* (Monthly). Washington, D.C.: GPO.

U.S. Department of Health and Human Services (Social Security Administration). 1980. *Work disability in the U.S.: A chartbook.* Washington, D.C.: GPO.

U.S. Department of Labor. 1981. *Employment and training report of the President.* Washington, D.C.: GPO.

U.S. Department of the Treasury (Internal Revenue Service). Various years. *Statistics of income: Individual tax returns.* Washington, D.C.: GPO.

U.S. Department of the Treasury. 1977a. *Report of the Commission on Private Philanthropy and Public Needs.* Washington, D.C.: U.S. Department of the Treasury.

U.S. Department of the Treasury. 1977b. *Blueprints for basic tax reform.* Washington, D.C.: GPO.

Varian, H. R. 1978. *Microeconomic analysis.* New York: Norton.

Varian, H. R. 1980. Redistributive taxation as social insurance. *Journal of Public Economics*, 14, 49–68.

Vroman, W. G. 1969. *Macroeconomic effects of social insurance on aggregate demand.* Washington, D.C.: U.S. Department of Health, Education, and Welfare.

Watts, H. W., and Rees, A. (eds.). 1976–1977. *The New Jersey Income-Maintenance Experiment*, Vol. 2. *Labor supply responses.* New York: Academic Press.

Watts, H. W., and Skidmore, F. 1977. An update of the poverty picture plus a new look at relative tax burdens. *Focus* (Institute for Research on Poverty newsletter). Vol. 2 (1). Madison, Wis.

Weisbrod, B. A. 1968. Income redistribution effects and benefit-cost analysis. In S. B. Chase (ed.), *Problems in public expenditure analysis.* Washington, D.C.: The Brookings Institution.

Wilcox, C. 1969. *Toward social welfare: An analysis of programs and proposals attacking poverty, insecurity, and inequality of opportunity.* Homewood, Ill.: Irwin.

Wilensky, H. L. 1975. *The welfare state and equality: Structural and ideological roots of public expenditures.* Berkeley, Calif.: Univ. of California Press.

Wilensky, H. L. 1981. Leftism, catholicism, and democratic corporatism: The role of political parties in welfare state development. In P. Flora and A. J. Heidenheimer (eds.), *The development of welfare states in Europe and America.* New Brunswick, N.J.: Transaction Books.

Williams, A. 1977. Income distribution and public expenditure decisions. In M. Posner (ed.), *Public expenditure.* Cambridge: Cambridge Univ. Press.

Williams, C. A., Jr., Turnbull, J. G., and Cheit, E. F. 1982. (5th ed.) *Economic and social security: Social insurance and other approaches.* New York: Wiley, Ronald Press.

Wilson, T. (ed.). 1974. *Pensions: Inflation and growth: A comparative study of the elderly in the welfare state.* Toronto: Heinemann.

References

Wilson, T., and Wilson, D. J. 1982. *The political economy of the welfare state*. London: Allen and Unwin.
Witte, E. E. (edited by R. J. Lampman). 1962. *Social security perspectives*. Madison, Wis.: Univ. of Wisconsin Press.
Woodhall, M. 1978. *Review of student support schemes in selected OECD countries*. Paris: Organisation for Economic Co-operation and Development.
Worrall, J. D. 1978. A benefit-cost analysis of the vocational rehabilitation program. *Journal of Human Resources, 13,* 285–298.
Worthington, M. D., and Lynn, L. E., Jr. 1977. Incremental welfare reform: A strategy whose time has passed. *Public Policy, 25,* 49–80.
Yanovsky, M. 1965. *Social accounting systems*. Chicago, Ill.: Aldine.
Young, D. R., and Nelson, R. R. (eds.). 1973. *Public policy for day care of young children: Organization, finance and planning*. Lexington, Mass.: Lexington-Heath.
Zymelman, M. 1976. *The economic evaluation of vocational training programs*. Baltimore: Johns Hopkins Press.

Author Index

Asterisks denote substantive references. Authors mentioned only in Guides to Reading are not in this index.

A

Aaron, H., 128*, 134, 153
Abramovitz, M., 96*, 132*
Akerlof, G., 118
Anderson, M., 82

B

Barlow, R., 121*
Barro, R., 134
Baumol, W., 118
Bender, S., 94*, 95*, 96*
Bismarck, O., 155
Bixby, A. K., 8, 26, 28
Blinder, A., 131
Boltho, A., 152
Boskin, M. J., 163
Boulding, K. E., 2*, 98, 152
Bowen, W. G., 121
Bradbury, K. L., 92, 168
Brandeis, E., 1*
Brazer, H. E., 121*
Break, G. F., 121*
Brehm, C. T., 128
Briggs, A., 73n
Brittain, J. A., 59
Brown, C. V., 120n
Browning, E. K., 64*, 94, 156
Browning, J. M., 94

Buchanan, J. M., 33
Budd, E., 34
Burkhauser, R., 131, 161, 163

C

Cagan, P., 134
Cain, G., 115n, 120, 121
Campbell, R. R., 163
Carter, J. E., 9*, 159*, 168
Cloward, R. A., 155
Cohn, E., 96*

D

Danziger, S., 41, 64*, 91–92, 128–130*, 134
Davis, L., 156
Denison, E. F., 94*, 96*, 112
Dewey, J., 99*
Douglas, P. H., 120*, 121*
Downs, A., 168
Dye, R. F., 59

E

Eisenhower, D. D., 69
Eisner, R., 34, 94–96*

217

F

Fabricant, S., 1*
Feldstein, M. S., 20, 133
Feldstein, P., 80
Fellner, W., 132*
Finegan, T. A., 121
Fischer, D., 118
Ford, G., 9*
Fox, A., 44
Freeman, R. B., 91
Friedman, M., 100
Friedman, R., 100
Fuchs, V., 110

G

Garfinkel, I., 120*, 121*, 125*, 126*, 127n, 161, 169
Gershuny, J., 100
Glennerster, H., 160
Goetschius, G., 110
Goldsmith, R., 1*
Golladay, F. L., 94
Goode, R., 25
Goodin, R. E., 73n
Gordon, R. H., 131
Gramlich, E., 68

H

Hansen, W. L., 168
Harris, R., 100
Hauptman, A. M., 47
Hausman, J., 121*, 122*
Haveman, R., 64*, 92, 94, 127n, 128–130*, 134
Hayek, F. A., 99*, 100*, 101*
Heckman, J., 120n
Hirschman, A. O., 100
Hoagland, G. W., 64*, 82
Hochman, H., 89
Hoffman, R., 24
Holden, K., 161
Hybels, J. A., 59

J

Jackson, L. R., 100
Johnson, C. M., 115n
Johnson, L. B., 9*, 82*
Johnson, W. R., 64*, 100
Jolly, R., 21

K

Keeley, M. C., 120n, 122
Kelly, L., 44
Kendrick, J., 21, 34
Kyrk, H., 18

L

Lampman, R. J., 3n, 18, 52, 88, 91n, 103–104, 111n, 125, 162–163, 168–169
Leavitt, T. D., 44
LeGrand, J., 167
Leimer, D. R., 44
Lesnoy, S. D., 44
Levitan, S. A., 68, 115n, 131n
Lindbeck, A., 110, 111n
Lowry, I., 168

M

MacCallum, G. C., 99
MacDonald, M., 51, 92, 136
MaCurdy, T., 120n
Manski, C. F., 168
Masters, S., 120*, 121*, 125*, 126*
Merriam, I., 1*, 148n
Mincer, J., 121
Moon, M., 63
Morgan, J. N., 59, 121*
Moss, M., 20
Mueller, D., 156
Munnell, A., 133–134*, 163
Musgrave, P. B., 90*, 109*, 119*
Musgrave, R. A., 90*, 109*, 119*

N

Nicholson, J. L., 20
Nixon, R., 9*, 168
North, D., 156

Author Index

O

Okner, B. A., 57*
Okun, A. M., 104
Olsen, E., 82

P

Paglin, M., 82
Pareto, V., 143
Pechman, J. A., 57*
Peltzman, S., 139
Pieper, R. J., 94*, 95*, 96*
Piven, F. F., 155
Plotnick, R., 41, 64*, 82, 92, 128–130*, 134
Pound, R., 75n
Poynter, J. R., 85

R

Radner, D., 34
Rawls, J., 99, 102*
Reagan, R. W., 9*, 158*
Rees, A., 122
Reynolds, M., 91*
Rivlin, A., 2*, 68
Robins, P. K., 122
Rodgers, J. D., 89
Ross, H. L., 127n
Ruggles, N., 34
Ruggles, R., 34

S

Sanders, T., 121*
Saving, T. R., 128
Sawhill, I., 92, 127n
Schmundt, M., 82
Schobel, B. D., 110*
Schultz, T. W., 6*, 77
Schulz, J. H., 44
Seers, D., 21
Seldon, A., 100
Simons, E. R., 94*, 95*, 96*
Skidmore, F., 125
Smeeding, T., 82, 88

Smolensky, E., 82, 91*
Snyder, W. W., 97
Spiegelman, R. J., 122
Steuerle, E., 24
Stiefel, L., 82
Stigler, G., 155

T

Taggart, R., 131n
Taussig, M. K., 91
Tawney, R. H., 98, 99*
Thurow, L., 82
Tobin, J., 76
Tollison, R. D., 33
Tullock, G., 33
Turner, J. A., 131

U

Uhr, E., 169

V

Vroman, W. G., 97

W

Warlick, J., 163
Watts, H., 120, 122, 125
West, R. W., 122
Whitehead, T. C., 34
Wicks, J. H., 110
Wilensky, H., 152, 155*
Wise, D. A., 168
Wise, D. E., 131
Witte, E. E., 1*
Wolfe, B., 128
Woodhall, M., 168
Wurzburg, G. K., 68

Y

Yanovsky, M., 34

Subject Index

A

Accounting
  framework of, 14, 18–22
  SCI, 20–22, 37–38
  social, 1, 2, 18–22, 34
  time period of, 29, 63–64, 87; see also Bias
Accounts
  current vs. capital, 21
  flow-of-funds, as social accounting system, 1, 18n
  sectoral, transfer items in, 37
  social, important distinctions in, 18–19
Administration of SCI programs
  loss of freedom and centralization of, 100–101
  social costs of, 109–111
Aged, see also Old Age Insurance; Retirement; Social security
  distribution of SCI benefits to, 61–64, 122–123
  and donor benefits, 88
  in Germany, 152
  historical changes in SCI benefits for, 70–73
  interfamily transfers to, 28
  and labor supply, 120, 124–127
  reduction of income inequality, 90
  SCI bias toward, 53–56, 63
  SCI contributions by, 59–60
  SCI growth and future increases in population of, 153, 157–158, 170
Aged poor, see Poor; Poverty

Age of majority
  definition of income-receiving unit and, 19–20
Aid to Families with Dependent Children (AFDC), see also Female-headed households; Women
  alternative methods of delivery of, 168–169
  benefit-reduction rates, 61–63
  benefits and beneficiaries of, 41–43, 45, 157
  as earnings-conditioned benefit, 118
  eligibility for, 45
  influence on family size of, 92
  labor supply effects of, 128–129
  nuclear family and, 19
  and welfare reform, 168
  mentioned, 9, 58
Alimony, as interfamily transfer, 28
Allocational efficiency, see Efficiency
Allocation of goods and services, see also Choice; Efficiency
  in economic theory, 142–143
  effects of SCI on, 136–140
  and income and substitution effects, 145
  SCI and private consumption goods, 30–31
Australia, pro-poor SCI system of, 161

B

Baby boom, 157, 163
Balance of Payments Accounts, 1

Basic Educational Opportunity Grants
    (BEOG), see also Education
  effect on enrollments, 80
  future changes in, 168
  included in SCI, 26
  mentioned, 46, 86, 140
Beneficiaries, see also Benefits; Donors;
    Secondary consumer income
  labor supply responses, by category,
    119, 125
  program administrators as, 110
  secondary, 88–89, 91
Benefit–cost analysis, see also Benefits, social; Costs, social
  global and SCI, 68–69
  as purpose of book, 2
  in SCI subdiscipline, 6
  weighting of social benefits in, 101–106
  weighting of social costs in, 140–145
Benefit-reduction rates
  and choice of retirement age, 131
  horizontal and vertical equity and, 104
  labor supply effects of, 118, 120–121
  as reduction to gross wage, 61–63
Benefit replacement rate, 44–45
Benefits, SCI
  bias in distribution of, 52–56
  cash, 2, 40–43, 69–73, 135
  classification of, 11
  earnings-conditioned, 117–118, 122–123
  excluded from taxation, 26–27
  and labor supply, 61–64, 129
  multiple receipt of, 41
  net incidence of, 61–64
  pattern of, 43
  private, 27
  sliding of, 88–89, 134
  targeting of, future choices in, 161–162
  as wealth, 133–134
Benefits, social
  balancing of, 7, 89
  defined, 3
  of SCI, summary and weighting of,
    101–106
Bias
  in distribution of benefits to special
    groups, 53–56
  of SCI system towards aged, 63
  of short accounting period, 20
Black market for food stamps, 136

Blacks, changes in inequality and, 90–91
Breadwinner
  loss of, 40–43, 45
  mentioned, 73–74
Break-even point, 3
  allocational effect of shifts in, 136
  response of, to change in income, 125
British National Health Service, 167
Business, see also Intermediaries
  SCI treatment of transfers to, in NIPA, 37

C

Capital, see also Human capital; Savings
  accumulation of, and future SCI
    choices, 166
  formation, competing with SCI, 159–160
  transfer of, 21
Capital gains, treatment in social accounts, 34
Capitalism, democratic, and freedom, 99
Cash benefits, see Benefits, SCI
Child allowance, see also Tax expenditures
  exemption for children as alternative to,
    10, 24
  in Germany, 150–152
  as substitute for AFDC, 157, 168
Choice
  distortion of, due to SCI, 141–142
  freedom of, 6, 100–107
  of future SCI growth, 159–162
  parental, and education, 167
  in provision of health care, 81
  and SCI mentalities, 162
Circular flow analysis, SCI in, 29
Coercion, see Choice; Participation
Collective bargaining, 36–37, see also Employee compensation; Labor contract
Comparisons, international, see International comparisons
Consumer income, see also Income; Primary income; Secondary consumer
    income
  as distinct from producer income, 10
Consumption value, of SCI goods, 144–145
Contract, see also Labor contract, Law
  defined, 36

Subject Index

freedom of, 36, 75n, 85
transfer as implicit, 88
Contributions, charitable, *see also*
    Philanthropy
  and efficiency, 89
  and income level, 152
  progressive income tax and, 59
  standards for, 86
  tax expenditures for, excluded from
    SCI, 26
Contributions, SCI, *see also* Taxes
  employer, 7, 21, 26–27, 38, 160
  fair sharing of, 86–90, 102
  historical changes in progressivity of,
    87–88
  incidence of, 21, 56–61
  new methods of financing, and SCI
    growth, 153, 169
Cost–benefit analysis, *see* Benefit–cost
    analysis
Cost effectiveness, *see also* Efficiency
  of alternative methods of reaching a
    goal, 2
Costs, *see also* Benefit–cost analysis
  of leisure and labor supply, 116
  loss of freedom as, 99–101
  optimal level of SCI, 110–111
  overhead, compliance, collection, and
    administrative, 109–111
  social, defined, 108
  social, and loss of labor time, 131
  summation and weighting of SCI, 140–
    145
Counterfactual, *see also* Benefit–cost
    analysis
  choice and significance of, 68–69
  compatibility of, in labor supply evalua-
    tion, 129–130
Coverage, *see individual programs*

D

Day care
  benefits for, 50–51
  as earnings-conditioned benefit, 119
  mentioned, 82, 100, 168
Deadweight loss, *see* Efficiency
Deductions, income tax, *see* Tax
    expenditures

Dependency ratio
  and future payroll tax increases, 163–
    166
  historical changes in, 153–155
Disability
  benefits and beneficiaries, 40–43, 45,
    122–123
  and changes in labor supply, 124–127
  reduction of insecurity with respect to,
    73
Disability Insurance (DI), 36, 70–73, 161
  labor supply effects of, 128–129
Donors
  benefits to, 88
  and donees, in transfer, 15
  employers as, in social insurance, 36
  substitution of SCI for private pur-
    chases of, 135
  tax expenditures to, 26

E

Earned income tax credit, *see also* Tax
    expenditures
  as part of NIT movement, 162
  rationale for inclusion in SCI, 24
  and reduction of poverty, 86
  and tax incidence, 59
  as wage subsidy, 116
Earnings-conditioned benefit, *see* Benefits,
    SCI; Means-tested benefits
Econometric modeling of labor supply,
    120n
Economic growth, *see* Growth, economic
Economic inquiry, moods of, 3–5
Economic security, 73–80, 159
Education, *see also* Basic Educational Op-
    portunity Grants; Human capital
  attainment, 94–96
  compulsory attendance, 76
  costs, 46, 76–80, 94–95, 139
  and economic growth, 94–96
  enrollment, 46–47, 78–79, 126, 168
  future SCI choices and, 167
  growth in local funding for, 79
  higher, 78–79, 139
  history, 78–79
  interest subsidies not included in SCI,
    47

Education (cont'd)
  and interfamily transfer, 76–77
  as investment, 20–21, 78
  and philanthropic organizations, 78–79
  private, 79, 137–139
  reduction of insecurity with respect to, 76–80
  SCI for, 46–47, 122–123
  SCI and reallocation of resources to provision of, 135–140
  subsidy for, timing of receipt, 20
  tuition subsidy and labor supply, 127–128
  voucher system of financing, 167
Efficiency
  allocational vs. distributional equity, 5–6
  vs. equity, 104
  gain, donor benefits as, 90
  involuntary SCI contributions and, 89
  loss, see Excess burden
  mentioned, 3
Eligibility, see *individual programs*
Employee compensation
  defined, 30
  and inflation, 97–98
  insurance as part of, 36, 75, 81
  nonwage items, treatment in NIPA, 37
  SCI contributions as part of, 86
  mentioned, 35–36
Employer contributions
  future choices of, and SCI, 160
  mandated, 7
Employers, see also Intermediaries
  as donors in social insurance, 36
  supply-side transfers and, 34
Employment-generating effects of purchases of goods and services, 1
Energy Assistance program, 168
Enrollment, see Education
Equality of opportunity, 6, 156
  as goal, 77–78, 105, 167
  and provision of SCI goods, 135
  reduction of social tensions, 98
  SCI and, 90
Equity, see also Efficiency
  and efficiency, 104
European economic community, 2
Evaluation, see also Benefit–cost analysis
  as instrument of policy analysis, 68

Excess burden, see also Efficiency
  and allocational effects of SCI, 145
Exchange, distinct from transfer, 10
Exemption, see also Tax expenditures
  tax expenditures for children under 18, 41–43
Externalities, 89

F

Fabians, mentioned, 155
Factor income, see Primary income
Family, see also Intermediaries, Nuclear families
  age of majority and definition of, 19–20
  SCI benefits as influence on, 92
  tax law, 23
Family income
  children and SCI benefits, 168–169
  and labor supply, 115, 130
  primary, and supplements to, 29
Female-headed households, see also Aid to Families with Dependent Children
  labor supply changes in, 124–127
  and leisure, 142
  and poverty, 84–85
  SCI benefits to, 122–123
Fertility, 170
  and age composition, 153
  and future OAI growth, 157, 165
  SCI effects on, 92
Fiscal policy, 6, 17–18, 97
Flow-of-funds accounts, see Accounts
Food, see also Food Stamp program
  SCI benefits for purchase of, 50–55 passim
  SCI and reallocation of resources to provision of, 135–140
Food Stamp program
  as alternative to poor laws, 85
  benefit-reduction rates and, 118
  benefits, 51, 54
  as earnings-conditioned SCI benefit, 119
  and family size, 92
  as in-kind grant to encourage allocation of food, 136
  labor supply effects of, 129
  and Medicaid, 137

and reducing income poverty, 85
as substitute for cash benefit, 81–82
summation of effects of, 140
mentioned, 7, 81–83, 127, 162, 168
Freedom, *see also* Choice
positive and negative, 99–101
Free-rider phenomenon, 89–90

G

Germany, Federal Republic of, 168
and American SCI growth, 156
SCI in, 148–152
G.I. Bill, 19, 79
Gini coefficient, 64, 91, 105
Goals
of SCI system, degree of attainment, 101–106
of SCI system, future, 156–157
of SCI system, stated, 73, 90–101
social, 2–3, 5, 68
Government, *see also* Intermediaries
functions of, 18
purchases of SCI goods and services, 18
Government, local, *see* State and local government
Government, state, *see* State and local government
Government expenditures
externalities as rationale for, 89, 135
political reaction against growth in, 9
SCI purchases of goods and services, 18
Great Depression
and early SCI growth, 147–148
mentioned, 169
Growth, economic
as SCI side effect, 94–98
weighting of social benefits from, 102
Guaranteed student loans, 47; *see also* Education

H

Health care, *see also* Hospital care; Insurance
as civil right, 81

deductibility from income tax as subsidy to, 136
distribution of SCI for, 122–123
financing, 80–81, 167
historic changes in SCI for, 81
as human capital, 95
international comparisons of, 149, 152
SCI benefits and beneficiaries, 47–49
SCI and reallocation of resources to, 135–140
utilization of, 47, 50, 52–53, 80
ways to arrest rapid growth in expenditures on, 166–167
Health insurance, *see* Insurance
Horizontal equity, 23, 86, 103–104, 162
Hospital care, *see also* Health care
containing costs of, 158
subsidies for, 93
total expenditures on, 47, 51
Hours of work, decline in, 114
Household, *see also* Income-receiving unit; Nuclear families
composition, SCI influence on, 92
female-headed, *see* Female-headed households
as income-receiving unit, 19
Housing, *see also* Imputed rent
assistance, labor supply effects of, 129
economic income from homeownership, 24–26
future choices in SCI financing of, 168
public, 81–83, 105, 119
SCI and reallocation of resources to, 135–140
tax expenditures for, 51
Housing allowance, 156
Human capital
in accounting framework, 21
and intergenerational gifts, 134
stock in, as sum of depreciated investment costs, 94–96

I

Imputed rent, *see also* Housing
as secondary income, 24–26
tax expenditures for, 51, 54, 136
Incidence, *see* Income distribution; Tax incidence

Income
  adjusted, and poverty, 83
  circular flow of, 29–31
  consumer, 10
  definitions of, and income distribution studies, 63–64
  national, transfer as part of, 37–39
  nonlabor, 111, 116–119, 121
  primary, see Primary income
  producer, 23, 34
  property, 34, see also Housing
  secondary, see Secondary consumer income; Secondary income; Transfer
Income distribution, 19; see also Income; Inequality; Redistribution
  American standard method of representing, 104–105
  and benefit sliding, 93–94
  effect of SCI on, 61–65
  incidence of SCI on, 93–94
  indicators of, limited use in political action, 105
Income effect, of taxes on labor supply, 116
Income inequality, see Inequality
Income loss
  fair sharing of burden and, 86
  future growth in programs to offset, 162–166
  offset of, effect on saving, 132
  percentage offset by SCI, 44–45
  reducing insecurity with respect to, 73–76, 101–102
Income maintenance
  federal budget surpluses and growth in, 159
  international comparisons of, 149, 152
Income poverty, see Poverty
Income-receiving unit, 105; see also Family; Household; Nuclear families
  alternative definitions of, 19
  and SCI redistribution, 64
Income tax, see also Taxes
  as automatic stabilizer, 97
  corporate, collection costs and, 109
  as method for offsetting income loss, 86
  as preferred SCI funding source, 86
  progressive, as substitute for public assistance, 8
  virtual income and progressive rates, 121

Indexing, of SCI benefits, and SCI growth, 157
Inequality, see also Income distribution; Redistribution
  vs. equity as goal, 104
  income, reduction of as side effect of SCI, 90–94
Inflation, 97–98
In-kind transfers, see also Food Stamp program; Education; Health care; Housing; Medicaid; Medicare
  allocational effects of, 136–137
  as method to reduce poverty, 85, 91
  not found in NIPA, 38
  and poverty line, 56
  public vs. private provision of, 81
  and response to recipients' needs, 82
Input–output tables, 1
Insecurity, see Income loss
Insurance, see also Social insurance
  commercial, 1, 35
  data sources for SCI benefits from, 27
  health, 37, 47–50, 80, 81, 137
  private, 7, 10, 35, 38, 41–43, 153
Insurance equity, 3, 76, 163
Interest, treatment in NIPA, 37
Interfamily giving
  collection costs of, 109
  direct, 27
  for education, 168
  incidence of, 59
  as part of SCI system, 14
  transaction costs of, 141
  treatment in NIPA, 38
Intergenerational transfers, 18, 166
Intermediaries
  in circular-flow analysis, 29–31
  financial, 1
  growth of SCI benefits by, 69–73
  of SCI, future choices of, 160
  as SCI sector, distinct from families, 20
Internal Revenue Service, 169
International comparisons
  of social security and social welfare expenditures, 1–2, 9, 36, 147–152
  tax expenditures and, 23–24
  use of SCI accounting framework for, 22
  mentioned, 9
International Labor Organization, 2

Subject Index

Interpersonal utility, and donor benefits, 88–89
Intrafamily transfers, 10, 18
Investment
  for education, 77–78
  and SCI growth, 132
  social, as goal of SCI, 103–104, 162

J

Japan
  SCI ratio in, 148–149
  social insurance as part of labor cost in, 36
Job training
  benefits for, 51, 54–55
  distinct from make-work job, 34
  future choices in, 156, 168
  overlap with education, 82
  payment for, 36

K

Keynesian economics, 4, 96–97

L

Labor contract, 35–36; see also Contract; Employee compensation
Labor cost, see Employee compensation
Labor force
  full-time vs. part-time participation, 112
  participation rates, 112–114
Labor productivity
  SCI and capital formation, 132
  SCI and loss of, 132–135
Labor supply
  backward bending curve, 116
  changes in, 114, 115, 129–131
  effects of cash vs. noncash benefits, 119
  effects of SCI on, 120–131
  lifetime measure of, 115n
  in market, 111ff.
  men, studies of, 121
  women, studies of, 121
Laissez-faire vs. welfare state, 99
Law
  common, 1, 74
  of contract, 36

lien, 86
related to social insurance, 74–75
Law of torts, see Torts
Legal services, 50–51
Leisure, 142
Life-cycle model of savings, 133
Lifetime, and income-accounting period, 20, 87
Local government, see State and local government
Loss of family breadwinner, see Breadwinner
Low-Income Energy Assistance program, 82
Lump-sum grants
  effects on labor supply, 116–118
  as feature of SCI system, 118–119

M

Marginal analysis, 7
Marginal tax rates, see Taxes
Marxian economics, 4, 155
Means-tested benefits, see also Benefit-reduction rates
  AFDC as, 45
  and distribution of SCI, 61
  as feature of SCI system, 118–119
  for food, housing, and social services, 81–82
  and reduction of insecurity, 74
  and replacement rates, 44
Medicaid, 8, 85, 140, 158; see also Health care; Public assistance; Social insurance
  and allocation of health care, 137
  benefit notch in, 118, 137
  as earnings-conditioned benefit, 119
  growth in, 80, 159–160
  labor supply effects of, 129
  mandating national minimums for, 169
  as related to tax expenditures, 26
Medicare, see also Aged; Health care
  allocation of health care, 137
  growth in, 80, 159–160
  labor supply effects of, 129
  mentioned, 140
Mentalities of SCI, defined, 3, 102–104, 162

Merit goods
  education and health care, 4, 78
  SCI for, 45–46
Migration, 93
Minimum wage law, 100
Mississippi, 90
Monopoly rents, 33

N

National Bureau of Economic Research, 1
National Defense Student Loans, 47
National Health Insurance, 47, 157; *see also* Insurance
National Income and Product Accounts (NIPA), 1, 18n; *see also* Accounts
  representation of transfers in, 37–38
Negative Income Tax (NIT), 3, 104, 162, 163
  opposition to, 103
  as replacement for AFDC, 160
  as tax expenditure, 23
New Jersey Income Maintenance Experiment, 122
Nuclear families, *see also* Family; Household; Income-receiving unit
  as leading transfer institution, 18
  needs of, 152
  SCI flows between, 31–32
  as SCI income-receiving unit, 19
Nursing-home care, 80, 137, 153, 158

O

Old Age Insurance (OAI), *see also* Aged; Retirement; Social security
  benefits and beneficiaries under, 41–44
  dependency ratios and, 153–155
  early acceptance of benefits, 130
  as earnings-conditioned SCI benefit, 119
  future of, 153, 157–158, 161, 166
  growth of, 153
  indexing of, 163
  and inflation, 98
  and interfamily transfers, 130
  and labor supply, 128–129, 131
  and loss of freedom, 100
  replacement rates, 44–45
  and savings, 133–134

Old Age, Survivor's, Disability, and Health Insurance (OASDHI), 110; *see also* Disability Insurance; Medicare; Old Age Insurance; Survivor's Insurance
Organisation for Economic Co-operation and Development (OECD), 2, 147–149; *see also* International comparisons

P

Pareto optimality, 143
Participation
  forced, mandatory programs and, 100–101
  rates, in SCI programs, 45
Payroll taxes, *see also* Taxes
  future increases in, 163–165, 169
  and future SCI growth, 157–158
Pell Grants, *see* Basic Educational Opportunity Grants
Pensions, private, *see also* Aged; Retirement
  cash benefits, 43–44
  coercion and, 100
  collection costs of, 109
  incidence of contributions for, 59
  as part of SCI, 27
  replacement rates and, 44
  and savings, 134
  as SCI growth project, 157
  and social security, 158, 166
  treatment in social accounts, 37
Pensions, public, *see* Old Age Insurance
Philanthropy, *see also* Contributions, charitable
  contributions for, incidence of, 59
  costs of raising funds for, 109
  as SCI institution, 10
Philosophies of SCI, *see* Mentalities of SCI
Physicians, *see also* Health care
  and demand for health care, 137
  growth in number of, 80
Planning Program Budget System, 2, 160
Policy analysis, 68
Political analysis, 153, 155–156
Poor, *see also* Poverty
  aged, 84–85
  bias of SCI toward, 63

Subject Index

burden of SCI contributions on, 59–60
composition of, 83–85
income of, 59–65
SCI benefits for, 52–56
working, 85
Poor laws, in England, 85
Population growth, 163–165
Poverty, *see also* Income distribution; Inequality; Poor
adjusted income, 82–83
in benefit–cost analysis of SCI, 145
economic growth and, 160
future choices in SCI program to reduce, 168–169
population composition and, 83
reduction of, as goal of SCI, 82–86
reduction of, by income tax, 86
Poverty line
adjusted for in-kind benefits, 56
alternative definitions of, 82–83
and benefits for poor, 52, 56
Primary income, 2
distribution of, in socialist economies, 22n
overlap of SCI and NIPA, 38
and representative family, 30
SCI and changes in distribution of, 16, 29–31, 33, 61–65, 91
and tax incidence for poor, 60
Producer income, *see* Income; Primary income
Productivity, *see also* Labor productivity
increases in, due to SCI, 101, 102
slowing of gains in, 8
Property taxes, *see* Taxes
Proposition 13, 9, 158
Proposition 2½, 158
Public assistance, *see also* Poor; Poverty
as earnings-conditioned benefit, 119
and labor supply, 85, 128
Medicaid as, 80
miscellaneous SCI as, 81
and poverty, 82
as program to offset income loss, 41–43
as SCI mentality, 162
in sectoral accounts, 37
stigma and low participation rate in, 45
Public choice model of SCI growth, 156
Public employees, 28
Public goods
and efficient allocation of resources, 104

excluded from SCI, 11, 16
redistribution as, 89
Public policy and methods of allocation of goods, 136–139

R

Rate of return, *see also* Human capital; Old Age Insurance
on education, 96n
and efficiency of SCI investments, 103
on OAI contributions, 165, 166
and SCI mentalities, 162
Redistribution, *see also* Income distribution; Tax incidence
and coercion by majority, 90
economic growth and increase in, 159
economic theory and optimality, 143
and inflation, 97
philosophies of programs for, 105
as a public good, 89–90
across risk classes, in insurance, 35
SCI and, 61–65
and secondary beneficiaries, 87–89
social security system and, 163–166
standard methods of study, 63–64
systems of, 2
Regulation
as function of government, 18
SCI and increase in, 100
Rental allowance, 169
Rents, monopoly, seen as transfer, 33
Replacement rates, *see also* Old Age Insurance
predicting future trends in, 163–165
variations by program, 44
Research and development, effect of SCI and inflation on, 132
Retirement, *see also* Aged; Old Age Insurance; Pensions, private
baby boom and, 163–165
benefits for, 40–43
and goal of SCI to increase leisure, 142
induced by OAI, 133–134
and migration decisions, influence of SCI, 92–93
reduction of insecurity with respect to, 73
Retirement age, 128, 131

Risk, *see also* Income loss
  of income loss, and future SCI growth, 158
  insurance as protection against, 35
  in the workplace, 74–75

S

Sales taxes, *see* Taxes
Savings, 166
  and labor supply, 115
  motives for, and capital accumulation, 133
  SCI effects on, 31, 134
  targets and accumulation, 133
School enrollments, *see* Education
Seattle–Denver Income Maintenance Experiment, 122
Secondary consumer income (SCI)
  benefit eligibility and labor supply, 118–119
  and capital formation, 132–133
  defined, 2, 10, 14, 22
  demand for and income level, 152
  distinct from exchange, 14–18
  evolution of system, 8
  federal role and, 169
  growth of, 6, 69–73, 153, 155–159, 170
  labor supply effects of, *see* Labor supply
  planning of, 160
  ratio, 159
  and savings behavior, 134
  side effects of, 6, 11, 73n, 90–101
  and social climate, 98–101
SCI benefits, *see* Benefits, SCI
SCI contributions, *see* Contributions, SCI
SCI economics
  as school, 6
  as subdiscipline, 3–8
SCI intermediaries, *see* Intermediaries
SCI, mentalities of, *see* Mentalities of SCI
SCI programs, *see also individual programs*
  choices of universal vs. selective, 161
  fragmentation of legislative responsibility for, 160–161
  "supply-side," to promote economic growth, 159
  variations in, and evaluation of labor supply effects, 128
SCI social costs, *see* Costs

SCI transfers, substitutes for one another, 7
Secondary income, *see also* Income; Primary income; Secondary consumer income
  as distinct from primary, 14
  distribution of, goals, 6
  as a flow, 10
Sectoral Accounts, *see* Accounts
Sectors, *see* Intermediaries
Social accounting, *see* Accounting
Socia; accounts, *see* Accounts
Social benefits, *see* Benefits, social
Social costs, *see* Costs
Social Democrats, 155
Social insurance, 1, 7, 78, 96, 102
  advent of, in United States, 75
  and coercion, 100
  and growth of SCI, 153
  inadequacy of, 85
  labor supply effects of, 120–131
  Medicare as, 80
  as mentality of SCI, 162
  to offset income loss, 41, 74, 102–103
  as part of labor contract, 36–37
  and poverty, 82
  treatment in sectoral accounts, 37–38
Socialism, democratic, 9
Socialized economy, as counterfactual to primary income distribution, 33–34
Social policy, 8
Social security, *see also* Disability Insurance; Medicare; Old Age Insurance; Survivor's Insurance
  Act, 1983 amendments to, 166
Social Security Administration (SSA), 1, 22, 28, 161
Social security wealth, and accounting time period, 20
Social services, *see* Welfare services
Social welfare expenditures, *see also* Secondary consumer income
  accounting for, 2
  defined, 22
  development of, 1, 8
  items excluded from SCI, 22
  and other public expenditures, 34
  as part of all transfers, 15
  Reagan administration efforts to reduce, 158
  SSA funding information, 28

Subject Index

Stagflation, 8–9, 97–98
State and local government
  and costs of education, 109
  historical changes in SCI by, 70–73
  provision of cash benefits by, 41–43
  and role in SCI financing, 160
  social welfare expenditures of, 2
Students, *see* Education
Supplemental Security Income (SSI)
  and disability, 45
  labor supply effects of, 129
  as reform of social security, 166
  as rejection of lien law, 85–86
  relation to replacement rates, 44
Survivor's Insurance (SI), 45
  influence on family size, 92
  labor supply and, 126
  and student benefits, 47, 79–80

T

Taxes
  American system of, 87
  and benefit-reduction rates, 61–63
  consumption-based substitute for SCI funding sources, 169
  costs of administration, collection, and compliance, 109
  credit for education, 167
  and deductibility of SCI goods, 136
  on earnings capacity, 118
  effects on saving, investment, and R&D, 132–133
  and excess burden concept, 144–145
  and future SCI choices, 162
  historical changes in, 70–73
  income, *see* Income tax
  labor supply effects, 116–118, 125–127
  payroll, *see* Payroll tax
  purchases of food and other goods, effects on, 135
  SCI benefits excluded from, 26–27
  as SCI funding source, 28
  shifting and size distribution of income, 93–94
Tax evasion, 111
Tax expenditures
  for aged and blind, 41–43
  conversion to direct outlays, examples, 24–26

  and growth of SCI, 147–148
  included in SCI, 10, 22–23, 28
  as increasing allocation to goods and services, 136
  as reducing income tax progressivity, 59
Tax incidence, 29; *see also* Redistribution
  consensus view of, 87–89
  and donor benefits, 87–89
  and lifetime receipt of SCI, 87
  and SCI accounting, 21
  among SCI recipients, 87
  sliding of benefits, 87–88
  and social insurance, 36–37
  theory of, 93–94
Tax savings, *see* Tax expenditures
Technology
  and health care, 80, 153
  new, and SCI, 6
Third-party payment, 137
Time period of accounting, *see* Accounting
Torts, 74, 103
Training, job, *see* Job training
Transfer, 31–37, 152
  in circular flow analysis, 29
  defined, 14–18 passim
  distinct from exchange, 2
  distinct from primary income, 10
  and donor benefits, 88
  excluded from SCI, 34
  improvement of social environment and, 98
  and income level, 152
  NIPA treatment of, 37–38
  as secondary flow in sectoral accounts, 37
  on supply side, 34
  and tax burden of poor, 60

U

Underground economy, 110
Unemployment, *see also* Income loss
  high rates in United States, 8–9
  income loss offset by SCI, 44–45, 73
  involuntary, 41, 131n
  and loss of health insurance, 47
Unemployment insurance (UI), 8, 127
  as automatic stabilizer, 96–97
  benefits and beneficiaries, 40–45

Unemployment insurance (cont'd)
  development of, 75
  effect of spell duration of unemployment, 128
  and labor supply, 128–129, 131
  philosophy of redistribution and, 105
  as transfer from all employees to unemployed, 36
United Kingdom, 168
United States Congress, 23, 160–161

V

Vertical equity, 86, 162
Veterans
  benefits for, 44, 46, 80
  labor supply effects of disability compensation, 129
  programs for, and expenditures, 157
Voting model of SCI growth, 156

W

Wage diversions, 29, 103
  accounting for public employee benefits, 28
  forced, 100
  implicit accounting for in NIPA, 38
  incidence of, 56–59
  as SCI contributions, defined, 21
  as SCI funding source, 56–61
Wage rates, 115–116; see also Benefit-reduction rates, Employee compensation

Wage subsidy
  labor supply effects of, 116–118
  shifting of, 94
Wealth effects of SCI benefits, 133–134
Wealth transfers, 18, 166
Welfare services, 50, 54–55
Welfare state, 73n, 96, 99, 120, 148
  and decline in productivity, 132
  development of, 9, 155
  social welfare expenditures and policies of, 33
Women, see also Aid to Families with Dependent Children; Female-headed households
  changes in fertility, 115
  changes in work at home, 115
  and family size, SCI influence on, 92
  future choice of targeting SCI on, 161
  and historical changes in inequality, 91
  labor force participation rate, 112–113
  labor supply of, 120–122, 124–127, 130
  utilization of health care, 50, 53
Worker's compensation
  cash benefits for, 42–43, 45
  development of, 74–75
  and growth of SCI health-care benefits, 80
  and health care, 47–49
  labor supply effects of, 129
Work incentives, see also Labor supply
  benefit designs for, 118
  and benefit-reduction rates, 125–130
  targeting of SCI benefits, 122–127
  trade-off between income redistribution and labor supply, 119
Working poor, see Poor